OSF/Motif™ Style Guide

Revision 1.2

(For OSF/Motif Release 1.2)

Open Software Foundation

D1444958

 P T R Prentice Hall, Englewood Cliffs, New Jersey 07632

Cover design
and cover illustration: **BETH FAGAN**

This book was formatted with troff

Published by P T R Prentice-Hall, Inc.
A Simon & Schuster Company
Englewood Cliffs, New Jersey 07632

The information contained within this document is subject to change without notice.

Printed in the United States of America
10   9   8   7   6   5   4   3   2

ISBN 0-13-643123-2

Prentice-Hall International (UK) Limited, *London*
Prentice-Hall of Australia Pty. Limited, *Sydney*
Prentice-Hall Canada Inc., *Toronto*
Prentice-Hall Hispanoamericana, S.A., *Mexico*
Prentice-Hall of India Private Limited, *New Delhi*
Prentice-Hall of Japan, Inc., *Tokyo*
Simon & Schuster Asia Pte. Ltd., *Singapore*
Editora Prentice-Hall do Brasil, Ltda., *Rio de Janeiro*

Contents

List of Figures

List of Tables

Preface

The *OSF/Motif Style Guide* provides a framework of behavior specifications to guide application developers, widget developers, user interface system developers, and window manager developers in the design and implementation of new products consistent with the OSF/Motif™ user interface. This *OSF/Motif Style Guide* is also closely consistent with Microsoft Windows, Presentation Manager, and Common User Access (CUA).

The *OSF/Motif Style Guide* establishes a consistent behavior among new products by drawing out the common elements from a variety of current behavioral models. The *OSF/Motif Style Guide* anticipates the evolution of graphical user interfaces as new technology becomes available and as the use of the Motif™ user interface spreads. Behavioral guidelines will be added over time as they become stable.

For specific details of coding the implementation into an application program, widget, or window manager, see the other volumes of the OSF/Motif documentation set.

Audience

This document is written for four audiences. The following text suggests the sections in this guide that are relevant to each audience. We recommend that you read through the entire *OSF/Motif Style Guide* once to familiarize yourself with all user interface design concepts and to ensure that you do not miss anything.

- Application Designers

  Should be familiar with the contents of Chapters 1, 6, and 8, and Appendixes A and B.

- Widget Designers

  Should be familiar with the contents of Chapters 1 through 6, 8, and 9, and Appendixes A and B.

- User Interface System Designers

  Should be familiar with the entire contents of this guide.

- Window Manager Designers

  Should be familiar with the contents of Chapters 1, 6, 7, and 8, and Appendix A.

Applicability

This is Revision 1.2 of this document. It applies to Release 1.2 of the OSF/Motif software system.

Purpose

The purpose of this guide is to explain how to create OSF/Motif compliant applications, window managers, controls, and systems.

Document Usage

This document is organized into nine chapters and two appendixes.

- Chapter 1 provides general user interface design principles. Everyone should read this chapter.

- Chapter 2 describes the input model. New widget designers and user interface system designers should read this chapter.

- Chapter 3 describes the navigation model. New widget designers and user interface system designers should read this chapter.

- Chapter 4 describes the selection model. New widget designers and user interface system designers should read this chapter.

- Chapter 5 describes the activation model. New widget designers and user interface system designers should read this chapter.

- Chapter 6 describes user interface component choices, layout, and interaction. Everyone should read this chapter.

- Chapter 7 describes window manager design. Window manager designers and user interface system designers should read this chapter.

- Chapter 8 introduces and briefly describes internationalization and localization concepts and issues as they relate to user interface design. Everyone should read this chapter.

- Chapter 9 provides reference information for concepts described in earlier chapters, and provides detailed information about components. This chapter should be read by new widget designers and can by used as a reference by everyone.

- Appendix A shows the correspondence between OSF/Motif widgets and components described in this guide.

- Appendix B contains the Level One Certification Checklist, which is based on this guide.

Related Documents

For additional information about OSF/Motif, refer to the following documents:

- The *Application Environment Specification — User Environment Volume* defines a stable set of routines for creating user interface applications.

- The *OSF/Motif User's Guide* explains how to interact with OSF/Motif based applications.

- The *OSF/Motif Programmer's Guide* explains how to write applications using the OSF/Motif widget set.

- The *OSF/Motif Programmer's Reference* provides detailed reference information for programmers writing Motif applications.

Typographic and Keying Conventions

This document uses the following typographic conventions:

Bold   **Bold** words or characters represent system elements that you must use literally, such as commands, flags, and pathnames. **Bold** words also indicate the first use of a term included in the glossary.

Italic   *Italic* words or characters represent variable values that you must supply.

< >   Angle brackets enclose the name of a key on the keyboard.

Components of the user interface are represented by capital letters on each major word in the name of the component, such as PushButton.

See **Compliance Conventions** later in this Preface for an explanation of the asterisks (*) that appear in the margins.

Keyboard Conventions

Since not all keyboards are the same, it is difficult to give style guidelines that are correct for every manufacturer's keyboard. To solve this problem, this guide describes keys using a **model keyboard** mechanism. Wherever keyboard input is specified, the keys are indicated by the engraving they have on the OSF/Motif model keyboard. The model keyboard does not correspond directly to any existing keyboard, rather it assumes a keyboard with an ideal set of keys.

In addition to the standard letter, number, and character keys, the OSF/Motif model keyboard is composed of the following special keys:

- The special printing characters **</>**, **<\>**, and **<!>**
- The standard modifier keys **<Ctrl>**, **<Alt>**, and **<Shift>**
- Ten function keys **<F1>** through **<F10>**
- The arrow keys **<↓>**, **<←>**, **<→>**, and **<↑>**
- **<Backspace>**
- **<Cancel>**
- **<Delete>**
- **<End>**
- **<Escape>**
- **<Help>**
- **<Home>**, **<Begin>**, or both
- **<Insert>**
- **<Menu>**
- **<PageDown>**
- **<PageUp>**
- **<Return>**
- **<Space>**
- **<Tab>**

The OSF/Motif model keyboard also contains the following optional keys, which, although useful, are either not necessary or may be created by combinations of other keys:

- **<CapsLock>**
- **<Copy>**
- **<Cut>**
- **<Enter>**
- **<ModeSwitch>**
- **<NumLock>**
- **<PageLeft>**
- **<PageRight>**
- **<Paste>**
- **<ScrollLock>**
- **<Select>**
- **<Undo>**

Throughout this guide, behavior is described in terms of model keyboard keys. When a behavior takes advantage of an optional key from the model keyboard, it is also described in terms of the required special keys. Each of *
the keys described on the OSF/Motif model keyboard must be available *
either as specified or using other keys or key combinations if the specified *
key is unavailable. A few of the more important alternative key bindings are described here for your convenience.

- If **<Cancel>** does not exist, **<Escape>** can be used in its place.
- If **<Help>** does not exist, **<F1>** can be used in its place.
- If **<Menu>** does not exist, **<Shift> <F10>** can be used in its place.
- If **<F10>** does not exist, **<Shift> <Menu>** can be used in its place.
- If **<Home>** or **<Begin>** does not exist, **<Alt> <←>** can be used in its place.
- If **<End>** does not exist, **<Alt> <→>** can be used in its place
- Wherever **<Select>** and **<Space>** can be used for a selection action, **<Ctrl> <Space>** can be used as well.

- Wherever **<Enter>** and **<Return>** can be used for activation, **<Ctrl> <Return>** can be used as well.

Mouse Conventions

Mouse buttons are described in this guide using a **virtual button** mechanism to better describe behavior independent from the number of buttons on the mouse. This guide assumes a 3-button mouse. On a 3-button mouse, the leftmost mouse button is usually defined as **BSelect**, the middle mouse button is usually defined as **BTransfer**, and the rightmost mouse button is usually defined as **BMenu**. Details about how virtual mouse buttons are usually defined are given in Section 2.2.

Compliance Conventions

Throughout the guide "must," "should," and "can" have special meanings. Guidelines with "must" in them are requirements for *OSF/Motif Style Guide* compliance. Any guideline with "must" is included in the "OSF/Motif Level One Certification Checklist" for *OSF/Motif Style Guide* compliance. Guidelines with "must" are marked in the margin with an asterisk (*). Guidelines with "should" in them are recommendations. We consider them important for interapplication consistency, but we do not require them for compliance. You should follow them as closely as you are able. Guidelines with "can" in them indicate optional elements of user interface style.

The process for how *OSF/Motif Style Guide* elements migrate from options to requirements is described in the "OSF/Motif Level One Certification Checklist" (see Appendix B).

Note that by default this guide assumes your application is being designed for a left-to-right language direction environment, and that the application is written in English. Many of these guidelines can, and in fact should, be modified based on both language and scanning direction.

Style Guide Support Level Process

As of the 1.2 release, regions of this guide are designated with a support level. This support level system, which closely parallels the current *Application Environment Specification — User Environment Volume* support level system, specifies the commitment OSF makes to the guidelines in that region. The higher the support level, the longer the warning period required before OSF can delete the guidelines, or make an incompatible change in the guidelines. (An incompatible change is one that might require compliant applications to be rewritten.) Support levels, therefore, serve as advisories for application developers because they indicate the length of time that a guideline is guaranteed to remain stable.

During the *OSF/Motif Style Guide* development process, OSF staff members propose support levels for guidelines, based on criteria defined later in this Preface. OSF members review and comment on these support levels and the rest of the document.

In general, membership review proceeds as follows:

1. OSF prepares a list of proposed changes to the *OSF/Motif Style Guide*, and circulates it to OSF members. This review period may last from one to several months.

2. Members submit comments.

3. OSF responds to members' comments in the next version of the document, or in a discussion that takes place in an electronic news group or at a meeting.

OSF considers all review comments during the development of the *OSF/Motif Style Guide* and brings important or controversial issues up for further discussion. However, the review process is not a voting process, and OSF does not wait for consensus among the membership before adding new interfaces to the *OSF/Motif Style Guide* or making other technical decisions.

AES Support Levels

This section defines the support levels assigned to the guidelines. As previously mentioned, support levels define OSF's commitment to interface definitions by indicating the warning period required to make an incompatible modification or deletion of the guideline. New *OSF/Motif Style Guide* revisions may introduce upwardly compatible changes at any time, regardless of the support level.

The support levels are as follows:

- Full use
- Trial use

The following sections explain each support level, and how guidelines move from proposed status (in drafts) to final status (in published versions).

Full Use

A full-use guideline has the highest support level, so it is the most protected from incompatible modification or deletion.

OSF assigns a support level of full use to guidelines for the following reasons:

- The guideline already exists in an approved de jure standard. (A de jure standard is one that is set by an official standards body.)
- The guideline as specified in the *OSF/Motif Style Guide* is considered stable and already in widespread use in applications.
- The guideline has been upgraded to full-use status after a period of trial-use status in an earlier *OSF/Motif Style Guide* revision.

There should rarely be a need to remove a full-use guideline, or make incompatible modifications to it. However, if this ever becomes necessary, a full-use guideline keeps its full-use status, but we will publish a warning describing the proposed future change in at least two successive revisions of the *OSF/Motif Style Guide* before we make the change. This provides time for applications to be altered to deal with a different guideline, and for implementations to prepare for the change.

For example, suppose it becomes necessary to modify a full-use guideline that appeared in Release 1.2 of the *OSF/Motif Style Guide*. The draft for Release 1.3 shows the guideline as "proposed-for-modification/removal." Assuming the review concludes that this change is appropriate, the guideline in Release 1.3 still has full-use status, but is accompanied by a warning. The warning states that the guideline is scheduled for modification after Release 1.4, and describes the modified behavior. Application developers can now allow for either the original or the modified guideline. Release 1.4 contains the same warning. Release 1.5 provides the modified definition only.

Trial Use

A trial-use guideline is easier to modify or delete than a full-use guideline. There are several reasons why OSF classifies guidelines as trial use instead of full use. A guideline may be under consideration for inclusion in a de jure standard and so may possibly change as a result of the standards process. Or, OSF may perceive that the guideline is new compared to other included guidelines and, therefore, the implementation and use of the guideline may suggest revisions in its definition.

If it becomes necessary to modify or delete a trial-use guideline, it keeps its trial-use status, with warnings about its removal or incompatible change, for one full revision of the *OSF/Motif Style Guide*. In the preceding example, if the guideline to be modified were a trial-use guideline, Release 1.3 would include the unmodified definition with a warning and description of the change, and Release 1.4 would include the modified definition only.

Proposed Usage Levels

Draft versions of the *OSF/Motif Style Guide* give newly added or changed guidelines a "proposed-for-*level*" status, where *level* is full- or trial-use. In final versions, these guidelines move from "proposed-for-*level*" status to *level* status. Most existing guidelines retain their support level from the previous revision. A few may carry a proposed-for-*change* status (described as follows). New guidelines carry a proposed-for-*level* status.

The following list defines more exactly the AES proposed-for-inclusion and proposed for-change levels.

Proposed-for-*level*-use

A review level leading to *level*-use inclusion on acceptance, and no change in status otherwise. This status may be used to propose a new guideline for *level*-use, or to move an existing guideline to a higher status.

Proposed-for-modification/removal

A review level for existing guidelines that OSF proposes to make an incompatible modification in or remove from the *OSF/Motif Style Guide*. If this proposal is accepted during the review process, a full-use guideline remains as is, with a warning, for two revisions; a trial-use or temporary-use guideline remains as is with a warning, for one revision. If the proposal is rejected, the guideline remains as is.

Proposed-for-correction

A review level for guidelines of any support level in which OSF wishes to correct a specification error. OSF will propose correcting a guideline if a definition was obviously wrong (and implementations and applications could never follow the specification as it is written), if clarification of an unclear section is required, or if an error makes a definition clearly internally inconsistent or inappropriate. Guidelines proposed for correction return to their original status, in corrected form, on acceptance of the correction. They return to their original status in uncorrected form on rejection of the correction. (Proposal for correction is not required for OSF to fix a typographical error.)

Proposed-for-enhancement

A review level for guidelines in which OSF wants to make an upwardly compatible change in definition. If accepted, the definition change is effective in the published revision after the draft in which the proposal for enhancement occurred.

Global Usage Level for Revision 1.2

To avoid confusion when reading this guide, the entire guide has a global usage level. Each guideline in this guide has this global usage level unless specifically set out differently. To initiate this usage level process, in this version of the *OSF/Motif Style Guide* all the guidelines have a usage level of *trial-use*.

Problem Reporting

If you have any problems with the software or documention, please contact your software vendor's customer service department.

Chapter 1

User Interface Design Principles

A user interface is simply the interface between an application and the user of an application. The primary goal of a user interface is to help user interface designers easily create applications that increase user effectiveness and satisfaction. By following the guidelines presented in this *OSF/Motif Style Guide*, you can create applications that are well designed and easy to use. These guidelines pertain to all sorts of applications, from spreadsheets and word processors to CAD tools.

To be effective, a user interface allows a user to interact with an application simply and naturally. Successful user interface designers keep the user in mind while designing an application. Keep the user in mind by following these two principles:

- Know the user.

- Empower the user.

The user of an application, above all, wants to get the job done. A user interface needs to be designed so the user can quickly and easily complete the tasks. Users want mastery over an application. Make it simple for the user to master the basics of your application. At the same time, you can include advanced methods of interaction with the application, shortcuts for the user. Users are curious and exploratory. They will find these shortcuts as they use and master the application. Such shortcuts need not be as intuitive as the regular methods of interaction.

This chapter discusses the following guidelines for creating user interfaces that are consistent and easy to use. Because of the particular nature of your client application, component, or window manager, or in response to customers' needs, you may not be able to apply all of these principles all of the time.

- Adopt the user's perspective.

- Give the user control.

- Use real-world metaphors.

- Keep interfaces natural.

- Keep interfaces consistent.

- Communicate application actions to the user.

- Avoid common design pitfalls.

1.1 Adopt the User's Perspective

Effective design starts with adopting the user's point of view, which is often difficult to do. Application designers tend to see an application as the implementation of functions. In contrast, the user sees an application in terms of its interface.

Good design is rooted in an understanding of the user's work. A well-designed application solves users' problems, makes their work easier, and offers them new capabilities. The two most effective ways to understand the user's work are to involve users in the design and to be a user yourself.

Input from users can help determine both appropriate functions and methods for presenting them. Involve users as early as possible in the design process because, as the design progresses and the schedule closes in, the possibilities for design change decrease.

You do not need a working prototype to involve users. In fact, you can even involve users while you are writing specifications. At this stage, you can watch users work in order to understand the environment in which your application will be used. Talk to these users about their work, their current tools, and their goals for new tools.

For example, if you are designing software to create and display charts and graphs during meetings, you might attend meetings at various customer sites, see how charts and graphs are currently used in meetings, and interview meeting participants to learn what they would like to see in a new tool. Once you have a working prototype of your application, invite users to test it to see if your interface meets the goals you established for it.

Try to use your application in real situations. Using an application can provide critical insights into user interface problems. Acquiring experience with the application can be difficult and time consuming, but it is a worthwhile exercise. Before you even create the interface for your application, you can use similar applications, even competitive products, to help you understand the user's tasks.

1.2 Give the User Control

Users want and need to be in control of the tools they use to perform their work. The user can be in control when an application is flexible and uses progressive disclosure.

1.2.1 Keep Interfaces Flexible

Providing multiple ways for users to access application functions and accomplish their tasks increases their sense of control. Flexibility enables users to select the best method of accessing a function based on the criteria they choose: experience level, personal preference, unique situation, or simply habit. For example, a user can access a function through a Pulldown Menu, direct manipulation of an object, a mnemonic key press, or a keyboard accelerator.

Your application should also be configurable. Allowing users to configure settings and select personal preferences enhances their sense of control and encourages them to take an active role in understanding your product and how it works. To be effective, the configurability of your application needs to be easily accessible.

1.2.2 Use Progressive Disclosure

Design your application so that the necessary and common functions are presented first and in a logical order. Make the more sophisticated and less frequently used functions hidden from immediate view, but still available. For example, use a DialogBox to hide settings that are not accessed often.

Decisions about the placement of functions are not easy to make. From the implementation standpoint, all functions are important. Often, however, a relatively small number of functions account for the majority of use. Make sure that these important functions are prominently featured in the presentation of the interface. Also remember that they can be prominent only if other functions are hidden.

1.3 Use Real-World Metaphors

A good user interface allows the user to transfer skills from real-world experiences. For example, PushButtons push, and Scales slide. This makes it easier for the user to infer how to use an application. When you design a new component, consider how a similar real-world control performs to incorporate the metaphor into the new component. Real-world metaphors can extend to groups of components as well, especially when making a computer-based user interface to replace a mechanical user interface.

1.3.1 Allow Direct Manipulation

Users need to be able to directly manipulate elements of the user interface and their applications. For example, the user needs to be able to directly scroll Text with a ScrollBar, rather than using a keyboard-driven command. Direct manipulation simulates the real world where the user employs tools to perform tasks on physical objects. Users control applications by directly manipulating graphical components similar to real-world controls, rather than entering a command on a command line. Direct manipulation reduces the amount of information the user needs to memorize.

Direct manipulation connects an action to an observable response from a component. Using direct manipulation, the user gets an immediate visible result from each action.

The direct manipulation model is an object-action model. That is, you first select an object or group of objects, then you perform an action on the selected objects. An object-action model allows the user to see what elements will be acted on before performing an action. It also allows multiple actions to be performed successively on the selected elements.

Although it is important to allow direct manipulation of the objects in your application, you must also support methods for interacting with your application by keyboard-only users. These methods can also be used by advanced users to perform some tasks more quickly.   *

1.3.2 Provide Rapid Response

Make your application respond to input as rapidly as possible. The immediacy of the visual response is crucial to the experience of direct manipulation. When using components, provide the application's response immediately and in proportion to the component's actions. The application * must also have a consistent speed of response. Delays, disproportionate responses, or inconsistent responses can render an otherwise well-designed application unusable. Performance problems make it difficult for the user to concentrate on the task at hand.

1.3.3 Provide Output as Input

Another feature of direct manipulation is that the output of one part of an application or the output of the application itself is also available as input. For example, if one action produces a list of filenames, another action can select them for use elsewhere.

The user manipulates objects by locating them and clicking on them rather than typing in their names. Design so that the only time the user needs to type a name is to create an object. A well-designed application reduces the amount of information the user needs to memorize to perform tasks.

1.4 Keep Interfaces Natural

You can extend the concepts of giving the user control and using real-world metaphors to arrange your application so that tasks flow naturally. Users need to be able to anticipate the natural progression of each task; through this anticipation, they are able to complete tasks more quickly.

Each screen object needs to have a distinct appearance that the user can easily recognize and quickly understand. At the same time, the style of the interface needs to graphically unify these elements and ensure a consistent and attractive appearance at any screen resolution.

1.4.1 Make Navigation Easy

Make navigation easy by providing a straightforward presentation of the overall work area and the mechanisms for moving through it. Moving easily and quickly within the work area gives the user a sense of mastery over the application. For example, ScrollBars are an effective way to indicate the position of the current view in relation to an area as a whole. In addition to providing positional feedback, ScrollBars allow the user to move through the area.

Arrange elements on the screen according to their use; an optimal arrangement assists the user's decision-making processes and reduces the possibility of errors. The best approach for arranging screen elements according to use is to involve users in the arrangement process. Present screen objects in an orderly, simple, and uncluttered manner.

Reduce mouse movement to simplify the actions of the user. For example, place secondary DialogBoxes near their parent DialogBox so that when the secondary DialogBox appears, the mouse pointer is over the default PushButton, unless the user needs to see the contents of the original DialogBox. Reducing mouse movement helps make an interface natural because, from the user's point of view, work involves a stream of thoughts, intentions, and tasks (some predefined and some that become apparent during the process) that all relate to some desired outcome or accomplishment. This stream of thought is disrupted when the user has to make unnecessary mouse movements, open and close DialogBoxes, or search for commands.

1.4.2 Provide Natural Shades and Colors

Minimize the contrast between screen objects in order to direct the user's attention. Appropriate use of contrast helps the user distinguish screen objects against the background of a window. Very dark screen objects on a light background, very bright objects on a dark background, and bright colors all command the user's attention. If there are many objects with strong contrast or bright colors on the screen, the user will have difficulty knowing where to look first because all these objects compete equally for attention.

Use color as a redundant aspect of the interface; that is, use it to provide additional differentiation among screen objects. Differentiation also comes from the shape and size of the screen objects. For example, in many parts of the world, stop signs are red octagons. You recognize the stop sign by both its shape and color.

1.5 Keep Interfaces Consistent

The main purpose of the *OSF/Motif Style Guide* is to ensure consistency. Consistency is important both among applications and within a single application. Consistency helps the user transfer familiar skills to new situations. The user can apply the knowledge learned from one application to another application, reducing the amount of learning and subsequent recall. Consistency within applications facilitates exploration of new functions. When components work in a manner that is consistent with other components, the user will be less afraid to try new functions. The new functions will seem familiar, comfortable, and appropriate. The guidelines in the *OSF/Motif Style Guide* allow you to create applications that are consistent in a diverse market and that help your applications succeed in the marketplace.

Intraapplication consistency means the following:

- Similar components operate similarly and have similar uses.

  For example, because Pulldown, Popup, and Option Menus are similar components, their operation and use should be similar. Choosing the proper component is described in Section 6.1. Component interaction is described in the reference section for each component and also in Section 6.3.

- The same action should always have the same result.

  For example, pushing the top arrow in a ScrollBar should always move the ScrollBar up. Interaction is described in Section 6.3.

- The function of components should not change based on context.

  For example, clicking a button should always perform the same action. Note that even though the action is the same, the result of the action can depend on context. A button in a file editor can begin editing one of a number of files. The button need not always edit the same file; rather, its consistent action is to edit the selected file. Interaction is described in Section 6.3.

- The position of components should not change based on context.

  Components should not generally be added and removed as needed. This makes it difficult to quickly find the desired component. Instead, you should make unneeded components nonfunctional and indicate this by deemphasizing (graying out) their labels. Component layout is described in Section 6.2.

- The position of the mouse pointer should not warp.

  The location of the mouse pointer should be determined by direct manipulation and should not be positioned arbitrarily by the application. Positioning the mouse pointer by the application causes the user to lose track of the pointer. Warping the pointer also causes problems with tablet style pointing devices that rely on absolute pointer positioning. The input model is described in Chapter 2.

Consistency among applications increases the user's sense of mastery. Experience with one application can be readily applied to another application, creating a positive transfer of knowledge. The task at hand, rather than learning a new application, becomes the focus of a computer session. When applications work in a manner that is consistent with other applications, users enjoy a feeling of immediate confidence in their ability to master the new program. Also, they are pleasantly surprised when trying new functions because, although new, the functions seem familiar.

Interapplication consistency means the following:

- Components look familiar.

  This does not mean that components look exactly the same, but that the internal layout of components should be the same. Elements of appearance such as color, size, and thickness of beveled edges are less important to application interoperability. Component design and layout are described in the reference section for each component and also in Section 6.4.

- Interaction is familiar.

  When interaction is different among applications, it confuses the user and makes it difficult to concentrate on the task of the application. This applies to the behavior of components, input methods, selection models, and keyboard navigation. Interaction is described in Section 6.3.

- Components are organized in a familiar manner.

  The user needs to be able to quickly find the proper component for each task. Organizing the components according to consistent guidelines helps the user do this. Application layout guidelines are described in Section 6.2.

1.6 Communicate Application Actions to the User

Effective applications let the user know what is happening with the application, but without revealing implementation details. Proper communication between the user and the application increases user satisfaction. There are three guidelines for communicating from the application to the user: provide feedback, anticipate errors, and provide warnings.

1.6.1 Give the User Feedback

Feedback lets users know that the computer has received their input. Give users feedback whenever they have selected a component or Menu item by highlighting the component or Menu item in some way. In addition, if certain operations take more than a few seconds, you should let the user know that the computer is working on that operation by providing a message or by changing the pointer to a working pointer.

1.6.2 Anticipate Errors

Anticipate the errors that are likely to occur. By anticipating errors, you can avoid them in your design, enable the support of recovery attempts, and provide messages informing the user of the proper corrective action. For example, one technique for avoiding excessive error messages is to dim interface components when they cannot be used.

Context-sensitive help aids understanding, reduces errors, and eases recovery efforts. Help information text needs to be clear, concise, and written in everyday language. Help information needs to be readily accessible and just as readily removable.

Many users are most comfortable with learning how to use software applications when they use a natural, trial-and-error method. An undo function supports learning by trial and error by minimizing the cost of errors. An undo function allows the user to retract previous actions, and fosters a spirit of exploration and experimentation that is essential.

1.6.3 Use Explicit Destruction

Explicit destruction means that, when an action has irreversible negative consequences, it should require the user to take an explicit action to perform it. For example, while a worksheet can be saved simply by clicking on a Save PushButton, erasing the worksheet should require clicking on an Erase PushButton and answering a warning question like "Are you sure you want to erase this worksheet?" with a button click in the warning DialogBox.

Warnings protect the user from inadvertent destructive operations, yet allow the user to remain in control of the application. Warnings also encourage the user to experiment without fear of loss. Operations that can cause a serious or unrecoverable loss of data should warn the user of the consequences and request explicit confirmation.

1.7 Avoid Common Design Pitfalls

The process of achieving good design presents many challenges and potential pitfalls. The following guidelines can help you avoid common pitfalls:

- Pay attention to details.

  The details of an application express the sense of craft that you applied to the application. The details of an elegantly designed interface both please users and facilitate their work. For example, aligning the PushButtons of two related and overlapping DialogBoxes makes it easier for the user to activate new settings in an apparently seamless operation. Consistent capitalization of Menu items and DialogBox labels is a design detail that reduces textual distractions for the user.

- Do not finish prematurely.

  A common design pitfall is assuming too early that a design is complete. This tendency is aggravated by schedule pressures and difficulty in pinpointing the inadequacies of a design. While it is important to begin designing early, it is also important to allow for redesigning for as long as possible. The first design of an application is not a solution but a fresh perspective from which to view interface design problems.

- Design iteratively.

  Interface design is best done iteratively. The development cycle of implementation, feedback, evaluation, and change avoids errors by allowing for early recognition and correction of unproductive designs.

- Start with a fresh perspective.

  Avoid the temptation to convert existing software by simply translating it to a new style of interface. Because direct manipulation changes the way the user works, a simple one-to-one translation is unlikely to be successful. Command line applications that are converted to direct manipulation need to be extensively reconsidered and revised. The structure of the function hierarchy and presentation needs to be completely redesigned.

- Hide implementation details.

  User interfaces need to hide the underlying software and present a consistent interface to the user. A good user interface does not allow implementation details of the application to show through; it frees the user from focusing on the mechanics of an application.

Chapter 2

Input Models

Consistent models increase the user's sense of control of a system. By implementing consistent models across systems and applications, you encourage that sense of control. This chapter describes the models OSF/Motif uses to interact with the components:

- The keyboard focus model, which determines which component on the screen receives keyboard events.

- The input device model, which describes how different input devices, such as the keyboard and the mouse, interact with applications.

The navigation, activation, and selection models, also important for system and application consistency, are described in Chapters 3, 4, and 5.

2.1 The Keyboard Focus Model

A typical workspace can contain many windows. Each window will receive input from the keyboard, the mouse, or both. The window that receives keyboard events has the input focus. Indeed, when keyboard input is directed to a window, it is actually received by some control within the window. The **keyboard focus** model determines which window in the workspace and which component within that window gets each keyboard input. The keyboard focus may also be referred to as the input focus.

In order to avoid conflicts, the window manager must allow only one   *
window to have the keyboard focus at a time. The window with the   *
keyboard focus must be highlighted in some way, usually by a change in   *
shade or color to the window border. Each application must allow only one   *
component at a time to have the keyboard focus within the window that has   *
the keyboard focus.

The keyboard focus model is defined by a focus policy. A focus policy is a specific mechanism for moving the focus among windows and components. The focus policy can be different between windows than it is within windows. This section only attempts to describe the focus policies; however, their impact on window managers, applications, and components is described in detail where it applies. It is sufficient at this point to note   *
that window managers, applications, and new components must support both   *
explicit and implicit focus policies. Chapter 7 describes in detail how to move the focus among windows that use explicit and implicit focus policies.

2.1.1 Implicit Focus

In the **implicit focus** policy, the keyboard focus tracks the mouse pointer. No explicit action (other than mouse motion) is performed to set the keyboard focus in the implicit focus model. When an implicit focus policy is used at the window level, keyboard events are sent to the window that the mouse pointer is in. When an implicit focus policy is used within a window, keyboard events are sent to the component that the mouse pointer is in. In implicit mode, the keyboard focus tracks the mouse pointer. Because of this, there is no way to move the keyboard focus from the keyboard using implicit mode. Implicit focus is sometimes referred to as pointer, track pointer, or track listener policy, or as being real-estate driven. In this focus policy, the location cursor for keyboard events does not need to be shown except in components like Text, in which keyboard input is common; however, the application can show it.

2.1.2 Explicit Focus

The **explicit focus** policy requires the user to explicitly select which window or component receives the keyboard focus. In explicit focus mode at the window level, a user moves the keyboard focus to a window by pressing **BSelect** while the mouse pointer is over the window. Simply moving the mouse pointer over a window does not give the window the keyboard focus. Because of this, explicit mode is often called click-to-type. In explicit mode within a window, a user generally moves the keyboard focus to a specific component within a window by pressing **BSelect** over the component. Pressing **BSelect** must not move focus to a component that is   * not traversable or does not accept input. Pressing **BSelect** in a component that is used only to change the visible portion of another component, such as a ScrollBar or Sash, should act on that component but should not move focus to it. In this focus policy, the location of keyboard focus must be   * shown by a location cursor.

In explicit mode, focus can also be moved among windows by the keyboard using **<Alt> <F6>**, **<Alt> <Tab>**, **<Alt> <Shift> <Tab>**, and **<Alt> <Shift> <F6>**.

In explicit mode, keyboard focus moves explicitly among the components in a window as well as among the windows. Moving the keyboard focus among components in a window using the keyboard is called **component navigation**. Keyboard events go to the component in the window with the keyboard focus. Keyboard focus is moved among components using **<Tab>**, **<Ctrl> <Tab>**, **<Shift> <Tab>**, **<Ctrl> <Shift> <Tab>**, **<F10>**, **<Menu>**, **<↓>**, **<←>**, **<→>**, and **<↑>**. Internal window navigation is described in detail in Chapter 3.

If the focus policy is implicit, an implementation can still enable keyboard-based operations that explicitly move the location cursor. It must at least   * implement the special cases for Menu traversal as described in Chapter 3. **<F10>** (or **<Shift> <Menu>** if **<F10>** is not available) moves the cursor to the MenuBar. **<Menu>** (or **<Shift> <F10>** if **<Menu>** is not available) pops up a Popup Menu.

2.2 The Input Device Model

User interface applications can take input from both pointing devices and keyboards. For whatever reason, a user may prefer to interact with an application by using either a keyboard or a pointing device. Some users may even be restricted to using only a keyboard. Because of these preferences and possible restrictions, all application functionality must be *
available from the keyboard alone.

Design your application so that the user can control it using a pointing device, the keyboard, or both. Although you can decide to make the pointing device the primary means of control, you must provide the user *
with keyboard methods to control the application. Designing applications for dual accessibility enables users to choose the input device they find best suited to their particular work situation and personal preferences.

Certain disabled users are unable to keep modifier keys pressed while typing another key. Underlying window systems should provide a mode in which a typed modifier key acts as if it remains pressed until the next nonmodifier key is typed.

2.2.1 Pointing Devices

A pointing device is a tool that lets the user move a pointer around on the screen. A pointing device also has some means of activating the object under the pointer. A pointing device allows the user to directly manipulate screen objects. Rather than entering a keyboard command for each action, a user can point to an object and directly manipulate it using the pointing device.

The most typical pointing device is a mouse, although a graphics tablet, track ball, joystick, and other tools also work as pointing devices. Throughout this guide we use the term mouse to refer to all pointing devices. You can use any pointing device in place of a mouse.

With a mouse, objects on the screen can be manipulated by combining the mouse pointer with the mouse buttons. This guide assumes that a mouse, or any pointing device, has three buttons:

BSelect   Used for selection, activation, and setting the location cursor. *
This button must be the leftmost button, except for left-handed *
users where it can be the rightmost button.

BTransfer Used for moving and copying elements. This button must be the middle mouse button, unless dragging is integrated with selection. Details about the effects of integrating **BTransfer** with **BSelect** are described in Section 4.3.5.

BMenu Used for popping up Menus. This button must be the rightmost button, except for left-handed users, where it can be the leftmost button.

If your pointing device only has two buttons, **BSelect** still must be bound to the leftmost button. There are a number of alternatives to properly binding **BTransfer** and **BMenu**:

- The mouse can be treated as a 3-button mouse if chording the two buttons is treated as the third button. Chording buttons means to press, click, or release two or more buttons simultaneously. The chorded buttons can be treated as the second or third button on a 3-button mouse, in which case the unchorded buttons are treated as the first and third, or first and second buttons, respectively.

- Alternatively, **BTransfer** can be bound to the rightmost button, and **BMenu** is then bound to **<Alt> BSelect**.

- Finally, **BMenu** can be bound to the rightmost button, and **BTransfer** is then integrated with the selection button.

As with a 3-button mouse, the actions of the rightmost and leftmost mouse buttons can be switched for left-handed users.

If your mouse has only one button, **BSelect** must be bound to it, **BTransfer** can be integrated with **BSelect**, and **BMenu** must be bound to **<Alt> BSelect**. Mouse-based primary and quick transfer mechanisms are unavailable using a 1-button mouse.

If your mouse has more than three buttons, the first three correspond to those on a 3-button mouse.

Users can combine mouse button press and release actions along with mouse movements to activate elements of applications and components.

Various mouse button actions are described as follows, along with this guide's usage conventions:

Press Indicates pressing a mouse button without releasing it. This mouse action is often used to select an object for action. This guide uses **BSelect Press** to indicate a press on the first mouse button.

Release Indicates releasing a mouse button after pressing it. This mouse action is often used to perform the action initiated by a press or a drag. This guide uses **BSelect Release** to indicate a release on the first mouse button.

Click Indicates pressing and releasing a mouse button without moving the pointer. This mouse action is used to select an object or perform an action. The activation action actually occurs on the release of the mouse button. This guide uses **BSelect Click** to indicate a click on the first mouse button.

Motion Indicates pressing a mouse button without releasing it and then moving the position of the pointer. The action of a drag operation tracks the position of the mouse pointer. The drag action ends with a release action. This mouse action is commonly used to select a range of objects, or move a selected object. This guide uses **BSelect Motion** to indicate a drag using the first mouse button.

MultiClick Indicates a number of clicks in quick succession. MultiClicks are often referred to by the actual number of clicks, as in double-click or triple-click. A double-click is often used to perform the default action of an object. This guide uses **BSelect Click 2** to indicate a double-click on the first mouse button, **BSelect Click 3** to indicate a triple-click, and so on. This guide uses **BSelect Click 2+** to indicate two or more clicks on the first mouse button.

MultiPress Indicates a number of clicks in quick succession without a final release. As in MultiClick, MultiPresses are often referred to by the actual number of presses. This guide uses **BSelect Press 2** and the variations mentioned in MultiClick to indicate MultiPress actions on the first mouse button.

MultiMotion Indicates a MultiPress action followed by moving the position of the pointer. The action of a MultiMotion operation tracks the position of the mouse pointer. The MultiMotion action ends with a release action. As in MultiClick, MultiMotions are often referred to by the actual number of presses. This guide uses **BSelect Motion 2** and the variations mentioned in MultiClick to indicate MultiMotion actions using the first mouse button.

2.2.2 Pointer Shapes

The shape of the mouse pointer provides the user with an important visual cue, indicating the functionality of the area in which the mouse pointer is currently located. You should not create new mouse pointer shapes for functions that already have mouse pointer shapes associated with them, except for localization, but you can create new mouse pointer shapes for functions not already associated with a pointer shape. You should not use a predefined shape to symbolize a function that it was not designed to represent.

A list of the defined pointer shapes follows, along with their usage and hotspots. A pointer's hotspot is the actual position on the pointer that tracks the movements of the mouse. As the pointer changes from one shape to another, the location of the hotspot must not move on the screen. The hotspot is the precise location on the pointer where mouse actions occur.

    The upper-left pointing arrow pointer is a general-purpose pointer. It is used in most window areas for single-object selection and activation. The hotspot for the arrow pointer should be in the point of the arrow.

    You can optionally use an I-beam pointer in any Text component. It is used to change the location of the text insertion cursor and to perform actions on text. If the I-beam is used, it can be hidden during the time between any keyboard action and a mouse movement. This helps the user distinguish the I-beam pointer from the text insertion cursor, which can also be an I-beam. The hotspot for the I-beam pointer should be on the vertical bar of the I-beam about one-third up from the bottom.

✖ The X pointer can indicate when the pointer is outside of any application area. The hotspot for the X pointer should be where the lines intersect.

The resize pointers indicate positions for area resize, and they remain during a resize operation. The direction of the arrow in the pointer indicates the direction of increasing size. The horizontal and vertical pointers indicate resize in either the horizontal or vertical direction. The diagonal pointers indicate resize in both the horizontal and vertical directions simultaneously. The hotspot for the resizing pointers should be on the elbow or the line at the position pointed to by the arrow.

The hourglass pointer, a working pointer, indicates that an action is in progress in the area, and that the pointer has no effect in the area. While the hourglass pointer is active, all mouse button and keyboard events are ignored in the area. The hotspot for the hourglass pointer should be located at the center of the hourglass, although it should not be used for activation. The hourglass pointer can be used interchangeably with the watch pointer.

The watch pointer, a working pointer, indicates that an action is in progress in the area, and that the pointer has no effect in the area. While the watch pointer is active, all mouse button and keyboard events are ignored in the area. The hotspot for the watch pointer should be located at the top of the watch, although it should not be used for activation. The watch pointer can be used interchangeably with the hourglass pointer.

The 4-directional arrow pointer indicates a move operation is in progress, or a resize operation before the resize direction has been determined. During a move operation, the object, or an outline of the object should move to track the location of the pointer. During a resize operation, the pointer is used to indicate a direction for resizing. The 4-directional arrow pointer should change to the appropriate resize arrow when the resize direction is determined, either by crossing an object boundary with the pointer or by pressing a keyboard direction key. The hotspot for the 4-directional arrow pointer should be at the spot where the arrows intersect.

+ The sighting pointer is used to make fine position selections. For example, in a drawing program it can be used to indicate a pixel to fill or the connecting points of lines. The hotspot for the sighting pointer should be at the spot where the lines intersect.

The caution pointer is used to indicate that action is expected in another area before input can be given to the current area, and that the pointer has no effect in the area. While the caution pointer is active, all mouse button and keyboard events are ignored in the area. The hotspot for the caution pointer should be located at the center of the caution symbol, although it should not be used for activation.

? The question pointer is used to request an input position or component from the user. This is often used to input an object for interactive help. The user requests interactive help, then the question pointer is displayed to allow the user to indicate what position or component help is requested for. The hotspot for the question pointer should be at the bottom of the question mark.

You can optionally use an arrow pointing to the upper-right corner to indicate a pending Menu action. This shape indicates that a Menu is popped up or pulled down and waiting for a Menu item to be activated or the Menu to be removed. The hotspot for this arrow pointer should be in the point of the arrow.

If you need to design a new mouse pointer shape, keep the following in mind:

- The shape of the pointer should give a hint to its purpose.
- The hotspot should be easy to locate, and obvious.
- The shape should be easy to see.
- The shape should not create visual clutter.

2.2.3 Gain and Acceleration

The details of how the pointer tracks the motion of the mouse are not handled at the level of the application, but they are worth noting here. There are two concepts that define how the pointer tracks the motion of the mouse: gain and acceleration.

Gain refers to the ratio of the distance the pointer moves to the distance the mouse moves. If the gain is increased, the mouse pointer moves farther for a given mouse movement. The gain should not change across the environment. Instead, if your application requires finer motion, it should include a zoom feature. A zoom feature changes the relative size of an area of your application. Zooming in on an area allows the user to make finer adjustments than normal. Zooming out from an area allows the user to move through the application more quickly.

Acceleration is a temporary change in the gain. It is commonly used to change the gain, based on the speed of the mouse movements. The acceleration could be set so that, if the mouse moves slowly, the gain is reduced to allow for finer adjustments of pointer position or, if the mouse moves quickly, the gain is increased to allow quicker screen movement. This can be very confusing to new users. Gain and acceleration are handled on a global scale in the system, outside of the application. Applications should not change the gain and acceleration characteristics of mouse movement.

2.2.4 Warp Pointer Only If Explicitly Enabled

The pointer position is intended only as input to applications. It is not intended as an output mechanism for applications. Changing the location of the mouse pointer is known as warping the pointer. Your application must   *
not warp the pointer, unless you provide the user with a means of disabling   *
this behavior.

Warping the pointer is confusing to users, and reduces their sense of control. Also, warping the pointer can cause problems for users of absolute location pointing devices (like graphics tablets). Graphics tablets map pointer device locations to absolute screen locations; so, if the pointer is warped, the pointer loses synchronization with the pointing device, making some screen locations impossible to reach. Note that for these types of devices, accelerating the pointer has the same effect as warping the pointer, but this can be handled by the pointer driver software.

Chapter 3

Navigation

Regardless of whether they use a mouse, a keyboard, or both, users need to move the location cursor to new positions. That is, they will need to navigate around the workspace. The model is simple for mouse users, and more complicated for keyboard users. This chapter describes the general navigation model for mouse and keyboard users, describes the more complicated Menu navigation model, and then describes navigation within scrollable components.

3.1 Mouse-Based Navigation

In mouse-based navigation, the mouse is used to move the focus among controls. If an implicit focus policy is in use, the keyboard focus simply follows the mouse pointer, and no other explicit action is required to change the focus.

With an explicit focus policy, pressing **BSelect** on a component must move * focus to it, except for components that are used to adjust the size and * location of other elements, such as ScrollBars. Pressing **BSelect** on these components need not move the focus. If not, after the mouse has acted on the component, the focus should remain on the component that previously had it. Pressing **BSelect** will also generally perform some selection or activation operation. Clicking **<Ctrl> BSelect** on an activatable component can move focus to it without any other effect.

The only exception to the simple model of pointer navigation is a Menu system because Menus are not available on the screen until activated. Activating a Menu causes it to be shown on the screen. There are three types of Menus: Pulldown Menus, Popup Menus, and Option Menus. The MenuBar is also a special kind of Menu. A **Menu system** consists of all the Menus cascading from a single CascadeButton, OptionButton, or Popup Menu. The **MenuBar system** consists of the MenuBar and all of its associated Menus.

A Pulldown Menu is generally activated by pressing **BSelect** on a CascadeButton, which displays the Pulldown Menu. A Popup Menu is generally activated by pressing **BMenu** in an area with a Popup Menu, which displays the Popup Menu. An Option Menu is generally activated by pressing **BSelect** on an OptionButton, which displays the Option Menu. A Pulldown Menu pulled down from a CascadeButton within a Pulldown, Popup, or Option Menu is called a Cascade Menu. A MenuBar is generally activated by moving the input focus to the MenuBar. Since a MenuBar is always visible, activating the MenuBar does not change its appearance. Navigating to a Menu is equivalent to activating a Menu.

Menus are activated in one of two ways: spring-loaded or posted. Spring-loaded means that the Menu is removed when the mouse button that activated it is released. Posted means that the Menu is not removed when the mouse button that activated it is released, but must be explicitly removed by another user action.

BSelect Press with the pointer on a Menu must activate the Menu in a ∗ spring-loaded manner. If the pointer is in an element with an inactive Popup ∗ Menu and the context of the element allows a Popup Menu to be displayed, ∗ **BMenu Press** must post (activate) the Menu in a spring-loaded manner. Note that the availability and contents of the Popup Menu can depend on the location of the pointer within the element, the contents of the element, or the selection state of the element. In the case where a Popup Menu can be ∗ posted by both an element and an element contained within it, the Popup ∗ Menu of the internal element must be posted.

Once a Popup Menu is posted, **BMenu** must behave just as **BSelect** is ∗ described for any Menu system. **BSelect** must also be available from within ∗ a posted Popup Menu system, and must behave just as in any Menu system. ∗ **BSelect Release** within a spring-loaded Menu system must activate the ∗

button under the pointer at the time of the release. If the release is on a *
CascadeButton or OptionButton and the associated Cascade Menu was *
already posted at the time **BSelect** was pressed, it should be unposted; *
otherwise, the associated Cascade Menu must be posted.

Whenever any Menu is popped up or pulled down, the location cursor must *
be placed on the Menu's default entry, or on the first entry in the Menu if *
there is no default entry. Support for default entries in Menus is optional.

A spring-loaded Menu must be removed when the mouse button that *
activated it is released, except when the button is released on a *
CascadeButton in the Menu hierarchy. While a spring-loaded Menu system *
is popped up or pulled down, moving the pointer within the Menu system *
must move the location cursor to track the pointer. If the pointer rests on a *
CascadeButton, the Menu must be pulled down and must also become *
traversable. The Menu must be removed, possibly after a short delay, once *
the pointer moves to a Menu item outside of the Menu or its CascadeButton. *
If the Menu system is part of a MenuBar, moving the pointer to any other *
element on the MenuBar must unpost the current Menu system and post the *
Pulldown Menu associated with the new element. Releasing the button *
must activate any component in the Menu system, including a *
CascadeButton. Note that releasing the mouse button during a spring-
loaded Menu operation in a CascadeButton, even a CascadeButton in the
MenuBar, causes the associated Menu to remain posted.

BMenu Click with the pointer in an area with a Popup Menu that was not *
previously posted must activate the Menu in a posted manner. **BMenu
Release** with the pointer in an area with a Popup Menu that was posted prior
to the associated **BMenu Press** should unpost the Menu.

A posted Menu remains visible until explicitly unposted. The keyboard
focus model is forced to explicit, and the Menu system can be traversed
using the keyboard as described later in this section.

If a mouse button is pressed outside of the Menu to unpost the Menu, the
button press can also be treated as follows:

- The button press can have no effect other than to unpost the Menu.

- The button press can be passed to the underlying component, either
  always or only if some condition is met. For example, it can be passed
  to the underlying component only if the component is in the same
  window as the Menu system.

- Whether or not the button press is passed to the underlying component, it can have some other effect. For example, it can raise and give focus to the underlying window.

If the button press that unposts a Menu is not also passed to the underlying component, subsequent events up to and including the button release must not be passed to the underlying component. *
*

Once a Pulldown or Option Menu is posted, **BSelect Press** in the Menu system must cause the Menu to behave as a spring-loaded Menu. Once a Popup Menu is posted, **BSelect Press** or **BMenu Press** in the Menu system must cause the Menu to behave as a spring-loaded Menu. Because of this, the pointer-driven activation behavior of spring-loaded Menus fully describes pointer-driven activation behavior in Menus. *
*
*

3.2 Keyboard-Based Navigation

The navigation model for keyboard users is more complicated than the pointer navigation model. As described earlier, keyboard navigation is only required when the focus policy is explicit. Since window managers, applications, and components must support the explicit focus policy, they must also support keyboard navigation. The keyboard navigation model is composed of the following: *
*

- A focus identifier (the location cursor)
- Navigating among windows
- Navigating within windows

3.2.1 Location Cursor

The window with the focus is identified by highlighting the window border as described in Chapter 7. Within the window with the focus, the component with the keyboard focus is identified by the location cursor. The term location cursor refers to any visual element that indicates the location where keyboard events are sent. The location cursor is not strictly a cursor. The name *cursor* simply refers to its use as indicating the location of input.

The location cursor is shown in a number of ways, depending on the type of component with the keyboard focus. Possible location cursor types and their uses are described in the following text. When designing new components, you should try to use one of the existing styles of location cursor, but you can create your own if it is appropriate.

Box   The box cursor should be the default location cursor. It is shown as a box drawn around the object. Figure 3-1 shows the first ToggleButton in a group with a box style location cursor.

Figure 3–1. A Box Style Location Cursor

Outline Highlight

This cursor style is similar to the box style cursor. The outline is shown of a component whose outline is not normally shown. This form of location cursor is commonly used within Menu systems to show the Menu item with the location cursor. Figure 3-2 shows a Menu with an outline highlight style location cursor.

Figure 3–2. An Outline Highlight Style Location Cursor

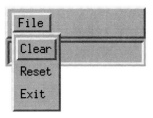

Text Cursor

In Text components, the text cursor acts as the location cursor to indicate that the Text component has the keyboard focus. Figure 3-3 shows possible text cursor shapes.

Figure 3–3. Text Cursor Shapes

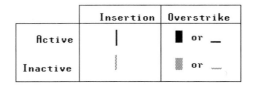

A text cursor must be shown differently when the Text does and   *
does not have the keyboard focus. This can be done by

- Darkening the cursor when the Text has focus and graying the
  cursor when the Text does not have focus

- Using a blinking cursor when the Text has focus and a static
  cursor when the Text does not have focus

- Showing the cursor when the Text has focus and hiding the
  cursor when the Text does not have focus

If the text cursor is hidden when the Text component does not have   *
the focus and if the component gets the focus, the text cursor must   *
reappear at the same position it had when the component lost focus.
A Text component can optionally include an outline highlight style
location cursor to reinforce the location of the keyboard focus.
Figure 3-4 shows a Text component with the keyboard focus.

Figure 3–4. A Text Cursor Style Location Cursor

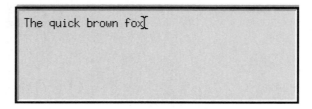

Item Cursor

A component that manages groups of elements, like a List, should
indicate that it has the keyboard focus with an item cursor style
location cursor. An item cursor highlights a single element, or
group of elements, that the component acts on. In the case of a List,
the item cursor should be a box around an element. In the case of a

Drawing area, it could be a box with resize handles around a drawn element. Components that use an item cursor to indicate keyboard focus can optionally include an outline highlight style location cursor to reinforce the location of the keyboard focus. Figure 3-5 shows a List component with the keyboard focus.

Figure 3–5. An Item Cursor Style Location Cursor

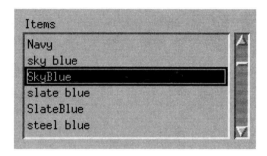

Fill   Some very small components, like a Sash for resizing Panes, should indicate the keyboard focus by filling. Where this is the case, there   *
must be no other meaning associated with the filled state. Filling avoids the problem caused by other styles of location cursor that make the small component too large. Figure 3-6 shows the first of two Sashes with the keyboard focus.

Figure 3–6. A Fill Style Location Cursor

Components must be designed and positioned within applications so that   *
adding and removing the component's location cursor does not change the   *
amount of space that the component takes up on the screen; that is, there is always room for the location cursor.

3.2.2 Window Navigation

A typical environment has several applications in operation simultaneously. Each application typically has a main or primary window that displays data and in which the user carries on primary interaction with the application. Applications can have additional windows to communicate context-specific interactions with the user of the application. These additional windows are called secondary windows, or transient windows. DialogBoxes are often used to create secondary windows.

The **window navigation** model can be divided into two levels:

- Moving among window families (among primary windows)
- Moving within a window family (among secondary windows)

A window family consists of a single primary window and all of its associated secondary windows. **<Alt> <F6>** and **<Alt> <Shift> <F6>** move the focus among windows in a window family. **<Alt> <Tab>** and **<Alt> <Shift> <Tab>** move the focus among window families. Window navigation is described in more detail in Chapter 7.

3.2.3 Component Navigation

Component navigation moves the location cursor, and therefore the keyboard focus, among components in a window. The window is divided into fields, and operations that use the **<Tab>** key move the cursor from one field to another. For this reason, fields are also known as tab groups. The directional keys **<↓>**, **<↑>**, **<→>**, and **<←>** are used for navigation within a field.

Menu systems, including the MenuBar, follow a different traversal model, described in Section 3.3.

A field can be an individual control, such as a Text control. In this case, the directional keys are used for internal navigation within the control. Alternately, a field can consist of a group of controls such as a RadioBox, which holds a group of RadioButtons. In this case, the directional keys are used to navigate among the component controls of the group.

The fields in a window are ordered. **<Tab>** generally moves the location cursor to the next field, and **<Shift> <Tab>** moves the location cursor to the previous field. However, a field can use **<Tab>** and **<Shift> <Tab>** for internal navigation. For example, within a multiline Text control, **<Tab>** is used to tab within the text. Consequently, **<Ctrl> <Tab>** must always navigate to the next field, and **<Ctrl> <Shift> <Tab>** must always navigate to the previous field. *

<Tab> (if not used for internal navigation) and **<Ctrl> <Tab>** must move the location cursor forward through fields according to the following rules: *

- If the next field is a control, **<Tab>** (if not used for internal navigation) and **<Ctrl> <Tab>** must move the location cursor to that control. *

- If the next field is a group, **<Tab>** (if not used for internal navigation) and **<Ctrl> <Tab>** must move the location cursor to a traversable component within the group. If the field contains a button that currently shows default highlighting, the location cursor should be placed on that button; otherwise, the first control in the field (the top-leftmost one in a left-to-right language environment) should get focus. *

If the next field contains no traversable components, **<Tab>** (if not used for internal navigation) and **<Ctrl> <Tab>** must skip the field. Note that Separators and Labels should not be traversable. The ScrollBars of ScrolledWindows also should not be traversable, particularly if a **<ScrollLock>** key is available on the keyboard. *

<Shift> <Tab> (if not used for internal navigation) and **<Ctrl> <Shift> <Tab>** must move the location cursor backward through fields in the order opposite to that of **<Tab>** (if not used for internal navigation) and **<Ctrl> <Tab>**. *

When a window acquires focus, the location cursor must be placed on the control that last had focus in the window, providing that all the following conditions are met: *

- The window uses an explicit keyboard focus policy. *

- The window acquires the focus through keyboard navigation or through a button press other than within the client area of the window. *

- The window had the focus at some time in the past. *

- The control that last had focus in the window is still traversable. *

If the component that last had focus is no longer traversable, or if the window has not previously had the focus, the location cursor should be placed on the component with which the user is most likely to want to interact. In a DialogBox, this is often a text control or a default button. If no such control exists, the location cursor should be placed in the first field in the window—in a left-to-right language environment, the top-leftmost field.

Developers should follow these general rules for field navigation:

- Fields should be traversed from the upper left to the lower right in a left-to-right language environment. In a right-to-left language environment, fields should be traversed from the upper right to the lower left.

- Field navigation must wrap between the first and last fields of the   * window.

- In a PanedWindow, each Pane should consist of one or more fields, and each Sash should be a field. Fields in a PanedWindow should be traversed in the following order:

  1. All fields in the topmost Pane

  2. The topmost Sash

  3. All fields in the next Pane toward the bottom

  4. The next Sash toward the bottom

  and so on, to the bottom of the PanedWindow.

Directional keys are used both for component navigation within a field and for internal purposes, including internal navigation, within a control.

When <↓> and <↑> are used for component navigation within a field, they   * must behave in the following way: *

- In a left-to-right language environment, <↓> must move the location   * cursor through all traversable controls in the field, starting at the upper   * left and ending at the lower right, then wrapping to the upper left. If the   * controls are aligned in a matrix-like arrangement, <↓> must first   * traverse one column from top to bottom, then traverse the column to its   * right, and so on. In a right-to-left language environment, <↓> must   * move the location cursor through all traversable controls, starting at the   * upper right and ending at the lower left.   *

- <↑> must move the location cursor through all traversable controls in   * the field in the order opposite to that of <↓>.   *

When <→> and <←> are used for component navigation within a field, they *
must behave in the following way: *

- In a left-to-right language environment, <→> must move the location *
cursor through all traversable controls in the field, starting at the upper *
left and ending at the lower right, then wrapping to the upper left. If the *
controls are aligned in a matrix-like arrangement, <→> must first *
traverse one row from left to right, then traverse the row below it, and so *
on. In a right-to-left language environment, <→> must move the *
location cursor through all traversable controls, starting at the lower left *
and ending at the upper right. *

- <←> must move the location cursor through all traversable controls in *
the field in the order opposite to that of <→>. *

Controls that use directional keys internally—such as Text, List, Canvas,
Sash, ScrollBar, and Scale—should be fields. If a control that uses *
directional keys internally does not act like a field, the directional keys must *
be used for both internal purposes and component navigation.

In particular, controls can use directional keys in one dimension for internal
purposes and in another dimension for component navigation. For example,
a vertically organized group of single-line Text controls can be grouped
together as a single field. <↓> and <↑> navigate among the single-line Text
controls in the field. <→>, <Ctrl> <→>, <←>, and <Ctrl> <←> navigate
among characters and words within an individual single-line Text control.

The directional keys modified with **<Ctrl>** can also be used for component
navigation, following the same rules specified above. If the directional keys
modified with **<Ctrl>** are used for component navigation, the unmodified
directional keys can be used for internal purposes.

For example, a table can consist of an array of single-word Text controls,
with <↑> and <↓> used to navigate up and down a column. <→> and <←>
can navigate among characters within an individual single-word Text
control, while **<Ctrl>** <→> and **<Ctrl>** <←> navigate horizontally among
the Text components in a row.

Within a control, the directional keys can be used in a variety of ways. In
list-like controls, or in graphics-like controls in which the elements are laid
out in a matrix-like arrangement, internal navigation using the directional
keys should move the cursor among elements using the same rules followed
for component navigation. However, if the control is scrollable, directional
navigation should not wrap between the first and last elements of the

control; a directional key that would otherwise cause wrapping should have no effect at the first or last element.

Additional internal navigation techniques may be needed in situations not covered by this guide, such as the following:

- Graphics-like controls in which the elements are densely populated or are organized into layers

- Applications that use 3-dimensional navigation

- Applications that organize elements hierarchically

In such cases, navigation models should not deviate unnecessarily from the standard navigation models.

Rather than move the cursor among elements, a graphics-like control can use a positional cursor. In this case, <↓>, <↑>, <→>, and <←> must internally navigate by moving the cursor one unit (for example, one pixel) at a time in the direction indicated by the key. In this model, the cursor is sometimes on an element and sometimes in the background of the control.

The use of the directional keys for internal navigation in text-like controls is described in the Text reference page in Chapter 9. In a control that displays a value, the directional keys can increment or decrement that value.

When the directional keys cause changes that are based on some unit, the directional keys modified by **<Ctrl>** can cause changes based on a larger unit. For example:

- In Text, <→> moves the cursor a character to the right, and **<Ctrl>** <→> moves the cursor a word to the right.

- In a Canvas, <→> can move a positional cursor one pixel to the right, and **<Ctrl>** <→> can move the cursor some number of pixels to the right.

- In a Scale, <→> can increment the Scale value by one unit indicated by minor tick marks, and **<Ctrl>** <→> can increment the Scale value by an amount corresponding to the distance between major tick marks.

If a control uses <→> and <←> for internal navigation, it must support the following behavior:

<Begin>   In a left-to-right language environment, this action must move the location cursor to the leftmost edge of the data or the leftmost element. In a right-to-left language environment, this action must move

the location cursor to the rightmost edge of the data   *
or the rightmost element.   *

\<End\>   In a left-to-right language environment, this action   *
must move the location cursor to the rightmost edge   *
of the data or the rightmost element. In a right-to-   *
left language environment, this action must move   *
the location cursor to the leftmost edge of the data   *
or the leftmost element.   *

If a control uses $\langle\uparrow\rangle$ and $\langle\downarrow\rangle$ for internal navigation, it must support the   *
following behavior: *

\<Ctrl\> \<Begin\>   This action must move the location cursor to one of   *
the following: *

- The first element   *

- The topmost edge of the data   *

- In a left-to-right language environment, the   *
  topmost left edge of the data; in a right-to-left   *
  language environment, the topmost right edge   *
  of the data   *

\<Ctrl\> \<End\>   This action must move the location cursor to one of   *
the following: *

- The last element   *

- The bottommost edge of the data   *

- In a left-to-right language environment, the   *
  bottommost right edge of the data; in a right-   *
  to-left language environment, the bottommost   *
  left edge of the data   *

Groups that are fields can also use **\<Begin\>**, **\<End\>**, **\<Ctrl\> \<Begin\>**, and
\<Ctrl\> \<End\> to move the location cursor to appropriate controls within
the group.

3.3 Menu Traversal

The Menu traversal model is different from the field traversal model. This
allows Menus to be traversable even when the focus policy is implicit. If a
Menu is traversed to while the focus policy in the application is implicit, the
focus policy must temporarily change to explicit. The focus policy must
revert to implicit whenever the user traverses out of the Menu system.

Traversing to a Menu system is the same as activating the Menu system. If
the MenuBar is inactive, **<F10>** must traverse to, or activate, the MenuBar
system. The location cursor must be placed on the first traversable
CascadeButton in the MenuBar. If there are no traversable CascadeButtons
in the MenuBar, **<F10>** must do nothing. Note that **<Shift>** **<Menu>** is
used on systems where **<F10>** is not available.

If the keyboard focus is on an element with an inactive Popup Menu and the
context of the element allows a Popup Menu to be displayed, **<Menu>** must
post (activate) the Popup Menu. The location cursor must be placed on the
default item of the Menu, or the first traversable item if there is no default
item. Note that the availability of the Popup Menu can depend on the
location of the cursor within the element, the contents of the element, or the
selection state of the element. Menus popped up from the keyboard should
be in the context of the insertion position of the element with the location
cursor. If there are no traversable items in the Popup Menu, it is up to the
system and the application whether to post the Menu or not. Note that
<Shift> **<F10>** is used on systems where **<Menu>** is not available.

If the keyboard focus is in an OptionButton, **<Select>** or **<Space>** must post
the Option Menu. The location cursor must be placed on the previously
selected item in the Option Menu. If the Option Menu is pulled down for
the first time, the location cursor must be placed on the default item in the
Menu. If there are no traversable items in the Option Menu, the application
should decide whether to post the Menu or not. If there is an active Option
Menu, **<Enter>**, **<Return>**, **<Select>**, or **<Space>** must select the current
item in the Option Menu, unpost the active Option Menu system, and return
the location cursor to the OptionButton.

Once a Menu system is posted, the Menu items can be traversed using <↓>,
<←>, <→>, and <↑>. A posted Menu system behaves somewhat like a
field, with the addition of traversing among Menus in the system. When a
Menu traversal action traverses to the next or previous component in a
Menu or MenuBar, the order of traversal and the wrapping behavior must be

the same as that of the corresponding component navigation action within a field, as described in Section 3.2.3. *

Two-dimensional Menus must not contain CascadeButtons. *

The following Menu traversal behavior must be supported: *

<↓>   This action must do the following: *

- If the component is in a vertical or 2-dimensional Menu, traverse down to the next traversable component, wrapping within the Menu if necessary. *

- If the component is in a MenuBar, and the component with the keyboard focus is a CascadeButton, post its associated Pulldown Menu and traverse to the default entry in the Menu or, if the Menu has no default, to the first traversable entry in the Menu. *

<↑>   If the component is in a vertical or 2-dimensional Menu, this action must traverse up to the previous traversable component, wrapping within the Menu if necessary, and proceeding in the order opposite to that of <↓>. *

<←>   This action must do the following: *

- If the component is in a MenuBar or 2-dimensional Menu, but not at the left edge, traverse left to the previous traversable component. *

- If the component is at the left edge of a MenuBar, wrap within the MenuBar. *

- If the component is at the left edge of a vertical or 2-dimensional Menu that is the child of a vertical or 2-dimensional Menu, unpost the current Menu and traverse to the parent CascadeButton. *

- If the component is at the left edge of a vertical or 2-dimensional Menu that is the child of a MenuBar, unpost the current Menu and traverse left to the previous traversable entry in the MenuBar. If that entry is a CascadeButton, post its associated Pulldown Menu and traverse to the default entry in the Menu or, if the Menu has no default, to the first traversable entry in the Menu. *

<→>   This action must do the following: *

- If the component is a CascadeButton in a vertical Menu, *
  post its associated Pulldown Menu and traverse to the *
  default entry in the Menu or, if the Menu has no default, *
  to the first traversable entry in the Menu. *

- If the component is in a MenuBar or 2-dimensional Menu, *
  but not at the right edge, traverse right to the next *
  traversable component. *

- If the component is at the right edge of a MenuBar, wrap *
  within the MenuBar. *

- If the component is not a CascadeButton and is at the *
  right edge of a vertical or 2-dimensional Menu, and if the *
  current Menu has an ancestor CascadeButton (typically in *
  a MenuBar) from which <↓> posts its associated *
  Pulldown Menu, unpost the Menu system pulled down *
  from the nearest such ancestor CascadeButton and *
  traverse right from that CascadeButton to the next *
  traversable component. If that component is a *
  CascadeButton, post its associated Pulldown Menu and *
  traverse to the default entry in the Menu or, if the Menu *
  has no default, to the first traversable entry in the Menu. *

For all Menu traversal actions, when the Menu is first posted, traversal
should go to the second traversable entry in the Menu if the Menu has no
default and the first traversable entry is a TearOffButton. Subsequent *
traversal actions must traverse to the TearOffButton in the same way as for *
other Menu entries.

The user can use keyboard actions to exit a Menu or a Menu system in the
following way:

- When a MenuBar system is active, **<F10>** should unpost the entire
  Menu system.

- When a Popup Menu system is active, **<Menu>** should unpost the entire
  Menu system. *

- In a Pulldown Menu, **<Cancel>** must either dismiss the Menu and move *
  the location cursor to the CascadeButton used to pull down the Menu, or *
  unpost the entire Menu system. *

- In a Popup Menu, Option Menu, TearOff Menu, or MenuBar, **<Cancel>**   *
  must unpost the Menu system.   *

- When **<F10>**, **<Menu>**, or **<Cancel>** is used to unpost an entire Menu   *
  system and an explicit focus policy is in use, the location cursor must be   *
  moved back to the component that had it before the Menu system was   *
  posted.

3.4 Scrollable Component Navigation

Certain components, such as List and Text, have built-in support for scrolling. However, any component or group of components can be associated with scrolling components or placed inside a ScrolledWindow and made scrollable.

A scrollable component generally has ScrollBars or some other type of scrolling component associated with it. When a component does not have a scrolling component associated with it, it generally should not be scrollable; however, components whose visible contents alone indicate that additional items exist beyond the bounds of the visible area, like Text, can be scrollable even if they do not have an associated scrolling component.

Any scrollable component must support the appropriate navigation and   *
scrolling operations. You must use the page navigation keys **<PageUp>**,   *
<PageDown>, **<PageLeft>** or **<Ctrl>** **<PageUp>**, and **<PageRight>** or   *
<Ctrl> **<PageDown>** for scrolling the visible region by a page increment.   *
A page is the portion of data that is visible, not any underlying structure of   *
the data. When scrolling by a page, you must leave at least one unit of   *
overlap between the old and new pages; for example, a line in a Text
component.

If the location cursor can be made visible, it must be. It should be moved   *
within the component so that it remains as near as possible to its original location in the viewport. However, if a navigation key (including directional and page navigation keys) is pressed while the **<ScrollLock>** key is down, the navigation key should be interpreted as specified for an associated ScrollBar—that is, it causes scrolling, while leaving the position of the cursor within the scrollable component unchanged. See the ScrollBar reference page in Chapter 9.

You should use the directional keys <↑>, <↓>, <←>, and <→> for moving the location cursor among elements, moving the location cursor by increments, or scrolling the visible region by regular increments. In general, keyboard operations should traverse through the entire scrollable component, not just through the visible portion.

When a mouse button is pressed initiating a selection operation within a scrollable component, and the pointer is then dragged outside of the scrollable component, the component should scroll toward the pointer. This is called autoscrolling. Drag and drop operations should produce similar scrolling behavior within scrollable components that force dragged elements to remain within the component. Releasing the button outside of the   *
component must not do any transfer in these cases. Parking the cursor on the edge of the scrollable component during the drag and drop operation should scroll the component toward the pointer.

When the location cursor is within a scrollable component, scrolling can move the cursor out of view; however, any keyboard operation that moves   *
the cursor to or in the component, or that inserts, deletes, or modifies items   *
at the cursor location must scroll the component so that the cursor is visible   *
when the operation is complete. When scrolling using the mouse, the location cursor can be allowed to scroll out of the visible region. When   *
scrolling using the keyboard, the location cursor must be moved so that it   *
remains within the visible region, if that is possible.

If a mouse-based scrolling action is in progress, <Cancel> must cancel the   *
scrolling action and return the slider to its position prior to the start of the   *
scrolling operation.

Chapter 4

Selection

The selection model determines how elements are selected from a group of elements. This chapter describes the selection models that are used by the various components of an application. OSF/Motif compliant applications use an object-action selection model. In an object-action selection model, the user first selects an object and then performs an action on it. The object-action selection model mimics real life, so it is a familiar process to the user and increases the user's sense of control over applications.

Objects include not only recognizable objects like windows, PushButtons, and List elements, but also component elements that are not always recognized as discrete objects, like individual letters of a text file. Applications can also treat a group of elements as a single element, either in a contiguous range or as a noncontiguous group. This chapter describes the following topics:

- Selection models, which determine how elements in a collection are selected for later action.

- Selection actions, which perform actions directly on a selection, such as cut, copy, and paste.

4.1 Selection Models

Selection is used to mark one or more of a group of elements simply for highlighting the elements, or so they can be moved, copied, or otherwise manipulated by the application.

Groups of elements can be organized into the following three types of collections:

- List-like collections
- Text-like collections
- Graphics-like collections

In list-like collections, when the pointer or location cursor is in the collection, the pointer or location cursor is considered to be on an element.

In text-like collections, when the pointer or location cursor is in the collection, the pointer or location cursor is considered to be between two elements. The name "text-like" refers to Text components in insert mode where the insertion cursor is always between two letters. List-like and text-like collections are usually ordered as linear collections; that is, the collections are treated as if the elements were connected as a series of elements in one dimension.

In graphics-like collections, the pointer and location cursor can be either on or between elements. Graphics-like collections are usually ordered as 2-dimensional collections. That is, the ordering of elements in the collection depends on both the horizontal and vertical position of the element within each collection.

The notion of "on" depends on the manipulation model presented by the control. For example, "on" can mean that the cursor is within the bounds of the element, or it can mean that the cursor is on the boundary of the element, or the element can have handles, and "on" means that the cursor is on one of the handles.

OSF/Motif compliant systems must support the five different selection   * models. Each model is used where appropriate in applications to limit the type of selections the user can make. For example, a List can limit selection to a single element where the user is only allowed to make one choice.

The five selection models are as follows:

Single Selection

> Used to select a single element in a collection. Clicking **BSelect** on an element selects it and deselects the previously selected element in the collection. Single selection is described in Section 4.1.1.

Browse Selection

> Used to allow browsing through single selection collections. Browse selection is also used to select a single element of a collection. Browse selection allows the user to browse through the elements by dragging **BSelect** through the elements in the collection. Browse selection highlights each element as it is traversed, and gives the application an opportunity to provide information about each element as it is highlighted. Releasing **BSelect** on an element selects it and deselects the previously selected element. Browse selection is described in Section 4.1.2.

Multiple Selection

> Used to select or deselect multiple elements of a collection. Clicking **BSelect** on an unselected element adds that element to the current selection. Clicking **BSelect** on a selected element removes that element from the current selection. Multiple selection is described in Section 4.1.3.

Range Selection

> Used to select a contiguous range of elements in a collection. Clicking **BSelect** on an element selects the single element and deselects any previous selection. **BSelect Motion** over a range of elements selects all the elements within the range and deselects any previous selection. Range selection is described in Section 4.1.4.

Discontiguous Selection

> Used for selecting multiple discontiguous ranges of elements in a collection. Clicking or dragging **BSelect** operates just as for range selection. Discontiguous selection also allows **<Ctrl> BSelect** to be used to add or remove selection ranges. Discontiguous selection is described in Section 4.1.5.

The choice of the selection model should be made on a collection-by-collection basis. Some components, like Text, enforce a selection model. Other components, like a List, allow the application or the user to determine the selection model.

Variants of these selection models may be needed for collections that are especially dense, when elements are organized in layers, when 3-dimensional selection is needed, when elements are hierarchically organized, or in other situations not covered by this guide. Selection models for such cases should not deviate unnecessarily from the standard selection models.

In all selection models, the selected element or group of elements should be visually highlighted in some way. Highlighting the selection can be done in the following ways:

- Using any one of the location cursor mechanisms

- Inverting the colors of the selection

- Drawing a solid or dashed box around the elements of the selection

The selection can also be an empty selection; that is, it is possible for no items to be selected in a collection. This commonly occurs in text-like collections where the location cursor is between two elements, or when the user has deselected all the elements.

4.1.1 Mouse-Based Single Selection

The single selection model is the simplest selection model. In the single selection model, when **BSelect** is clicked in a deselected element, the location cursor must move to that element, that element must be selected, and any other selection in the collection must be deselected.

4.1.2 Mouse-Based Browse Selection

The browse selection model is very similar to the single selection model. In browse selection, like single selection, only a single element is selected at a time. In the browse selection model, when **BSelect** is released in a selectable element, that element must be selected, and any other selection in the collection must be deselected. As **BSelect** is dragged through selectable elements, each element under the pointer must be selected, and the previously selected element must be deselected. The selection must remain on the element where **BSelect** is released, and the location cursor must be moved there.

The browse selection model gives the application an opportunity to provide information about each element as it is highlighted.

4.1.3 Mouse-Based Multiple Selection

Multiple selection allows the user to select or deselect multiple single elements of a collection. Clicking **BSelect** on an unselected element must   * add that element to the current selection in the collection. Clicking **BSelect**   * on a selected element must remove that element from the current selection   * in the collection. Clicking **BSelect** on an element must move the location   * cursor to that element.

With multiple selection, the user can select any group of elements in a collection, including discontiguous groups, all the elements, or none of the elements. Because multiple selection requires one mouse click for each element selected, although a simple model, it is not well-suited for selecting large groups of elements. **BSelect Motion** can optionally toggle a range of elements. (See Section 4.1.5 for a description of range toggling.)

4.1.4 Mouse-Based Range Selection

The range selection model allows the user to select multiple contiguous elements of a collection. The description of this selection model assumes that drag and drop is not integrated with selection. Integrating dragging and selection is described in Section 4.3.

In the range selection model, pressing **BSelect** must set an **anchor** on the   * element, or at the position where **BSelect** was pressed, and must deselect all   * elements in the collection. The anchor and the current position of the   * pointer determine the current range. As **BSelect** is dragged through the   * collection, the current range must be highlighted. When **BSelect** is   * released, the anchor must not move, and all the elements within the current   * range must be selected.

In text-like collections, elements are ordered linearly, and a **text pointer** is always considered to be between elements at a point near the actual pointer position. The anchor point must be the text pointer position when **BSelect** is   * pressed, and the current range must consist of all elements between the   * anchor point and the current text pointer position.

In graphics-like and list-like collections, a marquee, or highlighted
rectangle, is typically used to indicate the current range of the selection.   *
The current range must consist of those elements that fall completely within   *
the marquee. If a marquee selection is started when the pointer is on an
element, that element can be used as an anchor element, and should be used
as an anchor element if the collection is arranged as a list or matrix. If there   *
is an anchor element, the marquee must always be made large enough to   *
completely enclose it. Otherwise, an anchor point is used, which must be   *
the point at which **BSelect** was pressed, and must determine one corner of   *
the marquee. If the collection is arranged as a list or matrix, and the pointer
is on an element, the marquee should be extended to completely enclose the
element under the pointer. Otherwise, the marquee must be extended to the   *
pointer position.

Marquee selection can be implemented so that it is used only when **BSelect**
is pressed in the background; other selection models, not described in this
style guide, can be used when **BSelect** is pressed on an element. If marquee   *
selection is used, even if only when started in the background, clicking   *
BSelect on a selectable element must make it an anchor element, select it,   *
and deselect all other elements.

The user can extend the range selection using **<Shift> BSelect**. When   *
<Shift> BSelect is pressed, the anchor remains unchanged, and an extended   *
range for the selection is determined, based on one of the following   *
extension models:

Reselect   The extended range must be determined by the anchor   *
                         and the current pointer position, in exactly the same   *
                         manner as when the selection was initially made.   *

Enlarge Only   The selection can only be enlarged. The extended range   *
                         is determined by the anchor and the current pointer   *
                         position, but then must be enlarged to include the current   *
                         selection.   *

Balance Beam   A balance point is defined at the midpoint of the current
                         selection. When **<Shift> BSelect** is pressed on the   *
                         opposite side of the balance point from the anchor, this   *
                         model must work exactly like the reselect model. When   *
                         <Shift> BSelect is pressed, or a navigation action   *
                         modified by **<Shift>** is started on the same side of the   *
                         balance point as the anchor, this model must move the   *
                         anchor to the opposite end of the selection, and then must   *
                         work exactly like the reselect model. In graphics-like

collections, balancing the anchor is done separately in each dimension.

As **<Shift> BSelect** is dragged through the collection, the extended range should be highlighted, and selected elements outside of it should be dehighlighted. When **BSelect** is released, the anchor must not move, all the   *
elements within the extended range must be selected, and all the elements   *
outside of it must be deselected.

Text-like collections should use the balance beam model. The extension model used by other collections depends on the purpose of the collection.

In the range selection model, clicking **<Ctrl> BSelect** should move the location cursor to the position of the pointer without affecting the current selection.

4.1.5 Mouse-Based Discontiguous Selection

The discontiguous selection mechanism allows the user to make multiple simultaneous range selections. It is an extension of the range selection model. The description of this selection model assumes that drag and drop is not integrated with selection. Integrating dragging and selection is described in Section 4.3.

The behavior of **BSelect** in the discontiguous selection model must be   *
exactly the same as in the range selection model, and after setting the   *
anchor with **BSelect**, **<Shift> BSelect** must work exactly as in the range   *
selection model.

The primary difference between the range selection model and the discontiguous selection model is the use of **<Ctrl> BSelect**. In the range selection model, **<Ctrl> BSelect** is only used to move the position of the location cursor without disrupting the current selection. In the discontiguous model, **<Ctrl> BSelect** is used to toggle the selection state of an element or a range of elements.

If the current selection is empty, **<Ctrl> BSelect Click** can simply move the location cursor, but leave the anchor alone and leave all elements deselected. Otherwise, if **<Ctrl> BSelect** is clicked, the anchor and   *
location cursor must move to that point, and if **<Ctrl> BSelect** is clicked on   *
an element, the selection state of that element must be toggled, and that   *
element must become the anchor element.

<Ctrl> BSelect Motion must be used to toggle the selection state of a range *
of elements. The range itself must be determined exactly as for **BSelect** *
Motion. Releasing **<Ctrl> BSelect** must toggle the selection state of the *
elements in the range according to one of two models:

Anchor Toggle   Toggling is based upon an anchor element. If the *
range is anchored by a point, and is not empty, the *
anchor element must be set to the element within the *
range that is nearest to the anchor point. Toggling *
must set the selection state of all elements in the *
range to the inverse of the initial state of the anchor *
element. This is the model recommended for
toggling.

Full Toggle   The selection state of each element in the extended *
range must be toggled.

As **<Ctrl> BSelect** is dragged through the collection, highlighting should be
used to indicate the current range and the selection state of each element
that would result from releasing **<Ctrl> BSelect** at the current position.

After using **<Ctrl> BSelect** to toggle a selection, **<Shift> BSelect** or *
<Ctrl> <Shift> BSelect must be able to be used to extend the range of *
toggled elements. The extended range must be determined in exactly the *
same way as when **<Shift> BSelect** is used to extend a range selection.

When **<Ctrl> <Shift> BSelect** is released, the selection state of elements *
added to the range must be determined by the toggle model as previously *
described. If elements are removed from the range, they must either revert *
to their state prior to the last use of **<Ctrl> BSelect**, or change to the state *
opposite from the elements remaining within the extended range.

As **<Shift> BSelect** or **<Ctrl> <Shift> BSelect** is dragged through the
collection, highlighting should be used to indicate the current range and the
selection state of each element that would result from releasing **<Shift>**
BSelect or **<Ctrl> <Shift> BSelect** at the current position.

4.1.6 Keyboard Selection

Selections can be made by using the keyboard as well as the mouse. Two keyboard selection models are available: normal mode and add mode.

Normal mode is used for making simple contiguous selections from the keyboard. Normal mode is a navigation/selection mode where the location cursor is never disjoint from the current selection. In collections where the location cursor is on an element, the element with the location cursor is ordinarily selected; if it is not, pressing **<Select>** or **<Space>** moves the selection to the cursored element.

Add mode is used for making more complex and possibly disjoint selections. Add mode is a navigation/selection mode where the location cursor can move independent of the current selection. Even in collections that do not support discontiguous selections, add mode allows the selection to be unaffected by keyboard navigation.

Browse selections must only support normal mode. Single and multiple *
selections must only support add mode. Range selection must support *
normal mode and can also support add mode. Discontiguous selections *
must support both modes. The default mode for range and discontiguous *
selections must be normal mode. **<Shift> <F8>** must switch between add *
mode and normal mode if both modes are supported. When switching from
normal to add mode, if the cursored element is the only element selected in
the collection, it should be deselected. Mouse-based selection must not *
change based on the keyboard selection mode.

In editable components, add mode is a temporary mode that must be exited *
when an operation is performed on the selection or when the selection is *
deselected.

4.1.6.1 Keyboard-Based Single Selection

Collections using the single selection model must use add mode. In add *
mode, the navigation keys for the collection must move the location cursor *
independent from the selected element. If **<Select>** or **<Space>** is pressed *
on an unselected element, it must select the element with the location *
cursor, and it must deselect any previous selection in the collection.

4.1.6.2 Keyboard-Based Browse Selection

Collections using the browse selection model must use normal mode. The   *
navigation keys must move the location cursor and select the cursored   *
element, deselecting any other element. If the application has deselected all   *
elements or if the cursor is left disjoint from the selection, **<Select>** or   *
<Space> must select the cursored element and deselect any other element.

4.1.6.3 Keyboard-Based Multiple Selection

Collections using the multiple selection model must use add mode. The   *
navigation keys for the collection must move the location cursor   *
independent from the current selection. **<Select>** or **<Space>** on an   *
unselected element must add the element to the current selection. **<Select>**   *
or **<Space>** on a selected element must remove the element from the current   *
selection.

4.1.6.4 Keyboard-Based Range Selection

Collections using the range selection model must initially use normal mode.   *
This allows a keyboard-based behavior similar to dragging with the mouse.

In normal mode, navigation keys must move the location cursor and deselect   *
the current selection. If the cursor is on an element, it must be selected.   *
The anchor must move with the location cursor. However, in text-like   *
collections, a different model can be used in which the anchor must instead   *
remain at its current location, except that, if the current selection is not   *
empty, it must be deselected and the anchor must be moved to the location   *
of the cursor prior to navigation.

<Select> or **<Space>** (except in a Text component) must move the anchor to   *
the cursor, deselect the current selection, and, if the cursor is on an element,   *
select the element. Unless the anchor is on a deselected item, **<Shift>**   *
<Select> or **<Shift> <Space>** (except in Text) must extend the selection   *
from the anchor to the cursor, based on the extension model used by **<Shift>**   *
BSelect.

Using **<Shift>** in conjunction with the navigation keys must extend the
selection, based on the extension model used by **<Shift> BSelect**. If the
current selection is empty, the anchor must first be moved to the cursor. The
cursor must then be moved according to the navigation keys, and the
selection must be extended based on the extension model used by **<Shift>**
BSelect.

In add mode, **<Select>**, **<Space>**, **<Shift> <Select>**, and **<Shift> <Space>**
must work exactly as in normal mode. However, ordinary navigation must
simply move the location cursor, but must leave the anchor unchanged.
Shifted navigation must move the location cursor according to the
navigation keys, and the selection must be extended based on the extension
model used by **<Shift> BSelect**.

In Text, both **<Space>** and **<Shift> <Space>** must insert a space character.

4.1.6.5 Keyboard-Based Discontiguous Selection

Collections using the discontiguous selection model must initially use
normal mode. In the discontiguous selection model, add mode is not only a
separate model of interaction but also an extension to the range selection
model that allows the user to select discontiguous elements.

In normal mode, all keyboard operations must have the same effect as in the
range selection model. In normal mode, discontiguous selections cannot be
made using the keyboard.

In add mode, **<Select>** or **<Space>** must move the anchor to the location
cursor and initiate toggling. If the location cursor is on an element, the
selection state of that element must be toggled, but the selection state of all
other elements must remain unchanged. **<Shift> <Select>** or **<Shift>**
<Space> and shifted navigation operations must extend the selection
between the anchor and the location cursor, based on the toggle mechanism
used by **<Ctrl> BSelect**.

4.1.7 Canceling a Selection

<Cancel> must cancel or undo any incomplete motion operation used for   *
selection. Once <Cancel> is pressed to cancel a motion operation, the   *
application must ignore subsequent key and button releases until after all   *
buttons and keys are released. <Cancel> during a range selection should
leave all elements, except possibly for the cursored element, deselected.   *
<Cancel> while extending or toggling must leave the selection state of all   *
elements as they were prior to the button press.

4.1.8 Autoscrolling and Selection

If the user drags the pointer out of a scrollable collection during a motion-   *
based selection operation, autoscrolling must be used to scroll the collection   *
in the direction of the pointer. If the user presses <Cancel> with BSelect   *
pressed, the selection operation must be canceled as described in Section   *
4.1.7.

4.1.9 Selecting and Deselecting All Elements

There are two special keyboard-based selection mechanisms for selecting
(via <Ctrl> </>) and deselecting (via <Ctrl> <\>) all the elements in a
collection. <Ctrl> </> in a collection using multiple, range, or   *
discontiguous selection must select all the elements in a collection, place   *
the anchor at the beginning of the collection, and leave the location cursor   *
at its previous position.

Deselection differs between add mode and normal mode. In add mode,   *
<Ctrl> <\> must deselect all the elements in a collection. In normal mode,   *
<Ctrl> <\> must deselect all the elements in a collection, except the   *
element with the location cursor if the location cursor is being displayed. In   *
either case, it must leave the location cursor at its current location and move   *
the anchor to the location cursor. An application can deselect all elements
in a collection regardless of the state of add mode or the selection model.

4.1.10 Using Mnemonics for Elements

Collections can also support mnemonics associated with its elements if the
elements have labels. Pressing a mnemonic key while the collection has the *
keyboard focus must be equivalent to moving the location cursor to the *
element and pressing **<Select>** or **<Space>**.

4.2 Selection Actions

Each collection maintains its own selection. A selection need not contain
any elements, in which case it is said to be an empty selection. At any time,
there is one selection called the primary selection, which is the last
selection explicitly started by the user.

Clicking **BSelect** or **<Ctrl> BSelect** moves the primary selection to a
collection only when it results in making a selection that is not empty.
When **<Shift> BSelect** is clicked, an implementation can move the primary
selection to the component even if the resulting selection is empty. *
Dragging **BSelect**, **<Shift> BSelect**, or **<Ctrl> BSelect** must move the *
primary selection to the component if a button release during the pointer *
motion could have potentially selected any element.

A selection is said to be persistent if it is highlighted even when it is not the
primary selection.

Persistent
There are two variants of persistent selections: persistent always, in
which the current selection is always highlighted, and persistent on
focus, in which the current selection is only highlighted when it is the
primary selection or when the collection has the keyboard focus. In
either case, stronger highlighting should be used when the current
selection is also the primary selection. When focus is in the
collection, **<Alt> <Insert>** can be used to promote the current
selection to the primary selection.

Nonpersistent

> The collection only highlights a primary selection. When the primary selection is lost to another collection, the current selection is set to empty. When focus is in the collection, and it does not have the primary selection, **<Alt> <Insert>** can be used to restore the previous selection and make it the primary selection.

Collections that are never editable (such as noneditable Lists) should always use persistent selections. Collections that are editable can use either persistent or non-persistent selections.

When the user makes or changes a selection, the application can display information about the selection, but it should not perform any other action that uses the selected elements. For example, selecting a file from a List of files should not automatically open the file. Such actions should require additional user interaction.

4.2.1 Destination Component

The destination component is used to identify the component on which certain operations, primarily data transfer operations, act. There is only one destination component at a time. When using an explicit focus policy, the   * destination component must be the editable component that last had focus.   * When using a pointer focus policy, the destination component must be the * editable component that last received mouse button or keyboard input.

Special highlighting should be used to identify the destination component. In Text, a solid insertion cursor can be shown.

4.2.2 Operation Targets

Once a selection is made, the elements of the selection can be acted on using selection actions. Some common selection actions are delete, cut, copy, and paste, although your application is not limited to these. This section and the following one describe the way many selection operations work. Operations that transfer data are described in greater detail in Section 4.3.

The user may invoke an operation that can act on a selection in some component. A keyboard operation can be used, or a control can be activated, which performs the operation. There can be a number of components in a window to which the action could be applied, and it may not be clear which component is the target. This could be the case, for example, when selecting **Copy** from the **Edit** Menu, or when typing **<Ctrl> <Insert>**, the accelerator for **Copy**. For operations that act on selections, use the following hierarchy of rules to determine which component's selection to act on:

1. If the keyboard focus is in a component (or a Popup Menu of a component) that supports selections, the action must act on that component.   *
  *

2. Otherwise, if the keyboard focus is in a window (or a Menu of a window) with a main component that has a persistent selection, it should act on the main component.

3. Otherwise, if the keyboard focus is in the window (or a Menu of the window) that has the destination component, and the destination component contains a persistent selection that is not empty, it should act on the destination component.

4. Otherwise, if the keyboard focus is in the same window (or a Menu of the window) that has the primary selection, it should act on the component with the primary selection.

5. Otherwise, if the keyboard focus is in a window (or a Menu of a window) that has only one editable component with a persistent selection, then it can act on that component.

6. Otherwise, invoking the action should have no effect, except to signal an error or post a DialogBox.

Similarly, the user may invoke an operation that transfers data to a component or otherwise uses a component in some way, and, again, it may not be clear which component should be used. This could be the case, for example, when selecting **Paste** from the **Edit** Menu, or when typing **<Shift> <Insert>**, the accelerator for **Paste**. For operations that do not act on selections, use the following hierarchy of rules:

1. If the keyboard focus is in a component (or a Popup Menu of a component) that supports the action, the action must be applied to that component.   *
  *

2. Otherwise, if the keyboard focus is in a window (or a Menu of a window) with a main component that supports the action, it should be applied to the main component.

3. Otherwise, if the keyboard focus is in the window (or a Menu of the window) that has the destination component, and the destination component supports the action, it should be applied to the destination component.

4. Otherwise, invoking the action should have no effect, except to signal an error or post a DialogBox.

4.2.3 Selection Operations

This subsection describes some of the standard operations available through the **Edit** Menu and through standard keyboard bindings that operate on selections.

A collection can either enable or disable pending delete, which controls the circumstances under which the selection is deleted. By default, pending delete should be enabled.

Inserting or pasting elements into a selection, except for a primary transfer operation at the bounds of the primary selection, must first delete the selection if pending delete is enabled.

In normal mode, inserting or pasting elements disjoint from the selection must also deselect the selection, except for primary transfer operations whose source and destination are in the same collection. In add mode, the selection must not be deselected.

In editable list-like and graphics-like collections, **<Delete>** must delete the selected elements. In editable text-like collections, **<Delete>** and **<BackSpace>** must behave as follows:

- If the selection is not empty and the control is in normal mode, the selection must be deleted.

- If the selection is not empty, the control is in add mode, and the cursor is not disjoint from the selection, the selection must be deleted.

- If the selection is not empty and the control is in add mode, but the cursor is disjoint from the selection, **<Delete>** must delete one character forward, and **<BackSpace>** must delete one character backward.

- If the selection is empty, **\<Delete\>** must delete one character forward, *
  and **\<BackSpace\>** must delete one character backward.

More generally, any operation that deletes a region (for example, a word or
line) behaves as follows:

- If the selection is not empty and the control is in normal mode, the *
  selection must be deleted.

- If selection is not empty, the control is in add mode, and the cursor is not *
  disjoint from the selection, the selection must be deleted.

- If the selection is not empty and the control is in add mode, but the *
  cursor is disjoint from the selection, the operation must delete the *
  region.

- If the selection is empty, the operation must delete the region. *

If the region deleted (in add mode) partially overlaps the selection, then the *
overlapped part of the selection must be deleted.

Generally, whenever an action causes data to be removed from a
component, what to do with the space left by the data is up to the
component. In cases where the surrounding data can be reformatted to fill in
the space left by the removed data (such as in Text components), the delete
action should cause this reformatting. In this case, a clear action should
delete the data without reformatting any surrounding data. In Text
components, the clear action deletes the selected text and replaces it with
white space. In cases where the surrounding data cannot be reformatted to
fill in the space left by the removed data (such as in bitmap graphics), the
delete action should remove the data but not cause any reformatting. The
Cut entry from the **Edit** Menu should behave like the delete action.

In cases where an action adds data to a component, the effect the new data
has on the surrounding data depends on the component. In cases where the
surrounding data can be reformatted to allow the new data to fit in (such as
in Text components), insert actions should cause this reformatting. The
Paste entry from the **Edit** Menu should behave like insert actions.

\<Undo\> or **\<Alt\>** **\<BackSpace\>** should undo the last operation on a
selection.

4.3 Transfer Models

This section describes the four techniques available for transferring data:

Clipboard Transfer
> This technique transfers a selection from a source to the clipboard, and then subsequently from the clipboard to a destination.

Primary Transfer
> This technique transfers the primary selection directly to a destination without using the clipboard for intermediate storage of the data.

Quick Transfer
> This technique allows the user to indicate a range of elements (called a secondary selection) that are then transferred to the destination component.

Drag Transfer or Drag and Drop
> This technique allows the user to drag a selection or an unselected element from a source to a destination.

Clipboard and primary transfer operations can be invoked from Pulldown or Popup Menus and have standard keyboard bindings as well. Primary, quick, and drag transfer operations can also be invoked using **BTransfer**.

There are three transfer operations generally available:

- Copy, which copies elements from the source to the destination.

- Move, which moves elements from the source to the destination.

- Link, which inserts a link in the destination to elements in the source.

The default operation for primary and quick transfer using **BTransfer** is copy. The default operation for drag transfer is generally move, though it depends on the characteristics of the source and the destination. Modifiers can be used to force an operation different from the default: *

- **<Ctrl>** must force a copy. *

- **<Shift>** must force a move. *

- **<Ctrl> <Shift>** must force a link. *

If the move, copy, or link operation the user requests is not available, the * transfer operation must fail.

When data is moved or copied, it can change its appearance or representation. The destination can determine the representation of the transferred data as it chooses. For example, if a graphic element representing a file is transferred to a Text component, the name of the file (or possibly the contents, if it is a text file) can be inserted. If possible, the   *
source must transfer the format that the destination requests. Otherwise, the destination can use any heuristic to determine the best format to transfer the data in. That heuristic can even be, if the source cannot transfer in the preferred format, fail. If the destination decides that a transfer in its chosen format could possibly cause a loss of data between the source and the destination, the destination should notify the user of the possible loss of data and confirm the action before proceeding.

If there is a choice of the exact representation of data to be inserted, there should be some visual means that clearly indicates to the user which representation the application will use. If there is no such indication, then when the user performs the transfer operation, the application can post a Popup Menu or a DialogBox to allow the user to choose the representation.

A transfer can also cause the destination to take related actions. For example, transferring an element to a printer icon can cause the element to be printed.

The insertion position is the position in the destination at which transferred data is placed. The insertion position is determined in the following way:

- Some collections have a fixed insertion point (as in append-only text) or keep the elements in the collection ordered in a specific way. In those cases, the collection can determine where to place the data.

- If the collection does not have a fixed insertion point or keep elements   *
  ordered in a specific way, the insertion position for **BTransfer**-based   *
  primary and drag transfer operations must be the position at which the   *
  user releases **BTransfer**.

- If the collection does not have a fixed insertion point or keep elements ordered in a specific way, the insertion position for other transfer operations, including keyboard-based transfer operations, is determined as follows:

  — In text-like collections, the insertion position must be the location   *
    cursor, and the data must be pasted before it.

  — In list-like collections, the insertion position must be the element   *
    with the location cursor, and the data must be pasted before it.

— In graphics-like collections, the insertion position should be at the location cursor, but the exact placement of the data with respect to the location cursor is unspecified.

4.3.1 Clipboard Transfer

The clipboard transfer operations **Cut**, **Copy**, and **Paste**, are usually performed using the **Edit** Menu of an application. They also have standard keyboard bindings that must be available in every editable collection.

<Cut> or **<Shift>** **<Delete>** and the **Cut** entry of the **Edit** Menu must cut selected elements of the target component to the clipboard.

<Copy> or **<Ctrl>** **<Insert>** and the **Copy** entry of the **Edit** Menu must copy selected elements of the target component to the clipboard and can mark the selection for subsequent use with **Paste Link**.

A **Copy Link** entry of the **Edit** Menu can be used to place a link in the clipboard to selected elements of the target component so that the link can be placed in a destination by subsequent use of **Paste** or **Paste Link**.

See the rules for operations that act on selections in Section 4.2.2 for determining which component in a window is targeted by a **Cut**, **Copy**, or **Copy Link** operation.

<Paste> or **<Shift>** **<Insert>** and the **Paste** entry of the **Edit** Menu must paste the contents of the clipboard at the insertion position of the target component.

The **Paste Link** entry of the **Edit** Menu can place a link at the insertion position of the target component to the selection last marked by a **Copy** or **Copy Link** operation.

See the rules for operations that do not act on selections in Section 4.2.2 for determining which collection in a window is targeted by a **Paste** or **Paste Link** operation.

If the last data cut was the primary selection, pasting it can make it the primary selection if there is no current primary selection. Otherwise, pasting data should not select it. However, if the collection is in normal mode, the anchor and the cursor should be placed at opposite ends of the pasted data so that subsequent use of **<Shift>** **<Select>** or **<Shift>** **<Space>** can be used to select it.

If **Paste** or **Paste Link** is invoked using a component's Popup Menu, the data   *
must be pasted at the insertion position of the component. However, if the   *
Popup Menu is popped up over a selection, the selection must first be   *
deleted, even if pending delete is disabled, and the pasted data must replace   *
it, if possible.

If **Paste** or **Paste Link** is invoked from the **Edit** Menu or by a keyboard   *
operation, and the insertion position in the target component is not disjoint   *
from a selection, the pasted data must replace the selection contents if   *
pending delete is enabled.

4.3.2 Primary Transfer

Primary transfer can be invoked by clicking **BTransfer** or through standard
keyboard bindings. There are three primary transfer operations:

Primary Copy
> In an editable collection, **BTransfer Click**, **<Ctrl> BTransfer Click**,   *
> **<Alt> <Copy>**, and **<Alt> <Ctrl> <Insert>** must copy the primary   *
> selection to the insertion position, as defined in Section 4.3. (Note   *
> that the insertion position is usually different for mouse and keyboard   *
> operations.)

Primary Move
> In an editable collection, **<Shift> BTransfer Click**, **<Alt> <Cut>**,   *
> and **<Alt> <Shift> <Delete>** must move the primary selection to the   *
> insertion position, as defined in Section 4.3. (Note that the insertion   *
> position is usually different for mouse and keyboard operations.)

Primary Link
> In an editable collection, **<Ctrl> <Shift> BTransfer Click** must   *
> place a link to the primary selection at the insertion position, as   *
> defined in Section 4.3.

Transferring data to the destination by a **Primary Copy** or **Primary Link**   *
must not select it. However, if the source and the destination components
are different, and if the collection is in normal mode, the anchor and the
cursor should be placed at opposite ends of the transferred data, so that
subsequent use of **<Shift> <Select>** or **<Shift> <Space>** can be used to
select it.

A **Primary Move** must move the primary selection as well as the elements   *
selected; that is, the element moved to the destination must become selected   *
as the primary selection.

If a primary transfer operation is invoked using a component's Popup Menu,   *
the data must be transferred to the insertion position of the component.   *
However, if the Popup Menu is popped up over a persistent nonprimary   *
selection, the selection must first be deleted, even if pending delete is   *
disabled, and the transferred data must replace it. When a primary transfer   *
transfers data into a nonprimary selection, the transferred data must replace   *
the selection contents if pending delete is enabled.

When a **Primary Copy** or **Primary Link** is invoked by using **BTransfer**
with the pointer at the edge of the primary selection, by popping up a Popup
Menu at the edge of a primary selection, or by a keyboard operation when
the insertion position is at the edge of the primary selection, the data should
be transferred, and the selection should be left unchanged, even if pending
delete is enabled. If a **Primary Copy** or **Primary Link** is invoked inside
the primary selection, the operation should have no effect.

If **BTransfer** is pressed outside a primary selection, but at a position both
where a drag can be initiated and where data can be pasted by a primary
transfer, a user-settable timeout and motion threshold should be used in the
following way to distinguish drag initiation from primary transfer:

- If **BTransfer Motion** exceeding the motion threshold occurs following
  the **BTransfer Press**, a drag should be initiated.

- Otherwise, if the **BTransfer Release** follows the **BTransfer Press**
  within the timeout period, a primary transfer should be done.

- Otherwise, when the timeout period expires, a drag should be initiated.
  However, if **BTransfer Release** is then done without motion exceeding
  the threshold, the drag should be canceled.

If **BTransfer** is pressed within a draggable primary selection, the drag
should be initiated on the **BTransfer Press**.

4.3.3 Quick Transfer

Quick transfer is used to make a temporary (or secondary) selection and then immediately copy, move, or link that selection to the insertion position of the destination component. Quick transfer is implemented using **<Alt> BTransfer Motion**, with the standard modifiers used to force the various transfer operations.

Text components must support quick transfer.   *

There are three quick transfer operations:

Quick Copy

If a component supports quick transfer, **<Alt> BTransfer Motion** or   *
<Alt> <Ctrl> BTransfer Motion must temporarily select elements in   *
the specified range and, on release, must copy them to the insertion   *
position of the destination component.

Quick Cut

If a component supports quick transfer, **<Alt> <Shift> BTransfer**   *
Motion must temporarily select elements in the specified range and,   *
on release, must move them to the insertion position of the destination   *
component.

Quick Link

If a component supports quick transfer, **<Alt> <Ctrl> <Shift>**   *
BTransfer Motion must temporarily select elements in the specified   *
range and, on release, must place a link to them at the insertion   *
position of the destination component.

The range of the temporary selection must be determined by using exactly   *
the same model used when **BSelect Motion** determines the range of a   *
primary selection.

If the insertion position of the destination component is not disjoint from the   *
selection, the transferred data must replace the selection contents if pending   *
delete is enabled. Transferring data to the destination component by a quick   *
transfer must not select it. However, if the destination component is in
normal mode, the anchor and the cursor should be placed at opposite ends of
the transferred data so that subsequent use of **<Shift> <Select>** or **<Shift>**
<Space> can be used to select it.

Quick transfer can be used to transfer static text or graphics that are not
ordinarily selectable. For example, a portion of the text label of a
PushButton is not ordinarily selectable, since **BSelect Click**, **<Select>** or
<Space> activate the PushButton instead.

While dragging out the quick selection, the range should be highlighted in some way. The highlighting mechanism should be different from that used for the primary selection. In text, the highlight should be underlining.

If the pointer is dragged out of a scrollable collection while making the temporary selection, autoscrolling must be used to scroll the collection in the direction of the pointer. If **BTransfer** is released with the pointer outside of the collection, or if **<Cancel>** is pressed with **BTransfer** pressed, the highlighting must be removed and a transfer must not be performed.

4.3.4 Drag Transfer

Drag transfer, also known as drag and drop, provides a quick and simple model for transferring data within and between applications. Depending on where it is initiated, drag transfer can be used to transfer the selected elements of a collection, a single unselected element, an entire collection, and even unselectable static textual and graphics labels.

A user performs a drag transfer by pressing **BTransfer** in the source, moving the pointer to the destination (called the drop site), and releasing **BTransfer**. This transfers the data from the source to the destination. The usual modifier keys can be used to force a copy, move, or link:

- **<Ctrl> BTransfer Motion** must force a drag copy.
- **<Shift> BTransfer Motion** must force a drag move.
- **<Ctrl> <Shift> BTransfer Motion** must force a drag link.

If no modifier key is chosen, the default operation should be a move, although it depends on the characteristics of the source and the destination. In particular, the default should be copy if the source is not editable, or if the destination is a copying or transformation device; for example, if the drop occurs over an icon for a printer or a compiler.

When a drag move moves the primary selection, the primary selection should move to the destination, as well as the elements selected; that is, the element moved to the destination should become selected as the primary selection.

When a drag move moves a selection within the same component, the selection must move along with the elements selected.

In other cases, data transferred by a drag transfer must not become selected   ✻
at the destination. However, if the destination is in normal mode, then
except when drag copy and drag link transfer a selection within the same
component, the anchor and the cursor should be placed at opposite ends of
the transferred data so that subsequent use of **<Shift> <Select>** or **<Shift>**
<Space> can be used to select it.

Within a collection, drag transfer can be used to either drag a selected set of
elements, a single unselected element, or the entire collection. This is
determined in the following way:

- In text-like collections, initiating a drag in a selected region must drag   ✻
  the text selection (including all pieces if it is discontiguous).

- In list-like and graphics-like collections, initiating a drag on a selected   ✻
  element must drag the entire selection.

- In list-like and graphics-like collections, initiating a drag on an   ✻
  unselected element must drag just that element. If the collection   ✻
  contains a selection, the selection must not be affected (except if the   ✻
  drop occurs in the same collection).

- In graphics-like collections, initiating a drag in the background of a
  contiguous selected region can drag the selection. Otherwise,
  BTransfer Motion beginning in the background of a collection can drag
  the entire collection or, if the collection is scrollable, can be used to pan
  the collection.

If a drag is initiated in an unselected region and the pointer is over two   ✻
possible draggable elements, the drag must occur on the highest draggable   ✻
element in the stacking order. This also implies that with nested draggable
elements, the drag occurs on the smallest draggable element under the
pointer.

All collections should support drag transfer and should allow elements to be
dragged to or from other collections, including those in different
applications. A collection can support only drag (particularly if it is not
editable) or only drop.

If a collection only allows elements dragged from it to be dropped in the
same collection, then, during the drag, it can prevent the pointer from
moving outside of the collection. If so, and if the collection is scrollable,
holding the pointer at the edge of the collection should cause autoscrolling.

4.3.4.1 Drag Icons

When a drag operation is started, the pointer must be replaced with a drag *
icon. A drag icon provides visual feedback that a drag is in progress. It can
be composed of three parts:

- A source indicator

- An operation indicator

- A state indicator

Figure 4-1 shows move, copy, and link drag icons for graphical and textual
information. The bulk of the icon is the source indicator. When defining
new drag icons, you should follow the same rules as for defining new
pointers described in Section 2.2.2.

Figure 4–1. Drag Icons

All drag icons must include a source indicator. A source indicator should *
give a visual representation of the type of elements being dragged; for
example, horizontal lines in a rectangle for representing text. The source
indicator can include a fragment of the actual data being dragged, such as
the first few characters of some text.

An operation indicator shows whether the drag operation will result in a
move, copy, or link operation. Most drag icons should include an operation
indicator. An operation indicator can be shown either as a separate element
of the drag icon or as a variation of a graphic used for the source indicator.

The source of the dragged elements can also provide visual indications of
the result of a drop. For example, if the default operation for the dragged
elements is a move, the source can be hidden or deemphasized; or if the
default operation of the dragged elements is a link, a line can be drawn from
the source to the pointer.

A state indicator shows whether the current pointer location is over a valid drop site for the dragged elements. All drag icons can include a state indicator. A state indicator should be coincident with the hotspot of the pointer.

4.3.4.2 During a Drag

Systems should provide help operations during drag and drop. If a system provides drag and drop help, pressing **<Help>** (followed by releasing **BTransfer**) during a drag and drop operation should allow the posting of a DialogBox with the help information and the possible choices for concluding the drag and drop operation. The DialogBox should allow for canceling the drag and drop operation or for dropping the elements at the current location as a move, copy, or link.

Pressing **<Cancel>** during a drag operation must cancel the current drag   *
operation and return the system to the state prior to the start of the drag   *
operation.

It can be difficult during a drag and drop operation to make both the drag source and drop site visible to the user at the same time. A system can alleviate this problem by making it possible to navigate to drop sites that were not visibly available at the start of the drag operation. For example, a system can scroll a scrollable region when the pointer rests on the edge of that scrollable region. A system can open an icon view when the pointer rests on that icon. A system can also raise a window when the pointer rests in that window.

During a drag and drop interaction, the system should indicate dynamically whether the current pointer location is a possible valid drop site for the data that the user is dragging. This is done using drag-over effects, and drag-under effects. A drag-over effect is a change in the visual state of the drag icon. This change is usually represented in the drag icon's state indicator. If a drag icon has a state indicator, it should be coincident with the pointer's hotspot. The state indicator should be emphasized for valid drop sites and deemphasized for invalid drops sites. The state indicator can also indicate that there is no drop site under the pointer.

A drag-under effect is a change to the visual state of a possible valid drop site when the drag icon pointer is over the drop site. All drop sites should use some kind of drag-under effect. Drop sites can use a solid line around the site, or a raised or lowered beveled edge around the drop site as a drag-under effect. Drop sites can also change any visual component of the drop site, or even animate those changes, as a drag-under effect. For example, an icon representing a folder might show an animated image of the folder opening as a user drags a file onto it. Drop sites can also use other media (for example, audio effects) to provide feedback.

4.3.4.3 Ending a Drag

Releasing **BTransfer** (or **BSelect** when transfer and selection are   *
integrated) must end a drag and drop operation. In addition, as mentioned in   *
the previous section, pressing **<Cancel>** must also end a drag and drop   *
operation by canceling the drag in progress. When a user releases   *
BTransfer, the drop operation must occur at the location of the hotspot of   *
the drag icon pointer. The drop must occur into the highest drop site in the   *
stacking order. This also implies that in a group of nested drop sites the
drop occurs into the smallest drop site under the pointer.

However, if a drop occurs within a selection at any level, the transferred   *
data must replace the contents of the entire selection if pending delete is   *
enabled.

4.3.4.4 Drop Results

Every drop operation, even when there was a visual indication of a valid
drop site, can result in either success, failure, or partial failure (in the case
of dragging multiple elements). While the transfer is in progress, that is   *
until the drop site determines the success of the drag and drop operation, the   *
data must not leave the source. While the transfer is in progress, a transfer
icon representing the type of data being transferred should appear at the
drop site.

After a successful transfer, the data must be placed in the drop site and the   *
transfer icon must be removed. The removal of the transfer icon can be
accompanied by an animation that shows the icon transforming into the drop
site. For example, the transfer icon can melt into the drop site.

After a failed transfer, the data must remain at the drag source, the data must * not be placed in the drop site, and the transfer icon must be removed. The removal of the transfer icon should be accompanied by an animation that shows the icon returning to the source location. For example, the transfer icon can snap back to the location of the drag source.

When multiple elements are involved in a drag and drop operation, the success or failure of the operation can be determined for the group as a whole or for each individual element in the group. If the group is transferred as a whole, there should only be one transfer icon at the drop site while the transfer is in progress. If the elements in the group succeed or fail individually, there can either be a transfer icon for each element or one transfer icon for the whole group. In either case, if partial success or failure is allowed, the drop site should post a message for each individual failure or otherwise indicate which transfers succeeded or failed.

4.3.5 Integrating Selection and Transfer

Instead of using **BTransfer**, transfer operations can be integrated with **BSelect**. When **BSelect** is used for dragging operations, its use partially supersedes the use of **BSelect Motion** in the selection models described in Section 4.1. The following rules are designed to make the integration of selection and transfer less restrictive:

- In text-like collections, **BSelect Motion** starting in a selected region * must drag the text selection; starting outside the selected region, it must * be used for making selections.

- In list-like and graphics-like collections, **BSelect Motion** starting on a * selected element must drag the entire selection.

- In dense list-like or graphics-like collections, in which background * space around elements is not generally available and in which **BSelect** * **Motion** is used for browsing or for selecting or toggling a range of * elements, **BSelect Motion** starting on an unselected element must be * used for making selections.

- In less dense list-like or graphics-like collections, **BSelect Motion** in the   *
  background must be used for making marquee selections; if they are not   *
  supported, **BSelect Motion** can be used to drag the entire collection, or   *
  to pan if the collection is scrollable.

- **BSelect Click** must always be used for selection.   *

When **BSelect** is used for dragging, the **<Ctrl>** and **<Shift>** modifiers must   *
be used to force the transfer operation as for **BTransfer**. When **BSelect** is   *
only used for selection, the **<Ctrl>** and **<Shift>** modifiers have their usual   *
selection-specific meanings.   *

If **BMenu** is not available for Popup Menus, **<Alt> BSelect** must be used   *
instead.

If **BMenu** is available, then when transfer is integrated with selection,
<Alt> BSelect Click should be used for primary transfer, and **<Alt>**
BSelect Motion should be used for quick transfer, with **<Ctrl>** and **<Shift>**
forcing the transfer operation as usual.

Chapter 5

Component Activation

This chapter describes the component activation model, which determines how to act upon previously selected elements.

Once users select an object, they can perform an action on it by using the components available in the application, or by using one of the selection actions described in Chapter 4. Using components to perform actions on a selection is called activation.

Components are used to send information to the underlying application. For example, a Text component is used to send complicated information to the application, but most components (for example, PushButtons) are simply used to start an application process. In fact, even a complicated component like Text may need to tell the application that the user is finished entering information.

Components that start some application process are used following the activation model, which this chapter divides into the following areas:

- Basic activation
- Accelerators
- Mnemonics
- TearOff activation

- Help activation

- Default activation

- Expert activation

- Previewing and autorepeat

- Cancel activation

5.1 Basic Activation

The basic activation model mimics real-life button activation in that pressing on a button activates it. The user selects a button with the location cursor, which can be moved among components following the navigation model described in Chapter 3.

- Clicking **BSelect** on the button must activate the button.   *

- **<Select>** or **<Space>** on a button with the focus must activate the   *
  button.

- **<Select>**, **<Space>**, **<Enter>**, or **<Return>** on an activatable Menu   *
  entry with the focus must activate the entry.

When **BSelect** is pressed over a button, the appearance of the button must   *
change to indicate that releasing **BSelect** activates the button. If, while   *
BSelect is pressed, the pointer is moved outside of the button, the visual   *
state must be restored. If, while **BSelect** is still pressed, the pointer is   *
moved back inside of the button, the visual state must again be changed to   *
indicate the pending activation. If **BSelect** is pressed and released within a   *
button, the button must be activated, regardless of whether the pointer has   *
moved out of the button while it was pressed.

An implementation can allow **BSelect Click 2+** (multiple mouse button clicks) to be treated as a single mouse button click on a per-component basis; that is, all clicks except the first are discarded. In an application where double-clicks are used heavily, this can help prevent the user from unintentionally activating a button twice.

A selectable element of a collection can be activatable; for example, a link icon, or an audio annotation in Text. If so, **BSelect Click**, **<Select>**, and   *
<Space> (except in Text) must select it. **BSelect Click 2** must select and   *
activate it.

5.2 Accelerators

An accelerator is a key or key combination that invokes the action of some component regardless of the position of the location cursor when the accelerator is pressed. Accelerators are most commonly used to activate Menu items without first posting the Menu.

If the button with the accelerator is within a primary or secondary window, *
or within a Pulldown Menu system from its MenuBar, it must be activatable *
whenever the input focus is in the window or the MenuBar system. If the *
button with the accelerator is within a Popup Menu system, it must be *
activatable whenever the focus is in the Popup Menu system or the *
component with the Popup Menu.

Applications can provide accelerators for any button component. *
Implementations must support accelerators in PushButtons and *
ToggleButtons that are in Menus. If a button has an accelerator, the *
accelerator must be shown following the label of the button.

5.3 Mnemonics

A mnemonic is a single character that can be associated with any component that contains a text label. The label must contain the character, *
and the character must be underlined within the label, except in language *
environments in which underlining is unavailable. If a label does not *
naturally contain the character of the mnemonic, the mnemonic must be *
placed in parentheses following the label. Labels can also be sequentially numbered, and the number can serve as the mnemonic. Labels that are duplicated within an application should be given the same mnemonic. *
Mnemonics must be case insensitive for activation. Either an uppercase or lowercase letter can be underlined in the label.

When the location cursor is within a Menu or a MenuBar, pressing the *
mnemonic key of a component within that Menu or MenuBar must move the *
location cursor to the component and activate it. If a mnemonic is used for *
an OptionButton or for a CascadeButton in a MenuBar, pressing <Alt> and *
the mnemonic anywhere in the window or its Menus must move the cursor *
to the component with that mnemonic and activate it. Implementation must *
support mnemonics for OptionButtons, PushButtons in a Menu, *
ToggleButtons in a Menu, and CascadeButtons in a Menu or MenuBar.

Mnemonics can also be used to select and deselect elements within a component as described in Section 4.1.10.

5.4 TearOff Activation

Some Menus have TearOffButtons as their first elements. A TearOffButton is like a PushButton with the special interaction of converting a Menu into a DialogBox; that is, tearing off the Menu from its CascadeButton. TearOffButtons must follow the rules for the basic activation model described in Section 5.1. For example, pressing and releasing **BSelect** in a TearOffButton tears off the Menu and transforms it into a DialogBox.

TearOffButtons also have a second activation mechanism. Once a Menu with a TearOffButton is posted, pressing **BTransfer** in the TearOffButton must start a TearOff action. As long as **BTransfer** is held, a representation of the Menu must follow the movements of the pointer. Releasing **BTransfer** must end the TearOff action by unposting the Menu system, creating a new window at the current pointer location with the contents of the Menu, and give focus to the new window in explicit pointer mode. The contents of the new window should not include the TearOffButton.

Pulling down or popping up a Menu that is currently torn off should not affect the torn off Menu. If the same Menu is torn off again, using either basic activation or TearOff activation, the existing torn off window should be removed prior to the creation of the new window. A torn off Menu is closed by pressing **<Cancel>** while focus is in the window or by using the TearOff Menu's window Menu.

5.5 Help Activation

Help is generally invoked from selections in the **Help** Menu of the MenuBar. In addition, **<Help>** on a component must invoke any context-sensitive help for the component or its nearest ancestor with context-sensitive help available. Within DialogBoxes, applications should provide context-sensitive help for the DialogBox as a whole.

<Shift> <Help> should switch into context-sensitive help mode if it is available. In the context-sensitive help mode, the pointer shape changes to show the mode, and help is provided for the next component that the user selects, after which context-sensitive help mode is exited.

5.6 Default Activation

Any window can have a default action, although default actions are most frequently used in DialogBoxes. A DialogBox should have a default action associated with it. The default action in a window can change depending upon which component has the focus. The current default action should correspond to the action of some PushButton, called the current default PushButton of the window.

The current default PushButton must be highlighted in some way, usually by   *
displaying a border around it. When the focus is on a PushButton, its action   *
must be the default action, and the PushButton must show default   *
highlighting. If the default action in a window varies, some PushButton   *
must always have default highlighting, except when there is no current   *
default action.

In a DialogBox, default PushButtons should be in the bottom area of PushButtons of the DialogBox. However, if a particular default action is associated with a cluster of controls in a window, the corresponding default PushButton can be located adjacent to the cluster.

When an explicit focus policy is in use, and the focus is outside the window, default highlighting should be placed on the PushButton whose action corresponds to the default action that would result from moving the focus to the window by using keyboard navigation among windows.

The default action of a DialogBox is activated according to the following rules:

- If the focus is in a window, **<Enter>** and **<Ctrl> <Return>** must invoke   *
  the default action, and, if the focus is in a component in a window other   *
  than multiline Text, **<Return>** must invoke the default action. These   *
  actions must have no other effect on the component with the focus,   *
  unless the default action has some effect.

- In list-like and graphics-like collections, when the location cursor is not on an activatable element, **BSelect Click 2** should act like **BSelect Click**, followed by invocation of the default action.

- When the focus is on a ToggleButton not used for expert activation, **BSelect Click 2** should activate the ToggleButton and then perform the default action.

Except in the middle of a button motion operation, **<Cancel>** anywhere in a *
DialogBox must be equivalent to activating the **Cancel** PushButton in the *
DialogBox.

5.7 Expert Activation

Some activatable elements, usually PushButtons and ToggleButtons, can have **expert activation** actions associated with them. **BSelect Click 2** (that is, double-clicking the element) should activate any expert action for the element. Expert actions should only be available in a Panel of PushButtons or in a Panel of RadioButtons where one of the RadioButtons is always on. *
When the focus is on a button used for expert activation, there must be no *
default action available, unless the default and expert actions are the same.

The expert action should include the regular action of the component in a more global manner. For example, a Panel of RadioButtons in a drawing application could include a tool for turning on the erase cursor. Selecting the RadioButton turns on the erase cursor. Double-clicking the RadioButton could erase the drawing area.

If a component with an expert action is selectable, activating the expert *
action must first select the component and then perform the expert action.

To support new users and keyboard-only users, expert actions must only be *
shortcuts to application features available elsewhere.

5.8 Previewing and Autorepeat

Two special actions can be used with activation: previewing and autorepeat. When **BSelect** is pressed and held over a PushButton or ToggleButton, the application can present information in some way that describes the effect of activating the button. This is called **previewing**. The information must be *
removed when the user releases **BSelect**. Applications should provide a means to disable previewing for experienced users.

PushButtons can also **autorepeat**; that is, when **BSelect** is pressed and held, the PushButton activates and continues to activate at regular intervals until the PushButton is released. Autorepeating buttons should continue to repeat even when the pointer moves outside the button while the button is pressed; however, applications can suspend the activation of the button until the pointer is moved back inside of the button. While the button is active, it should be drawn in the active state.

5.9 Cancel Activation

<Cancel> is available in most contexts to stop or cancel the current interaction. **<Cancel>** has an impact on the following contexts:

- Pressing **<Cancel>** during a mouse-based selection or drag operation *
  must cancel the operation.

- Pressing **<Cancel>** during a mouse-based scrolling operation must *
  cancel the scrolling action and return the system to its state prior to the *
  start of the scrolling operation.

- Pressing **<Cancel>** anywhere in a DialogBox must be equivalent to *
  activating the **Cancel** PushButton, if one exists, except during a mouse- *
  based selection or drag operation, in which case it should cancel the *
  operation.

- Pressing **<Cancel>** in a Pulldown Menu must either dismiss the Menu *
  and move the location cursor to the CascadeButton used to pull it down *
  or unpost the entire Menu system. **<Cancel>** in a Popup Menu, Option *
  Menu, TearOff Menu, or MenuBar must unpost the Menu system.

- Pressing **<Cancel>** while the focus is in a torn off Menu window must *
  close the torn off Menu window.

Chapter 6

Application Design Principles

This chapter is directed at application designers, rather than the people who write the algorithms of an application, although they are often one in the same. Application designers are the people who design the interface between the application algorithms and the user. In designing user interfaces, an application designer chooses the proper controls or groups of controls, or components, to pass data between the base application and the user, lays out those components naturally, and ensures that user interaction with the components and the layout are easy to use.

This chapter describes the three elements of application user interface design, as well as the principles for designing new user interface components. The four major sections of this chapter are as follows:

- Choosing components
- Layout
- Interaction
- Component design

6.1 Choosing Components

The user interface of an application is made up of components that perform two simple functions: presenting the application information to the user, and allowing the user to enter data for the application. Components can be divided into six types: basic controls, field controls, basic groups, layout groups, framing groups, and DialogBox groups. The groups are containers for controls and groups of controls. Groups can be nested.

The component types that should be available in a user interface toolkit are described in the following lists. The details of these components are described in the reference section in Chapter 9 of this guide. The correspondence of these components to widgets available in the OSF/Motif toolkit is described in Appendix A.

- **Basic Controls**

  Separator   Draws a separating line within windows, between Menu items, and between Panes of a PanedWindow. A Separator does not allow application interaction.

  Label   Displays static text and images. A Label presents application information to the user.

  PushButton   A button used to activate an operation. A PushButton contains a Label that indicates the operation of the button. The Label can contain text or an image.

  CascadeButton   A button used to display a Pulldown Menu. A CascadeButton contains a Label that indicates the Menu to be displayed. CascadeButtons can also contain an arrow graphic after the Label to distinguish it from PushButtons and to indicate the direction of the cascading Menu.

OptionButton

A button used to display an Option Menu. An Option Menu allows for a one-of-many selection. An OptionButton contains a Label that indicates the current state of the Option Menu and a bar graphic to distinguish it from a PushButton.

ToggleButton

A button with two states: on and off. A ToggleButton contains a Label that indicates the active state. Normally, preceding the Label is a graphic indicator of the state of the ToggleButton.

CheckButton

A ToggleButton in a group of ToggleButtons where any number of the ToggleButtons can be on at a time. The graphic indicator for a CheckButton is usually a filled square to indicate the on state or an empty square to indicate the off state. On color systems, the filled color can be distinct from general application colors to visually distinguish the on state.

RadioButton

A ToggleButton in a group of ToggleButtons where only one of the ToggleButtons can be on at a time. The graphic indicator for a RadioButton is usually a filled diamond or circle to indicate the on state or an empty diamond or circle to indicate the off state. On color systems, the filled color can be distinct from general application colors to visually distinguish the on state.

TearOffButton

A button used for tearing off a Menu to create a dialog representation of the Menu contents. A TearOffButton tears off a Menu in place when activated, or is dragged to tear off and move in one action. A TearOffButton usually contains a dashed line graphic representing perforations.

- **Field Controls**

Sash	Used to set the boundary between two components. A Sash is usually a small square on the boundary between two components. The separated components are called Panes, and a group of Panes, Separators, and Sashes is called a PanedWindow.
Scale	Used to set or display a value in a range. A Scale is usually composed of a slider, moving within an element that indicates the size of the range, and a Label that indicates the current value. The position of the slider indicates the value relative to the range. The slider is moved directly by using the mouse pointer or by using the arrow keys. A Scale can also have buttons with arrow graphics for moving the slider with the mouse.
ScrollBar	Used to scroll the visible area of a component. A ScrollBar is usually composed of a slider, moving within an element that indicates the full size of the component, and buttons with arrow graphics for moving the slider with the mouse. The slider indicates the relative position and size of the visible area of the component. The slider is moved directly by using the mouse pointer or by using the arrow keys.
List	Used for selecting elements from a list of elements. A List can allow multiple items to be selected or can be constrained to only allow one item to be selected at a time. A List is usually composed of a vertical list of items. A List can also have both horizontal and vertical ScrollBars for scrolling the visible portion of the list of items.
Text	Used for displaying, entering, and modifying text. There are single line and multiple line variants. Multiline Text can have both horizontal and vertical ScrollBars for scrolling the visible portion of the text area.

Canvas	Used for displaying, entering, and modifying graphics. A Canvas can have both horizontal and vertical ScrollBars for scrolling the visible portion of the drawing area.

• **Basic Groups**

Panel	Organizes a collection of components in a horizontal, vertical, or 2-dimensional layout. A Panel is usually composed of just one type of button.
Menu	Organizes a collection of buttons, Labels, and Separators in a horizontal, vertical, or 2-dimensional layout within a separate Menu window. There are three types of Menus: Pulldown, Popup, and Option. A Menu is only available while it is pulled down or popped up.
MenuBar	Organizes a collections of CascadeButtons in a horizontal layout at the top of a MainWindow.

• **Layout Groups**

Composition	Organizes a collection of components in an arbitrary layout.
PanedWindow	A linear grouping of components, Separators, and Sashes. Sashes are used to set the boundary between two components. The separated components are called Panes and can contain any components.

• **Framing Groups**

Frame	Draws framing decorations around a component.
ScrolledWindow	Frames a component and adds ScrollBars for scrolling the visible area of the component.
MainWindow	Organizes the contents of a primary window. A MainWindow frames the client area and can optionally include ScrollBars, a MenuBar, a command area, and a message area.

- **DialogBox Groups**

  A DialogBox group can either be nested within another group or organizes the contents of a secondary window. Although a DialogBox can contain any component, a simple DialogBox is composed of a Label and a Panel of PushButtons for supplying a response to the DialogBox. The OSF/Motif toolkit provides a number of ready-designed DialogBoxes for common uses: CommandDialog, FileSelectionDialog, MessageDialog, PromptDialog, and SelectionDialog. Several types of MessageDialog are available: ErrorDialog, InformationDialog, QuestionDialog, WorkingDialog, and WarningDialog.

6.1.1 Guidelines for Choosing a Main Component Group

At the highest level, components are organized into MainWindows, Menus, and DialogBoxes. Correctly deciding which component group to use for which parts of an application is one of the most important tasks of an application designer.

Every application must contain at least one MainWindow. The * MainWindow can contain a MenuBar, ScrollBars, a command area, a message area, and the client area. The client area of the MainWindow contains the framework of an application. The client area should contain all the components needed to perform the primary actions of the applications. For example, in a text editor application, the MainWindow usually contains a text editing area; in a graphics editor application, the MainWindow usually contains a graphics editing area and the components for changing drawing functions. Components that are used constantly throughout the application should be contained in the MainWindow's client area. Components that are used intermittently or infrequently should be placed in Menus or DialogBoxes.

The advantages of Menus are that they are readily available, quickly accessed and dismissed, and easy to browse through. The most commonly used Menus should be placed in the MenuBar in the MainWindow to increase these advantages. Because Menus are readily available, and quickly accessed and dismissed, they should be used for components that are frequently used. The time delays of bringing up a DialogBox for frequently used components can greatly reduce user productivity. Because Menus are easy to browse through, they should also be used for components that are commonly accessed by most users.

The advantages of Menus also cause some disadvantages. A Menu is a very short-lived component group. It is displayed only while the user makes a selection. Once the user makes a selection, the Menu disappears. So a Menu is not well-suited for making several selections at once.

Adding a TearOffButton to a Menu can allow that Menu to remain available even after a user selection. By activating a TearOffButton, the user changes the current Menu into a simple DialogBox with the same contents as the Menu. A Menu with a TearOffButton allows the user to make multiple selections because the user can cause it to stay posted after a selection. A TearOffButton is useful when it is unclear whether you should include a set of buttons in a Menu or DialogBox.

Menus, other than TearOff Menus, are also modal; that is, while a Menu is posted, the user cannot interact with other elements of the application. Because of this, unless a Menu can be torn off, it should not be used for components that the user may want to have available while interacting with other elements of the application.

The other disadvantage of Menus is they can only contain buttons and Labels. Menus should be used for performing simple actions and setting values, but are not suitable for more complicated functions like text entry.

DialogBoxes are used for two general purposes: to present information to the user and to take user input. Applications should use DialogBoxes to present transient information to the user, like warnings, cautions, or conformations to actions. DialogBoxes that present information to the user are called Message DialogBoxes. Message DialogBoxes are often placed on the screen by applications without a request from the user. Because Message DialogBoxes can disrupt a user's work, applications should present constantly updated information in the client area of the MainWindow. Also, applications can present minor cautions, incidental notes, and simple help in the message area of the MainWindow.

The advantages of using DialogBoxes to take user input are that they are long-lived and can contain any components. Because they are long-lived, they can be used to perform more than one action at a time and can remain available while the user interacts with other parts of the application. Applications should use user-input DialogBoxes like small applications. DialogBoxes should be used to perform tasks ancillary to the application, where the user can take more than one action before dismissing the DialogBox. Applications should also use DialogBoxes where the task requires more complicated interaction than is available in a Menu, like file selection.

Table 6-1 summarizes the suggested uses for MainWindows, Menus, and DialogBoxes.

Table 6–1. Suggested Window Types

For These Cases	Use This Main Component Group		
	MainWindow	Menu	DialogBox
Primary application actions	X	—	—
Ancillary application actions	—	—	X
Components used intermittently	—	X	—
Components used frequently	X	X	—
Components used seldomly	—	—	X
Components accessed by most users	—	X	—
Simple actions	X	X	—
Complex actions	X	—	X
Presenting transient information	—	—	X
Presenting updating information	X	—	—
Presenting minor information	X	—	—

6.1.2 Guidelines for Choosing Interactive Methods

Choosing the correct components for a task is usually simple. In most cases, a task seems to naturally belong to a component; for instance, scrolling a region with a ScrollBar or choosing a value from a range with a Scale. Each component's general purpose is described in Section 6.1, as well as in the reference section in Chapter 9. In some cases, though, it is difficult to decide between two controls or groups of controls that could perform the same task. The following subsections give some guidelines for choosing among some common similar components:

- Choosing a single-choice component

- Choosing a multiple-choice component

- Choosing among Menus and Panels

- Choosing between Text or Canvas, and a Label

6.1.2.1 Choosing a Single-Choice Component

A single-choice component allows the user to select a single item from a group of items. Applications should use a single-choice component to limit the user to one choice; for example, choosing among available pen widths in a drawing program. The available single-choice components are as follows:

- RadioBox

- OptionButton

- List

You should choose a single-choice component based on the number of items to choose among, the space available for the selection area, and the permanence of the selection. For a small number of items, the best component is a RadioBox or an OptionButton. RadioBoxes should usually contain no more than 5 or 6 items. Option Menus, which are connected to OptionButtons, should usually contain no more than 10 to 12 items. If there is very little space available in your application, you should use an OptionButton over a RadioBox, since the OptionButton takes up very little space.

When the number of items to choose from gets larger than a RadioBox or OptionButton can easily handle, you should use a List. You should also use a List when the items to choose from can change. For application consistency, the choices in a RadioBox or OptionButton should not change, but, if they do, you should use an OptionButton over a RadioBox. If a RadioBox or OptionButton choice becomes unavailable, it should be disabled rather than removed. Section 6.3.1.6 describes disabling components in detail.

6.1.2.2 Choosing a Multiple-Choice Component

A multiple-choice control or group of controls allows the user to simultaneously choose multiple items from a group of items. Applications should use multiple-choice components, rather than a series of single-choice actions, where the user may want to select more than one item from a group.

The available multiple-choice components are as follows:

- CheckBox

- List

As with single-choice components, the main factor when choosing which one to use is the number of items in the group. For small groups of fewer than seven static elements, applications should use a CheckBox. Applications should otherwise use a List. Note that a List component can be used as a single-choice or multiple-choice component.

6.1.2.3 Choosing Among Menus and Panels

Popup Menus should only be considered as shortcuts to application features because they are hidden in the application. Features hidden in Popup Menus are difficult to find for beginning users of an application because they provide no cue to their existence; however, they can provide rapid access to frequently used functionality once the user learns their contents. Applications should use Popup Menus to allow users to remain focused on their work areas and when there is not enough space in the client area for a Panel of buttons.

Popup Menus contain a set of buttons that can be used in the same way as a Panel of buttons or a Pulldown Menu. The primary difference is availability. A Popup Menu is only visible when requested by the user. At all other times it is hidden, providing no cue to its existence. When the user requests a Popup Menu, the application displays it at the location of the pointer. Buttons and Pulldown Menus, on the other hand, are always visible, but users need to move the focus away from their main work to activate them. Another difference is that buttons take up screen space while Popup Menus do not. Pulldown Menus provide a good compromise in space and availability versus Popup Menus and Panels.

Applications should use a Panel of buttons when the user makes frequent or multiple selections and when space in the client area allows. Whenever the choice between Popup Menus and Panels is difficult, applications should favor Panels.

A good compromise solution to these problems is a TearOff Menu. A TearOff Menu is a Pulldown Menu until the user wants it torn off into a DialogBox. After the Menu is torn off, the user can position it and use it in the same way as a Panel. TearOff Menus are especially useful because they contain a set of PushButtons that are not part of the main function of an application, allowing the user to activate the PushButtons multiple times in a row; for example, a font size Menu in a text editing application. In this case, the user can use the Pulldown Menu to change the font size of a single selected word or tear off the Menu into a Panel to perform a number of font size changes in the document. After finishing the font size changes, the user can dismiss the font size Panel.

6.1.2.4 Choosing Between Text or Canvas, and a Label

A Label is a simple mechanism for displaying text or graphics. A Label does not have any mechanisms for the user to edit its contents, or the overhead required for editing. Applications should use a Label for displaying text or graphics that do not need user editing. Applications should use a Text or Canvas when the text or graphics needs to be edited. On some systems, the contents of a Label are not selectable. If the user needs to select the contents of some noneditable text or graphics, applications should use a Text or Canvas and disable editing rather than using a Label.

6.2 Layout

The previous section described the components that are available for building an application. This section describes how to combine those components into a coherent application that encourages a user's sense of control. The guidelines presented in this section will help you create applications that are both consistent within themselves and with other OSF/Motif compliant applications.

This section discusses the following client area design topics:

- Common client areas
- Grouping components
- Menu design
- DialogBox design
- Designing drag and drop

Design the layout of your application windows according to the natural use order and the natural scanning order of the people who will be using your application.

First design for the natural use order. Consider the tasks that the user will perform with your application. The components should be positioned so that moving among the components is simple and quick while performing the most common tasks—the less pointer movement, the better. This is also true for keyboard traversal—the fewer keystrokes required to perform a task, the better.

The natural scanning order is most important when arranging small groups of components to help the user find the correct component for the task. You should put the most important and most used commands first. In most cases, this order is from left to right and from top to bottom. For users in right-to-left language environments, the natural scanning direction is from right to left and from top to bottom.

6.2.1 Common Client Areas

Your application is presented in windows. The windows can be either MainWindows, DialogBoxes, or Menus. The contents of these windows are the application client areas. Some of these client areas have common features that are described in this section. The following subsections describe in detail the contents of the MainWindow and the common MainWindow areas:

- Command area
- Message area
- ScrollBars
- MenuBar

Following this is a description of some common Popup Menus and DialogBoxes. These common client areas provide a familiar base for users new to your application to begin working.

6.2.1.1 MainWindow

Figure 6-1 shows a MainWindow with its client areas.

Figure 6–1. A Typical MainWindow and Its Common Client Areas

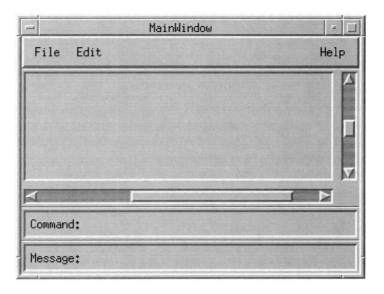

MainWindows contain the framework for your application. The principal component of a MainWindow is typically a scrollable work area. The application can also provide a group of useful controls, arranging these along the top, bottom, or side of the work area.

In a text editing application, a MainWindow usually contains the text. In a spreadsheet application, a MainWindow usually contains the spreadsheet. In a mail browsing application, a MainWindow usually contains a list of mail messages and an area for viewing a message. Every application must have at least one MainWindow.   *

Some applications may want more than one MainWindow; for example, applications with more than one primary function, like the query and update features of a database, and applications with more than one instance of the same primary function, like a graphics editor working on multiple figures. When an application has multiple MainWindows that serve the same primary function, each window should be treated as a separate application.   *
Each window must close and iconify separately. When an application has   *

multiple MainWindows that serve different primary functions, each window   *
must be iconifiable separately, but it is up to the application to decide   *
whether each closes separately or whether closing one window closes the   *
entire application. You should take special care to identify, using the
window manager title bar or a prominent internal Label, which DialogBoxes
belong to each MainWindow.

6.2.1.2 Command Area

Even though user interface applications are oriented toward direct
manipulation of graphical elements, your application can provide an area for
a user to enter a typed command. This can be particularly useful when
updating an existing command-based application to an application based on
a graphical user interface.

If your application includes a command area, it should run from border to
border across the MainWindow. If the MainWindow includes a message
area at the bottom, the command area should be placed just above the
message area; otherwise, it should be placed at the bottom of the
MainWindow.

The command area often consists of one or both of the following
components:

- A command entry area, consisting of a command entry field or a
  CommandBox

- A group of PushButtons for common window actions

6.2.1.3 Message Area

Your application can provide a message area in the MainWindow for
presenting application messages. Your application should not use a message
area for warnings or messages requiring immediate action. These should be
displayed in a DialogBox.

The message area can be used to provide brief help, either in response to a
request from the user or, as the focus changes, to indicate the purpose of the
component with the focus.

If your application includes a message area, it should run from border to border across the bottom of the MainWindow, below any ScrollBars or the command area. Your application can display and remove the message area as needed.

6.2.1.4 ScrollBars

An application can use ScrollBars in its MainWindow to provide a means for viewing an area larger than the MainWindow. Your application defaults should place ScrollBars on the bottom and right sides of the application. (ScrollBar placement can be a user preference.) You should place ScrollBars below the MenuBar and above any command or message area. ScrollBars should not scroll the MenuBar, command area, or message area. The ScrollBars can be displayed and removed as needed.

6.2.1.5 MenuBar

A MenuBar is a basic group that organizes the most common features of an application. The MenuBar must be a horizontal bar at the top edge of the *
application just below the title area of the window frame. The MenuBar contains a list of Menu topics in CascadeButtons with Pulldown Menus connected to them. A MenuBar must contain only CascadeButtons, because *
other buttons inhibit Menu browsing. Each Menu topic should have a single-letter mnemonic indicated by underlining.

The following Pulldown Menus provide general functions common to most applications. Remember that these Menu guidelines, like all the guidelines in this *OSF/Motif Style Guide*, apply only in a left-to-right language environment in an English-language locale. You need to make the appropriate changes for other locales.

File   The **File** Menu should contain components for performing actions on the files, such as opening, saving, closing, and printing. It should also contain components for performing actions on the application as a whole, such as quitting. If the Label **File** is not appropriate to the context of your application, you can choose a different, more appropriate Label. The **File** Menu should have a mnemonic of **F**.

Selected   The **Selected** Menu should contain components for performing actions on the objects represented by the current selection of the application, such as opening or printing a selected item. This Menu is often similar to the **File** Menu, except that it acts on the objects denoted by the current selection. For example, in a directory browser, **Open** in the **File** Menu could (using a DialogBox) prompt the user for the name of a directory to open for browsing, while **Open** in the **Selected** Menu opens the file whose icon is currently selected in the browser. The **Selected** Menu should not contain editing functions normally found in the **Edit** Menu. The **Selected** Menu should have a mnemonic of **S**.

Edit   The **Edit** Menu should contain components for performing actions on the current data of the application, such as an undo action or making global substitutions in a block of text. It should also include components for interacting with the system clipboard, such as cut, copy, and paste. The **Edit** Menu should have a mnemonic of **E**.

View   The **View** Menu should contain components for changing the user's view on the data. Components in the **View** Menu should not actually change the data. The exact contents of the **View** Menu are application specific but can include components that change the appearance of the data, the amount of data that is displayed, or the order in which the data is displayed. The **View** Menu should have a mnemonic of **V**.

Options   The **Options** Menu should contain components for a user to customize the application. The exact contents of the **Options** Menu are application specific. The **Options** Menu should have a mnemonic of **O**.

Help   The **Help** Menu should contain components that provide user help facilities. The components in the **Help** Menu usually bring up a DialogBox with help information. Every application should have a **Help** Menu. The **Help** Menu should have a mnemonic of **H**.

While we recommend that you include the common Menus in the MenuBar of your application, your choice of Menu titles and items depends on the nature of your application. If your application requires it, you should design more relevant titles and selections, but do not change the meanings of items used in the common Menus.

If any of the common Menus are present, they must be arranged in the   *
following order with respect to each other, ranging from left to right across   *
the MenuBar in a left-to-right language environment: *

> **File** Menu   *
> **Selected** Menu   *
> **Edit** Menu   *
> **View** Menu   *
> **Options** Menu   *
> **Help** Menu   *

You can omit any of these Menus if they are not relevant to the application.
You can also intersperse other, application-specific, Menus among these
Menus. However, if a **File** Menu is present, it must be the first Menu and   *
must be placed at the far left of the MenuBar. If a **Help** Menu is present, it   *
must be the last Menu and must be placed at the far right of the MenuBar.

The recommended contents of the **File**, **Edit**, and **Help** Menus follow. The
contents of the **Selected**, **View**, and **Options** Menus are application specific
and are not specified here. Each of these common Menus can contain a
TearOffButton.

6.2.1.5.1 File Menu Contents

Figure 6-2 shows a sample **File** Menu. The common Menu contents are
described following the figure. Note that you should only include those
functions actually supported by your application. The **File** Menu can
contain a TearOffButton.

Figure 6–2. The File Menu and Its Selections

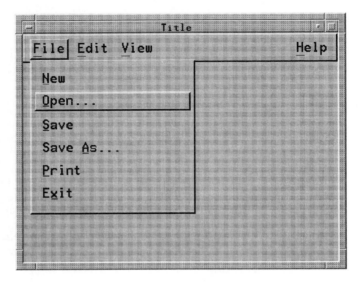

New   Must create a new file. This operation must clear existing *
               data from the client area. If completion of the operation *
               will obliterate current changes to the file, you must display *
               a DialogBox, asking the user about saving changes. This *
               action must have the mnemonic **N**.

Open . . .   Must open an existing file. This operation must prompt the *
               user for the name of the file with a DialogBox. The title bar
               should be updated with the name of the newly opened file. *
               If completion of the operation will obliterate current *
               changes to the file, you must display a DialogBox, asking *
               the user about saving changes. This DialogBox should be
               displayed after the user selects a new file. This action must *
               have the mnemonic **O**.

Save   Must save the currently opened file without removing the *
               existing contents of the client area. If the currently opened *
               file has no name, **Save** must prompt for a filename with a *
               DialogBox. This action must have the mnemonic **S**.

Save As . . .   Must save the currently opened file under a new name *
               without removing the existing contents of the client area. *
               This operation must prompt for the name of the file with a *

DialogBox. If the user tries to save the new file under an   *
existing name, **Save As** must alert the user with a   *
DialogBox if a possible loss of data would occur. This   *
action must have the mnemonic **A**.

Print   Must schedule a file for printing. If your application   *
requires specific printing information before printing, the   *
operation must first request that information with a   *
DialogBox, and the entry title must be followed by an   *
ellipsis. Printing information can also be specified for the
application in the **Options** Menu. This action must have   *
the mnemonic **P**.

Close   Can be supplied in applications that have multiple
independent primary windows. This action must not be   *
supplied in applications with a single primary window or   *
multiple dependent primary windows. This action must   *
only close the current primary window and its associated   *
secondary windows; that is, the window family. This action   *
must have the mnemonic **C**. You can include this action
even though it is similar to the **Close** action in the window
Menu. This ensures that users have a way to close the
primary window even if they are not running a compliant
window manager. Applications must prompt the user to   *
save any unsaved changes if the action would cause loss of   *
data.

Exit   Must end the current application and all windows   *
associated with it. This action is equivalent to closing all
primary windows of the application. This action must have   *
the mnemonic **X**. You should include this action even
though it is similar to the **Close** action in the window Menu.
This ensures that users have a way to end the application
even if they are not running a compliant window manager.   *
Applications must prompt the user to save any unsaved   *
changes if the action would cause loss of data. If your
application does not have a **File** Menu, put **Exit** at the end
of the first Pulldown Menu.

You should include Menu items in the order described. If you add new
Menu items, you should insert them near similar elements.

6.2.1.5.2 Edit Menu Contents

Figure 6-3 shows a sample **Edit** Menu. The common Menu contents are described following the figure. Note that you should only include those functions actually supported by your application. The **Edit** Menu can contain a TearOffButton.

Figure 6–3. The Edit Menu and Its Selections

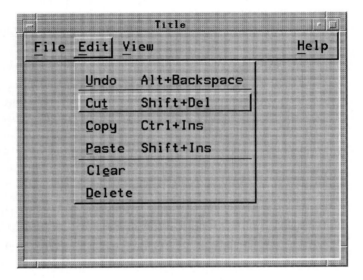

Undo Alt+Backspace

Must reverse the most recently executed action. To provide a *
visual cue to the user, the **Undo** selection title should be
dynamically modified to indicate what is being undone. For
example, if the most recently executed action was a paste, the
action name would be **Undo paste**. Your application should
be able to undo all of the actions in the **Edit** Menu. This *
action must have the mnemonic **U**.

Cut Shift+Del

Must remove the selected portion of data from the client area *
to the clipboard. This action must choose the component to *
act on by following the rules in Section 4.2.2 for operations *
that act on selections. This action must have the mnemonic **T**.

C̲opy   Ctrl+Ins

> Must copy the selected portion of data to the clipboard without *
> removing the original data from the client area. This action *
> must choose the component to act on by following the rules in *
> Section 4.2.2 for operations that act on selections. This action *
> must have the mnemonic **C**.

Copy Lin̲k

> Must copy a link of the selected portion of data to the *
> clipboard without removing the original data from the client *
> area. This action must choose the component to act on by *
> following the rules in Section 4.2.2 for operations that act on *
> selections. This action must have the mnemonic **K**.

P̲aste   Shift+Ins

> Must paste the contents of the clipboard into a client area. *
> This action must choose the component to act on by following *
> the rules in Section 4.2.2 for operations that do not act on *
> selections. This action must have the mnemonic **P**.

Paste L̲ink

> Must paste a link of the data represented by the contents of the *
> clipboard into a client area. This action must choose the *
> component to act on by following the rules in Section 4.2.2 for *
> operations that do not act on selections. This action must have *
> the mnemonic **L**.

Cl̲ear

> Must remove a selected portion of data from the client area *
> without copying it to the clipboard. The remaining data is not
> compressed to fill the space that was occupied by the cleared
> data. This action must choose the component to act on by *
> following the rules in Section 4.2.2 for operations that act on *
> selections. This action must have the mnemonic **E**.

D̲elete

> Must remove a selected portion of data from the client area *
> without copying it to the clipboard. This action must choose *
> the component to act on by following the rules in Section 4.2.2 *
> for operations that act on selections. This action must have *
> the mnemonic **D**.

Select All   Ctrl+/

> Must make the primary selection consist of all the elements in *
> a component of the client area. This action must choose the *
> component to act on by following the rules in Section 4.2.2 for *

operations that do not act on selections. If the action uses an accelerator, it should be **<Ctrl> </>**.

Deselect All   Ctrl+

Must remove from the primary selection all the elements in a *
component of the client area. This action must choose the *
component to act on by following the rules in Section 4.2.2 for *
operations that do not act on selections. If the action uses an
accelerator, it should be **<Ctrl> <\\>**.

Select Pasted

Must make the primary selection consist of the last element or *
elements pasted into a component of the client area. This *
action must choose the component to act on by following the *
rules in Section 4.2.2 for operations that do not act on *
selections.

Reselect   Alt+Insert

Must make the primary selection consist of the last selected *
element or elements in a component of the client area. This *
action must choose the component to act on by following the *
rules in Section 4.2.2 for operations that do not act on *
selections. The action must be available only in components *
that do not support persistent selections and only when the *
current selection is empty. If the action uses an accelerator, it
should be **<Alt> <Insert>**.

Promote   Alt+Insert

Must promote to the primary selection the current selection of *
a component of the client area. This action must choose the *
component to act on by following the rules in Section 4.2.2 for *
operations that act on selections. This action must only be *
available for components that support persistent selections. If
the action uses an accelerator, it should be **<Alt> <Insert>**.

You should include Menu items in the order described. If you add new Menu items, you should insert them near similar elements.

If you use accelerators for **Undo**, **Cut**, **Copy**, and **Paste**, you must use either *
one or both of the models presented in the following two tables.

Table 6–2. Edit Menu Accelerators, Model 1

Edit Menu Item	Accelerator
Undo	\<Alt> \<BackSpace>
Cut	\<Shift> \<Delete>
Copy	\<Ctrl> \<Insert>
Paste	\<Shift> \<Insert>

Table 6–3. Edit Menu Accelerators, Model 2

Edit Menu Item	Accelerator
Undo	\<Ctrl> \<Z>
Cut	\<Ctrl> \<X>
Copy	\<Ctrl> \<C>
Paste	\<Ctrl> \<V>

In addition, if your keyboard has **\<Undo>**, **\<Cut>**, **\<Copy>**, and **\<Paste>** keys, these should be supported as accelerators for the corresponding Menu items as well.

6.2.1.5.3 Help Menu Contents

There are two acceptable models for the contents of the **Help** Menu. This guide allows either model.

Figure 6-4 shows a sample of the first model for the **Help** Menu. The common Menu contents for this model are described following the figure. Note that you should only include those functions actually supported by your application. The **Help** Menu can contain a TearOffButton.

Figure 6–4. The Help Menu and Its Selections (First Model)

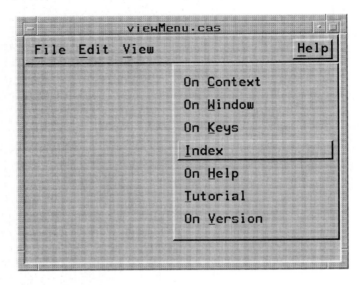

On Context   Shift+Help

> Must initiate context-sensitive help by changing the *
> shape of the pointer to the question pointer described in *
> Section 2.2.2. When the user moves the pointer to the *
> component help is wanted on and presses **BSelect**, any *
> available context-sensitive help for the component must *
> be presented, and the pointer reverts from the question *
> pointer. This action must have the mnemonic **C**. If the *
> action uses an accelerator, it must be **<Shift> <Help>**.

On Help

> Must provide information on how to use the *
> application's help facility. This action must have the *
> mnemonic **H**.

On Window

> Must provide general information about the window *
> from which help was requested. This action must have *
> the mnemonic **W**.

On Keys

> Must provide information about the application's use of *
> function keys, mnemonics, and keyboard accelerators. *
> This action must have the mnemonic **K**.

Index

> Must provide an index for all help information in the *
> application. This action must have the mnemonic **I**.

The index can provide search capabilities.

Tutorial
    Must provide access to the applicatic . tutorial. This   *
    action must have the mnemonic **T**.

On Version
    Must provide the name and version of the application.   *
    This action must have the mnemonic **V**. It can provide
    other information as well.

Figure 6-5 shows a sample of the second model for the **Help** Menu. The
common Menu contents in the model are described following the figure.
Note that you should only include those functions actually supported by
your application. The **Help** Menu can contain a TearOffButton.

Figure 6–5. The Help Menu and Its Selections (Second Model)

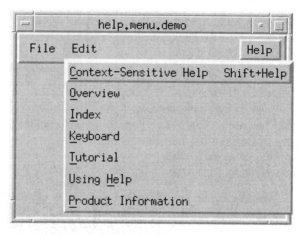

Context-Sensitive Help   Shift+Help
    Must initiate context-sensitive help by changing the   *
    shape of the pointer to the question pointer described   *
    in Section 2.2.2. When the user moves the pointer to   *
    the component help is wanted on and presses **BSelect**,   *
    any   available   context-sensitive   help   for   the   *
    component must be presented, and the pointer reverts   *
    from the question pointer. This action should be   *
    followed by a separator. This action must have the   *
    mnemonic **C**. If the action uses an accelerator, it must   *
    be **<Shift> <Help>**.

Overview   Must provide general information about the   *
application window from which help was requested.   *
This action must have the mnemonic **O**.

Index   Must provide an index for all help information in the   *
application. This action must have the mnemonic **I**.
The index can provide search capabilities.

Keyboard   Must provide information about the application's use   *
of function keys, mnemonics, and keyboard   *
accelerators. This action must have the mnemonic **K**.

Tutorial   Must provide access to the application's tutorial. This   *
action must have the mnemonic **T**.

Using Help   Must provide information on how to use the   *
application's help facility. This action must have the   *
mnemonic **H**.

Product Information

Must provide the name and version of the application.   *
This action must have the mnemonic **P**. It can provide
other information as well.

Applications should place additional **Help** Menu items between **Index** and
Using Help.

Help is usually provided in DialogBoxes but can also appear in the message
area. You should include Menu items in the order described. If you add
new Menu items, you should insert them near similar elements.

6.2.1.6 Popup Menus

A Popup Menu is a Menu that is associated with another element. It is
usually hidden from the user and is posted using **BMenu** and **<Menu>**. It is
used to organize actions that are specific to its associated element, but it
should not be the only place in an application where those actions are
available; that is, Popup Menus should be a redundant element of a user
interface whose main purpose is to provide the experienced user with a
quick way to perform common tasks on individual elements.

The following common actions provide general functions common to Popup
Menus in many applications. While we recommend that you include these

common actions in your Popup Menus consistently with the descriptions here, your choice of items depends on the nature of your application. If your application requires it, you should design more relevant titles and selections, but do not change the meanings of items used in the common Popup Menus.

Even within a single control, such as a Canvas, the contents of a Popup Menu can depend on the position within the control, or the state of the elements at that position, such as whether the Menu is popped up from within a selected range of elements. When **BMenu** is used to pop up the Menu, the location of the pointer when **BMenu** is pressed is what matters. When **<Menu>** is used to pop up the Menu, what matters is the position of the location cursor within the control.

Note that you should include only those functions actually supported by your application. Remember that these Menu guidelines, like all the guidelines in this guide, apply only in a left-to-right language environment in an English-language locale. You need to make the appropriate changes for other locales.

Propertie_s_

Must display a properties DialogBox that the user can use to   *
set the properties of the component. If the Menu is popped up
over a selection, it can display the properties of the selection.
If the Menu is popped up over an unselected item, it can
display the properties of that item. If the Menu is popped up
over the background, it should display the properties of the
collection, except over a part of the background considered to
be in the selection. This action should have the mnemonic **S**.

_U_ndo Alt+Backspace

Must reverse the most recently executed action. To provide a   *
visual cue to the user, the **Undo** selection title should be
dynamically modified to indicate what is being undone. For
example, if the most recently executed action was a paste, the
action name would be **Undo paste**. This action should have
the mnemonic **U**. This action should have the same
accelerator as the corresponding entry in the **Edit** Menu.

Primary Move Alt+Shift+Delete

Must move the contents of the primary selection to the   *
component. This action must only be used in an editable   *
component. If the action uses an accelerator, it should be
<Alt> <Shift> <Delete>, **<Alt> <Ctrl> <X>**, or both. In
addition, if the keyboard has a **<Cut>** key, this action should

support **<Alt> <Cut>** as an accelerator. If more than one format can be moved from the primary selection, **Primary Copy** can cascade a Menu of possible transfer formats, in which case it should not have an accelerator.

Primary Copy   Alt+Ctrl+Insert

Must copy the contents of the primary selection to the *
component. This action must only be used in an editable *
component. If the action uses an accelerator, it should be **<Alt> <Ctrl> <Insert>, <Alt> <Ctrl> <C>,** or both. In addition, if the keyboard has a **<Copy>** key, this action should support **<Alt> <Copy>** as an accelerator. If more than one format can be copied from the primary selection, **Primary Copy** can cascade a Menu of possible transfer formats, in which case it should not have an accelerator.

Primary Link

Must place a link to the primary selection in the component. *
This action must only be used in an editable component. If the link can be viewed in more than one way, **Primary Link** can cascade a Menu of possible viewing representations.

Cut

Must cut elements to the clipboard and can mark them for use *
in a subsequent **Paste Link** operation. If the Menu is popped *
up in a selection, the entire selection must be cut. If the Menu is popped up over an unselected element, just that element should be cut. If the Menu is popped up in the background, the entire collection can be cut. This action should have the mnemonic **T**.

Copy

Must copy elements to the clipboard and can mark them for *
use in a subsequent **Paste Link** operation. If the Menu is *
popped up in a selection, the entire selection must be copied. If the Menu is popped up over an unselected element, just that element should be copied. If the Menu is popped up in the background, the entire collection can be copied. This action should have the mnemonic **C**.

Copy Link

Must copy a link of elements to the clipboard and can mark *
them for use in a subsequent **Paste Link** operation. If the *
Menu is popped up in a selection, a link to the entire selection *
must be copied. If the Menu is popped up over an unselected *
element, a link to just that element should be copied. If the

Menu is popped up in the background, a link to the entire collection can be copied. This action should have the mnemonic **K**.

P̱aste   Shift+Insert

Must paste the contents of the clipboard to the component.   *
This action must only be used in an editable component. This
action should have the mnemonic **P**. This action should have
the same accelerator as the corresponding entry in the **Edit**
Menu.

Paste Ḻink

Must paste a link of the contents of the clipboard to the   *
component. This action must only be used in an editable   *
component. This action should have the mnemonic **L**.

Cḻear   Must remove a selected portion of data from the client area   *
without copying it to the clipboard. If the Menu is popped up   *
in a selection, it must delete the selection. If the Menu is
popped up over an unselected element, it should delete that
element. If the Menu is popped up over the background,
except over a part of the background considered to be in the
selection, it can delete all the elements. The remaining data is
not compressed to fill the space that was occupied by the
cleared data. This action should have the mnemonic **E**.

Ḏelete   Must remove a selected portion of data from the client area   *
without copying it to the clipboard. If the Menu is popped up   *
in a selection, it must delete the selection. If the Menu is
popped up over an unselected element, it should delete that
element. If the Menu is popped up over the background,
except over a part of the background considered to be in the
selection, it can delete all the elements. This action should
have the mnemonic **D**.

Select All   Ctrl+/

Must make the primary selection consist of all the elements in   *
the collection with the Popup Menu. If the action uses an
accelerator, it should be **<Ctrl> </>**.

Deselect All   Ctrl+

Must deselect the current selection in the collection with the   *
Popup Menu. If the action uses an accelerator, it should be
<Ctrl> <\\>.

Select Pasted

>   Must make the primary selection consist of the last element or *
>   elements pasted into the collection with the Popup Menu.

Reselect Alt+Insert

>   Must make the primary selection consist of the last selected *
>   element or elements in the component with the Popup Menu. *
>   The action must be available only in components that do not *
>   support persistent selections and only when the current *
>   selection is empty. If the action uses an accelerator, it should
>   be **<Alt> <Insert>**.

Promote Alt+Insert

>   Must promote the current selection to the primary selection. *
>   This action must only be available in components that support *
>   persistent selections. If the action uses an accelerator, it
>   should be **<Alt> <Insert>**.

If an action invoked from a Popup Menu, such as **Primary Copy**, inserts or *
pastes data in a collection, the data must be pasted at the insertion position *
of the component. However, if the Popup Menu is popped up over a *
selection of an editable collection, the selection must first be deleted, even *
if pending delete is disabled, and the pasted data must replace it.

If an action invoked from a Popup Menu acts on a group of elements, it *
behaves according to the following rules:

- If the Menu is popped up in a selection, it must act on the entire *
  selection.

- If the Menu is popped up on an unselected element of a list or graphics
  collection, it should act on just that element.

- If the Menu is popped up in the background, except in a part of the
  background considered in the selection, it can act on the entire
  collection. However, if the operation is destructive, it must first prompt *
  for verification.

Appropriate words, such as **Selection** or words denoting the type of a single
element of the collection as a whole, should be added to a Label to specify
which elements are affected. For example, if a Popup Menu contains the
entry **Copy Selection**, the current selection is copied to the clipboard
regardless of where in the collection the Menu is popped up.

A Popup Menu item should have an accelerator only if the result of typing
the accelerator would be equivalent to popping up the Menu by pressing

<Menu> and then selecting the Menu item. If **Cut Selection** is included in a Popup Menu, it should use the same accelerators as **Cut** in the **Edit** Menu. If **Copy Selection** is included in a Popup Menu, it should use the same accelerators as **Copy** in the **Edit** Menu.

6.2.1.7 DialogBoxes

Applications use DialogBoxes to interact with the user about application details not directly related to the primary purpose of the application. Applications display DialogBoxes only when needed to convey a message to the user, or when the user requests it to provide input to the application. They follow the same general layout guidelines as a MainWindow. Additional guidelines for DialogBox design are given in Section 6.2.4, as well as in the reference section in Chapter 9.

The following DialogBoxes provide general functions common to many applications.

6.2.1.7.1 CommandDialog

A CommandDialog should be used to enter keyboard commands. It should not interrupt the user's interaction with the application; that is, it should not be modal. It should include a CommandBox as shown in Figure 6-6.

Figure 6–6. A CommandDialog

6.2.1.7.2 FileSelectionDialog

A FileSelectionDialog should be used to enter the name of a file for processing. It should not interrupt the user's interaction with the application; that is, it should not be modal. It should include a FileSelectionBox as shown in Figure 6-7.

Figure 6–7. A FileSelectionDialog

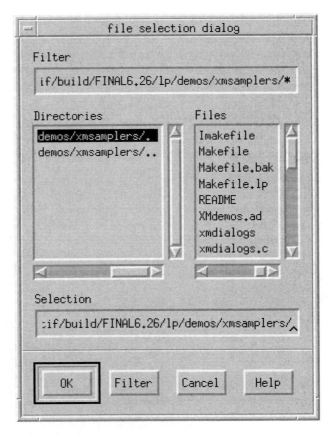

6.2.1.7.3 PromptDialog

A PromptDialog should be used to prompt the user for input. It can interrupt the user's interaction with the application; that is, it can be application modal. It should include a message, a text input area, and one of the following button arrangements as shown in Figure 6-8.

OK Cancel
OK Cancel Help
OK Apply Cancel
OK Apply Cancel Help
OK Apply Reset Cancel
OK Apply Reset Cancel Help

Figure 6–8. A PromptDialog

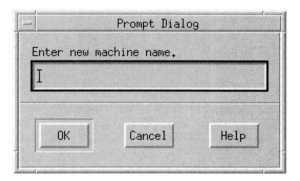

6.2.1.7.4 SelectionDialog

A SelectionDialog should be used to allow a user to make a selection from a list of choices. It can interrupt the user's interaction with the application; that is, it can be application modal. It should contain a SelectionBox as shown in Figure 6-9.

Figure 6–9. A SelectionDialog

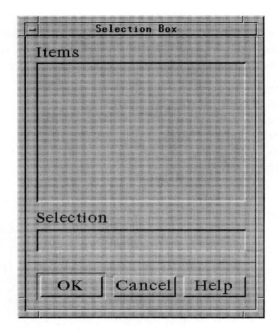

6.2.1.7.5 MessageDialog

A MessageDialog should be used to convey a message to the user. It should
include a message and one of the following button arrangements:

OK
OK Help
OK Cancel
OK Cancel Help
Yes No
Yes No Help
Yes No Cancel
Yes No Cancel Help
Cancel
Cancel Help
Retry Cancel
Retry Cancel Help

There are a number of different types of MessageDialogs: ErrorDialog, InformationDialog, QuestionDialog, WorkingDialog, and WarningDialog.

An ErrorDialog should be used to convey a message about a user error. It should stop user interaction with the application until it is dismissed; that is, it should be application modal. It should include an error symbol, a message, and one of the following button arrangements as shown in Figure 6-10:

OK Cancel
OK Cancel Help

Figure 6–10. An ErrorDialog

An InformationDialog should be used to convey information to the user. It   *
must not interrupt the user's interaction with the application; that is, it must   *
not be modal. It should include an information symbol, a message, and one
of the following button arrangements as shown in Figure 6-11:

OK
OK Help

Figure 6–11. An InformationDialog

A QuestionDialog should be used to get a user response to a question. It should interrupt the user's interaction with the application; that is, it should be application modal. It should include a question symbol, a message, and one of the following button arrangements as as shown in Figure 6-12:

Yes No
Yes No Help
Yes No Cancel
Yes No Cancel Help

Figure 6–12. A QuestionDialog

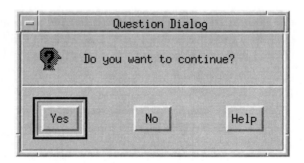

A WarningDialog should be used to alert the user to a possible danger. It should interrupt the user's interaction with the application; that is, it should be application modal. It should contain a warning symbol, a message, and one of the following button arrangements as shown in Figure 6-13:

Yes No
Yes No Help
OK Cancel
OK Cancel Help

Figure 6–13. A WarningDialog

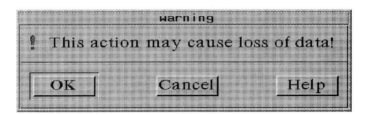

A WorkingDialog should be used to show work in progress and give the user an opportunity to cancel the operation. It should not interrupt the user's interaction with the application; that is, it should not be modal. It should contain a working symbol, a message, and any of the following sets of buttons in order as shown in Figure 6-14:

Close
Cancel or **Stop**
Pause Resume
Help

A WorkingDialog should also include a progress indicator if that information is available.

Figure 6–14. A WorkingDialog

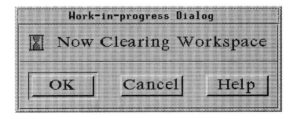

6.2.2 Grouping Components

The following subsections describe how you should group components by using the group components described in Section 6.1:

- Grouping similar components
- Arranging components for fixed layout
- Arranging components for resizing layout
- Arranging components for aligned layout
- Arranging components in PanedWindows

Separators are a good tool for visually separating groups of components. You should use Separators in your application any place where the border between two groups of components is not obvious by some other means, such as for a significant change in component types, framing, or a division by space.

6.2.2.1 Grouping Similar Components

Components similar in appearance and function group together naturally. You should organize similar components together. Similar PushButtons, as in a Menu, and a Panel of CheckButtons, as in a list of options, are good examples of where grouping is important. Without grouping, related actions are difficult to find. One of the most important cases is a Panel of RadioButtons. Without grouping, when you turned on one RadioButton, you might not see the previous button turn off. You can also associate a title with a group of components to better associate the group and its purpose.

6.2.2.2 Arranging Components for Fixed Layout

Components that are grouped using a Composition group component can be positioned as they best fit, both physically and visually. This is often the case in the MainWindow client area, and is also useful when the layout of the components is important to the application.

When you lay out components in this manner, remember that your application can be resized by the user. This can be compensated for in a number of ways. If the area has a fixed size and is not appropriate to scroll, like a control panel, you can either clip the area or turn off resizing. If the area has a fixed size and is appropriate to scroll, you should include ScrollBars for scrolling the viewable area.

6.2.2.3 Arranging Components for Resizing Layout

Composition component groups can also be positioned so that the position and size of each component is relative to the Composition component group or other components in the group. This style of layout permits the components to change size proportionally to any change in the size of the Composition component.

Sometimes a window is resized too small to be useful. Your application can either simply ignore this, clip the region once all the components are at their minimum size, remove less useful components to make room for more shrinking, or replace all the components with a message that indicates that the minimum size is reached, stating that the user needs to enlarge the window to continue working in it.

6.2.2.4 Arranging Components for Aligned Layout

Panels can arrange components aligned horizontally, vertically, or in two dimensions. Buttons are usually aligned in Panels horizontally along the bottom of the client area, either in a MainWindow or in a DialogBox. ToggleButtons should be arranged in vertical Panels so the graphics align and look neat. A common use of Panels is in building Menus or RadioBoxes; that is, a set of RadioButtons. Two-dimensional Panels are commonly used in graphics programs to present drawing styles and in spreadsheets to contain cells.

Your application should use Panels to provide the best organization for large groups of similar components. Panels should be placed in a Composition component group to allow for proper user resizing either by using ScrollBars or by resizing the elements of the Panel.

6.2.2.5 Arranging Components in PanedWindows

PanedWindows provide a way for the user to simply adjust the size of components relative to one another. You should use PanedWindows to separate user tasks in an application with limited space. This allows the user to ignore elements of the application that are unused.

PanedWindows can also be used to present two simultaneous views of the same data. For example, a text editor can use multiple Panes, with a separate Text component in each Pane to allow the user to write in one section of a document while looking at another. The user can then resize the Panes to show more or less of either block of text.

PanedWindows can be composed of either vertical (one on top of the other) or horizontal (side by side) sets of Panes, Separators, and Sashes. Users can resize Panes by dragging the boundary between them. Making one Pane bigger makes the other Pane smaller, while the overall size of the window remains the same.

6.2.3 Menu Design

Menus are the primary means of organizing most of an application's features. Because of screen size limitation and visual simplicity, Menus organize components used frequently by users and components used in most application sessions.

There are four types of Menus:

- Pulldown Menus

- TearOff Menus

- Popup Menus

- Option Menus

Pulldown Menus are pulled down from a CascadeButton. CascadeButtons should always be available in the context that they are needed. Menus can also contain CascadeButtons so that Menus can be nested. The MenuBar is a horizontal collection of CascadeButtons.

TearOff Menus are a combination of a TearOffButton and another Menu, usually a Pulldown Menu. A TearOffButton contains a dashed line graphic representing perforations. TearOffButtons must be the first element within a   *

Menu. When the TearOffButton is activated, the Menu changes into a DialogBox. A TearOff Menu is useful when you do not want the Menu to disappear after a Menu selection.

Popup Menus are context sensitive, but give no cue to their existence. They are popped up when the user presses **BMenu** over a component with an associated Popup Menu. Popup Menus should only be used to provide shortcuts, since new users of an application may not realize or remember that they exist. Even within a single control, such as a Canvas, the contents of a Popup Menu can depend on the position within the control, or the state of the elements at that position, such as whether the Menu is popped up from within a selected range of elements.

Option Menus provide a means of selecting from a set of choices while taking up very little space. An Option Menu is popped up from an OptionButton, which is distinguished by a bar graphic on the right side of the button.

Menus are composed of titles, elements, mnemonics, and accelerators. A Menu's title should be unique to avoid confusion. The title should clearly indicate the purpose of the Menu.

- A Pulldown Menu's title is taken from the Label in the CascadeButton.

- A Popup Menu's title should be placed at the top of the Popup Menu and separated from the Menu elements by a Separator.

- An Option Menu's title is usually a Label to the left of the OptionButton, but it can be at the top of the Option Menu itself.

Most basic controls can be Menu elements including Labels, Separators, PushButtons, ToggleButtons, and CascadeButtons. The elements can be identified by either a text label or a graphic. A Menu must be wide enough   * to accommodate its widest element.

A mnemonic provides a quick way to access Menu elements from the keyboard. While the location cursor is in a Menu or MenuBar, pressing the mnemonic letter of an element activates that element. The MenuBar's and any Option Menu's mnemonics can be used by pressing **<Alt>** with the mnemonic letter. An element's mnemonic should be the first character of the element's Label. If that character conflicts with another mnemonic in the Menu, another character in the Label should be used. The mnemonic of an element should be underlined in the element's Label. When the appropriate mnemonic letter does not appear in the element's Label, it should appear in parentheses after the Label.

An accelerator provides a way to access Menu elements from the keyboard without posting the Menu. Accelerators are useful to the experienced user for saving time when using frequently used components. You should provide accelerators primarily as a matter of utility, not design conformity.

If a keyboard accelerator exists for a Menu entry, it should appear following the Menu's Label, justified on the same line. The accelerator and the selection should be separated by enough space to make them visually distinct.

You should use the following guidelines when designing Menus and Menu systems:

- Keep Menu structures simple.
- Group like Menu elements together.
- List Menu selections by frequency of use.
- List Menu selections by order of use.
- Separate destructive actions.
- Provide mnemonics and accelerators.
- Use TearOffButtons in frequently used Menus.

6.2.3.1 Keeping Menu Structures Simple

Applications should keep Menu structures simple. One of the primary benefits of Menus is the ease of access to the elements of the Menu. While cascading submenus help the application and the user organize Menu elements, each level of a submenu reduces the ease of access to the Menu elements. Multiple levels of cascading submenus can also quickly create visual clutter. Whenever you consider using a cascading submenu, you should consider using a DialogBox or more Pulldown Menus instead.

6.2.3.2 Grouping Like Menu Elements Together

Applications should group Menu elements into logical groups. This helps the user locate specific Menu elements. You should first try to place a new Menu element into the common Menu groups described in Section 6.2.1.5. If that is not appropriate, you should group new Menu elements according to function, with the more frequently used element appearing first. You should also use Separators between logical groups of elements.

6.2.3.3 Listing Menu Selections by Frequency of Use

As in other client areas, applications should order Menu elements according to the frequency of usage, positioning the most frequently used elements near the top of the Menu.

6.2.3.4 Listing Menu Selections by Order of Use

More important to Menu design than the frequency of use is the order of use. Applications should order Menu elements according to the order of usage. For example, the **Copy** element should be placed before **Paste.** This helps the user's interactions flow smoothly.

6.2.3.5 Separating Destructive Actions

Applications should separate destructive actions from frequently chosen selections. This is to avoid accidental selection of the destructive element. Destructive elements, like **Delete** or **Clear**, should be placed at the end of a Pulldown Menu and separated from other elements by a Separator.

6.2.3.6 Providing Mnemonics and Accelerators

Applications should provide mnemonics and accelerators to Menu elements. Try to choose mnemonics and accelerators that are easy to remember by using letters from the element's title. Note that mnemonics and accelerators only add to the utility of your applications. They never detract from the basic ability of a new user.

Applications should provide accelerators for frequently used Menu items. In general, accelerators should not be assigned for every Menu item in an application. It is preferable to assign accelerators that have some mnemonic value, although accelerators that use function keys are acceptable.

Applications should not use accelerators that are a combination of the modifier **<Alt>** and letter keys to avoid conflicts with mnemonics. For example, **<Alt> <E>** as an accelerator for **Exit** conflicts with the use of **<Alt> <E>** to pull down the **Edit** Menu since it is the mnemonic for the **Edit** CascadeButton in the MenuBar.

Similarly, applications that involve text entry should not use accelerators that are combinations of the modifier **<Shift>** and letter keys to avoid conflict with the text entry commands. Applications that expect field controls to have bindings that include combinations of the modifier **<Ctrl>** and letter keys, such as text editors, should also avoid these combinations.

Accelerator bindings that use only one modifier are preferable to bindings that use two or more modifier keys.

6.2.3.7 Using TearOffButtons

Applications should use TearOffButtons in Menus whose elements are used many times in a row. If the semantics of the entries in a Popup Menu depend on where in a component it is popped up, the Menu should not include a TearOffButton, unless context-sensitive entries are disabled when the Menu is torn off. Menu entries in a torn off Menu should be enabled or disabled as appropriate when the state of the application changes.

After a user tears off a Menu, the Menu elements are placed in a DialogBox that is titled with the Menu title, and the Menu is unposted. The TearOffButton should be removed from the DialogBox, but, if it remains, it can be used to close the DialogBox.

6.2.4 DialogBox Design

When designing a DialogBox, you should follow all the same layout principles as for other applications areas. DialogBoxes are usually transitory. The user usually wants to simply respond and get back to the primary tasks of the application. To help the user respond quickly, there are a number of common DialogBox actions. By using and ordering these actions consistently, you provide the user with cues to quickly respond to each DialogBox.

When a DialogBox is displayed, all components within the DialogBox should reflect the current state of the application. For example, if the DialogBox is used for changing the current font in a text editor, the DialogBox should be initially displayed with the current font. If the DialogBox is modeless, then any changes to the application should be updated in the DialogBox.

DialogBoxes can limit how a user can interact with other windows in order to force the order of interaction. These limitations, which are called modes, are described in the following text.

Modeless   Allows interaction with the secondary window and all other windows.

Primary modal   Does not allow interaction with any ancestor of the window.

Application modal   Does not allow interaction with any window created by the same application even if the application has multiple primary windows.

System modal   Does not allow interaction with any window on the screen. This includes windows from all other applications and any icon box. To indicate a system modal secondary window, the pointer should change shape to a caution pointer whenever it leaves the system modal secondary window.

Remember that the guidelines presented in this section, like all the guidelines in this guide, apply only in a left-to-right language environment in an English-language locale. You need to make the appropriate changes for other locales.

6.2.4.1 Common DialogBox Actions

While your application can sometimes require special DialogBox actions, most share common actions. The common actions provide a consistent means for the user to quickly respond to DialogBoxes and get back to the primary application tasks. The common actions should be presented in a horizontal collection of PushButtons at the bottom of the DialogBox, separated from the rest of the DialogBox by a Separator.

No DialogBox will contain all of the common actions in the following list. You should use the ones appropriate to your application or determine new actions so they do not conflict with the common actions listed. If you create a new action, you should give it an active-voice label that indicates its purpose. An active-voice label describes the action that pressing the button causes. The actions are listed in the approximate sequence in which they should appear in DialogBoxes as follows:

Yes   Must indicate an affirmative response to a question posed in the   *
DialogBox and then close the window. While **Yes** is not an active-voice label, it implies a positive response to a question in a QuestionDialog or a WarningDialog. Only use **Yes** if it is a clear answer to the question.

No   Must indicate a negative response to a question posed in the   *
DialogBox and then close the window. While **No** is not an active-voice label, it implies a negative response to a question in a QuestionDialog. Only use **No** if it is a clear answer to the question.

OK   Must cause the application to apply any changes and perform   *
related actions specified by the components in the DialogBox and   *
then dismiss the DialogBox. While **OK** is not an active-voice label, its usage is too common to change.

Close   Should cause the current DialogBox to be closed without performing any of the actions specified by the components in the DialogBox. This action is usually only available in a DialogBox that provides status information, such as a WorkingDialog. This Label can also be used if the actions in the DialogBox cannot be reversed, in which case this Label replaces **Cancel** after the first irreversible action is performed.

Apply   Must apply any changes and perform related actions specified by   *
the components in the DialogBox.

Retry   Must cause the task in progress to be attempted again. This action   *
is commonly found in message boxes that report an error.

Stop   Must end the task in progress at the next possible breaking point.   *
This action is commonly found in a WorkingDialog.

Pause   Must cause the task in progress to pause. This action is   *
commonly found in a WorkingDialog and should be used in
combination with **Resume**.

Resume   Must cause a task that has previously paused to resume. This   *
action is commonly found in a WorkingDialog and should be used
in combination with **Pause**.

Reset   Must cancel any user changes that have not been applied to the   *
application. It must also reset the status of the DialogBox to the   *
state since the last time the DialogBox action was applied or to   *
the initial state of the DialogBox.

Cancel   Must close the DialogBox without performing any DialogBox   *
actions not yet applied to the application. Pressing **<Cancel>**   *
anywhere in the DialogBox, except during a cancelable drag   *
operation, must perform the action of this button.

Help   Must provide any help for the DialogBox.   *

If a DialogBox action causes an error, the DialogBox should not be
dismissed before the error is displayed. Instead, the DialogBox should
remain available after the error is dismissed to give the user a chance to
correct the error and reuse the DialogBox. If the actions to be performed by
OK or **Apply** depend on the state, then these Labels should be replaced by
ones that indicate the action to be performed.

6.2.4.2 Arranging Common Actions

You should arrange PushButton actions in DialogBoxes in the same way you
arrange other PushButtons, according to order and frequency of use. The
common action PushButtons should be ordered as presented in the previous
section. Positive responses to the DialogBox should be presented first,
followed by negative responses, and canceling responses. **Help** should
always be the last action on the right.

The following rules should be used when determining what default buttons to place in a DialogBox:

- Modal DialogBoxes should use one of the following button arrangements unless superseded by another rule:

  OK Cancel
  OK Cancel Help

- Modeless DialogBoxes should use one of the following button arrangements unless superseded by another rule:

  OK Apply Cancel
  OK Apply Cancel Help
  OK Apply Reset Cancel
  OK Apply Reset Cancel Help

- Information DialogBoxes should use one of the following button arrangements:

  OK
  OK Help

- Question DialogBoxes should use one of the following button arrangements:

  Yes No
  Yes No Help

  It is possible that both the **Yes** and **No** actions of a Question DialogBox will perform an action. If this is the case, the Question DialogBox should use one of the following button arrangements:

  Yes No Cancel
  Yes No Cancel Help

- Warning DialogBoxes should use one of the following button arrangements:

  Yes No
  Yes No Help
  OK Cancel
  OK Cancel Help

- Working DialogBoxes should contain any of the following sets of buttons in order:

Close
Cancel or **Stop**
Pause Resume
Help

6.2.4.3 Determining DialogBox Location and Size

Your application determines the size and location of its DialogBoxes. You should size and place DialogBoxes so that they do not obscure important information in other windows of your application. The initial size of a DialogBox should be large enough to contain the dialog components without crowding or visual confusion, but otherwise should be as small as possible. DialogBoxes should follow the same rules for resizing as a MainWindow as described in Section 6.2.2.3.

You should place DialogBoxes on the screen so they are completely visible.

In general, you should place DialogBoxes close to either the component that caused it to be displayed, the current action, or the information needed to respond to it. When a DialogBox relates to an item in an underlying window, you should position the DialogBox to the right of the item. If there is not enough room to the right of the item, try to position the DialogBox to the left, below or above the item, in that order, depending on screen space available. You should only obscure related information as a last resort.

If a DialogBox does not relate to items in the underlying windows, the DialogBox should be placed centered in the application's work area.

If two DialogBoxes need to overlap, you should offset the top DialogBox to the right and below the title of the lower DialogBox. Use your best judgement, knowing that the screen area for DialogBoxes is limited.

While the previous suggestions seem simple enough, they cannot always be followed completely. Therefore, DialogBoxes, once displayed, should be movable so that the user can relocate them as needed to see information in underlying windows.

6.2.5 Designing Drag and Drop

By default, applications allow the user to drag text from just about everywhere and drop it into any writable Text component. If you want to use the features of drag and drop to and from other components in your application, you need to design these features into your application.

The most important decision you need to make in designing drag and drop into your applications is which elements you want to make draggable and which components you want to allow drops onto. When making this decision, keep in mind that drag and drop not only transfers data within an application but also between applications. Therefore you need to consider the impact of unfamiliar data being dropped into your application, and in which formats you want to allow your own application's data to be transferred out. The following subsections discuss the following other application considerations when designing drag and drop into your application:

- Drag icon design

- Drag source effects

- Drag-under effects

- Providing help on drop sites

- Determining transfer formats

- Indicating drop failure

6.2.5.1 Drag Icon Design

At the start of a drag operation, the pointer is replaced with a drag icon. The drag icon is defined by the application for each draggable element and can be composed of the following:

- A source indicator

- An operation indicator

- A state indicator

The source indicator should give a visual representation of the primary data type of the draggable element; for example, horizontal lines in a rectangle

for representing text or a color palette for representing a color tool. All drag   *
icons must include a source indicator. Figure 6-15 shows move, copy, and
link drag icons for graphics and textual information.

Figure 6–15. Drag Icons

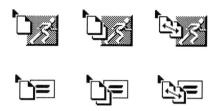

The operation indicator shows whether a drop will result in a move, copy, or
link of the transferred data. Most drag icons should include an operation
indicator, but an operation indicator should only be included in the drag icon
when the result of the drop operation is a data transfer. The operation
indicator can be shown either as a separate element of the drag icon or as a
variation of the graphic used for the source indicator.

The state indicator shows whether the current pointer location is over a
valid drop site for the dragged elements. The state indicator can show three
different states:

- Valid drop site — The hotspot of the drag icon is over a valid drop site
  for the data the user is dragging. A drop at this point usually results in a
  successful transfer.

- Invalid drop site — The hotspot of the drag icon is over a drop site, but
  the data the user is dragging is not compatible with the drop site. A drop
  at this point results in a failed transfer.

- No drop site — The hotspot of the drag icon is not over a drop site. A
  drop at this point results in a failed transfer.

All drag icons can include a state indicator. The state indicator should be
coincident with the hotspot of the pointer. The state indicator can be a
separate element in the drag icon or a change in the visual representation of
the drag source.

When defining new drag icons for your application, you should follow the
same rules as for defining any other new pointers described in Section 2.2.2.

6.2.5.2 Drag Source Effects

The source of the dragged elements can also provide visual indications of the result of a drop. For example, if the default operation for the dragged elements is a move, the source can be hidden or deemphasized; or, if the default operation of the dragged elements is a link, a line can be drawn from the source to the pointer.

6.2.5.3 Drag-Under Effects

A drag-under effect is a change to the visual state of a possible valid drop site when the drag icon pointer is over the drop site. All drop sites should use some kind of drag-under effect. Drop sites can use a solid line around the site, or a raised or lowered beveled edge around the drop site, as a drag-under effect. Drop sites can also change any visual component of the drop site, or even animate those changes, as a drag-under effect. For example, an icon representing a folder might show an animated image of the folder opening as a user drags a file onto it.

6.2.5.4 Providing Help on Drop Sites

Help on drag and drop operations should be provided by the drop site under the drag icon pointer at the time help is requested. If a drop site gets a help request during a drag and drop operation, the drop site application should post a DialogBox with help information about the results of a drop at that location and the choices for the completion of the drag and drop operation. The DialogBox should allow for canceling the drag and drop operation or dropping the elements at the current location as a move, copy, or link.

The drag and drop help DialogBox should be an Information DialogBox with a message describing the possible results of a drop at that location. The first button in the row of buttons at the bottom of the DialogBox should contain the default transfer option (**Move**, **Copy**, or **Link**) or **OK** for the single transfer action described in the text of the DialogBox.

If the user has not specified a transfer option using modifier keys, and more than one is possible, then:

- If there is a valid move transfer option, the DialogBox should contain the move transfer option on a button labeled **Move**.

- If there is a valid copy transfer option, the DialogBox should contain the copy transfer option on a button labeled **Copy**.

- If there is a valid link transfer option, the DialogBox should contain the link transfer option on a button labeled **Link**.

- The DialogBox should not include an **OK** button.

Drag and drop help DialogBoxes must contain a **Cancel** button for   *
canceling the drag and drop operation in progress. The DialogBox can contain a **Help** button for providing further help on the DialogBox actions.

6.2.5.5 Determining Transfer Formats

After a drop operation, the application containing the drop site determines the best format to use to transfer the data, based on the data types that the drag source can send. The drop site can use any heuristic to determine this format.

If multiple transfer formats (in the case of links, multiple view formats) are acceptable in the drop site, the drop site application should let the user choose the correct transfer format either through a customization feature or through a DialogBox that lists the possible choices. The DialogBox should be a Question DialogBox asking the user to choose the best transfer format.   *
The DialogBox must provide a choice of available transfer formats. The choice can be provided as a row of buttons along the bottom of the DialogBox, or in a RadioBox within the QuestionDialog. Using either   *
method, there must be a **Cancel** button in the bottom row of buttons in the   *
DialogBox. The DialogBox can also include a **Help** button that provides help on the results of a drop at the current location. If the DialogBox uses a RadioBox to present the format choices, the most likely format should be first and initially selected, formats that are currently invalid should be set insensitive, and the DialogBox must include an **OK** button in the bottom   *
row of buttons for accepting the RadioBox choice. A Popup Menu can be used instead of a DialogBox to let the user choose the format.

6.2.5.6 Indicating Drop Failures

In most cases, the system indicates drop failure automatically. If your application allows partial success on transfers, it should post messages about partial failure that provide enough information for the user to recover from the failures.

6.3 Interaction

This section gives guidelines for creating applications with consistent interactions. When an application behaves as expected and the user is not surprised by the results of the actions, the user can complete tasks quicker. The following subsections present the following guidelines for good application interaction:

- Suppling indications of actions
- Providing feedback
- Allowing user flexibility

6.3.1 Supplying Indications of Actions

The first step to consistent interaction is to provide cues to the result of every action. This means that actions of components should be indicated by the component's shape, label, and graphics. It also means that the actions and interactions of components should remain consistent, so the user always knows what to expect.

Lastly, it means that interactions should be simple. As interactions become complicated, it also becomes difficult to visually represent the interaction. Complicated interactions and components create the possibility for more errors. Even the most complicated concepts can be clarified by careful organization, so, if your application's interactions seem complicated, consider reorganizing them for simplicity.

6.3.1.1 Using Common Components

Users expect components to behave consistently across all applications. PushButtons always perform an action. OptionButtons always provide selections. Because of this, when users want to perform an action, they look for a PushButton, usually in a Menu. They do not look for an OptionButton. You should use the components that are provided when appropriate, rather than create new ones. You should not alter the look of a component so drastically that its type is unrecognizable.

6.3.1.2 Using Intuitive Labels

One of the best indicators of the action of a component is its Label. The Label can be either text or a graphic. You should choose your Labels carefully to indicate the action of each component.

Components that perform actions should be labeled with active verbs. Components that present options should be labeled with nouns. You should also label component groups, including Panels, with nouns to indicate the contents of the group.

Consider the use of graphics as Labels with two cautions. Graphic Labels cannot be nouns or active verbs, so choose a graphic whose meaning is clear in the context of the component. Also remember that, while graphic symbols are very language independent, they can be highly culture specific. In some cultures, a mailbox graphic can indicate a mailer action; but, since mailboxes are not common in all cultures, an envelope graphic may be better, or you can provide a mechanism for changing the graphic based on the locale.

6.3.1.3 Using Graphics to Show Action

Many components also include a small graphic symbol following the Label to indicate the action of the component. CascadeButtons should use an arrow graphic that points in the direction the cascading Menu will appear. OptionButtons should use a rectangle graphic to distinguish them from PushButtons.

Any component that needs more information to complete its action should include an ellipsis following the Label. This additional information should be requested in a DialogBox. The ellipsis should not be used to indicate that the component will post a DialogBox. The ellipsis should be included only if the purpose of the DialogBox is to gather more information needed to complete the requested task. For example, the Menu choice **Print** would use an ellipsis if a DialogBox is posted requesting print characteristics prior to the printing action, but the Menu choice **Help** would not use an ellipsis even though the help information is presented in a DialogBox.

All previously mentioned graphics should follow the text or graphic of the Label. In left-to-right language environments, the graphic should be on the right. In right-to-left language environments, the graphic should be on the left. Note that the graphic indicating the state of a ToggleButton precedes the Label in a left-to-right language environment.

6.3.1.4 Showing Default Actions

Your application should use default values for common settings or obvious selections. Default values should be shown in the on state. For example, the default value for a Text area should be in the Text area in the selected state whenever text entry is requested; the default selection in a List should be set in the selected state whenever a list selection is requested; or the default RadioButton should be filled in a Panel at application start-up time. In any case, once the state is changed, the new state should take the place of the default until the state is reset. Your application can decide whether to save its state after being closed.

Groups of controls, such as a DialogBox, can also have a default action. The default action is usually activated by pressing **<Enter>** or **<Return>**. The default action of a component group should be distinguished from the other selections by an extra border as shown in Figure 6-16.

Figure 6–16. A Default PushButton

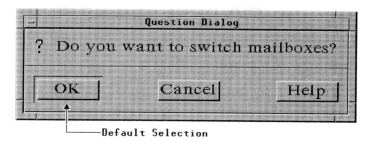

The **OK** PushButton should be the default PushButton in modal DialogBoxes and modeless DialogBoxes that are transient. The **Apply** PushButton should be the default PushButton in a modeless DialogBox that is likely to be displayed for multiple actions.

Using the keyboard to navigate through the PushButtons, the button with the location cursor should become the default PushButton. This ensures that pressing **<Enter>** or **<Return>** over a PushButton invokes the correct PushButton. When the location cursor leaves the PushButtons, the original default button should once again become the default.

6.3.1.5 Avoiding Component Modes

A component has modes when its action changes based on some previous action or the state of the application. This is very confusing to the user, who was expecting the original action of the component. Components in your application should not have modes. Your application should use multiple components rather than modal components.

6.3.1.6 Showing Unavailable Components

As the state of your application changes, certain components become inappropriate. For example, the **Minimize** selection in a window Menu is inappropriate when the window is already minimized. In such cases, you should make the inappropriate components unavailable. This is also called *disabling* the components. Disabled components should be visually deemphasized, usually by graying the Label of the component.

You should not remove unavailable components from the application client areas. The components should remain visible to remind the user of their existence and to ensure application consistency. Figure 6-17 shows a disabled Menu element.

Figure 6–17. A Disabled Menu Element

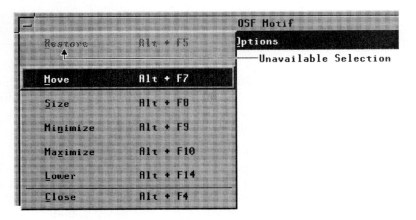

You should disable Menu items and components to help avoid errors. In general, you should disable the lowest level component that results in an irreversible error state. For example, consider a graphics editor that has a DialogBox that is used for aligning selected graphics objects. If the user might want to see the choices in the DialogBox even if the choices are not available, this DialogBox should be displayable at all times; its Menu item should not be disabled. If there are no graphics objects to align, the DialogBox should still be displayed, but its **OK** and **Apply** buttons should be disabled. Once graphics objects are selected, the **OK** and **Apply** buttons should become enabled.

Menu items that are inappropriate and that result in error messages should be disabled. Some examples are the **Edit** Menu's **Cut** and **Copy** actions when nothing is selected. The **Edit** Menu's **Undo** entry should be disabled if the last operation cannot be undone.

Menu items that perform no action need not be disabled. For example, the **New** entry in the **File** Menu need not be disabled immediately after it is invoked. It can be selectable repeatedly, even though it performs no new action, because it does not result in an error state.

A Menu item that displays a modal DialogBox should be disabled if it would cause an error either on display of the box, or on clicking the **OK** or **Apply** buttons in the DialogBox. Since the DialogBox is modal, nothing can be changed in the application to correct the error until the box is dismissed, and it should not be displayable until the application is in a state that makes the action of the DialogBox possible.

Menu items that display modeless DialogBoxes should never be disabled. If a box is modeless, the user can change the state of the application at any time to make the DialogBox useful. If the action cannot be completed because some necessary information is not yet available, then the **OK** and **Apply** buttons should be disabled.

After a TearOff Menu is torn off, an application can disable elements that are not appropriate in the torn off state. Elements in a torn off Menu can be disabled in the same manner as elements in any other Menu or DialogBox.

You should avoid frequently disabling and enabling components in situations where the state change would cause a distracting flashing. For example, editing a Text component in a DialogBox can cause some buttons to be inappropriate at each invalid text value. In this case, you should display an error message if the **OK** or **Apply** button is clicked for an inappropriate text value. Of course, the error message should explain the valid text values.

6.3.2 Providing Feedback

Another important element to user interaction is providing feedback about the current state of the application. This is done, as described in the previous section, by using labels and graphics and by keeping the interface consistent. Your application should also dynamically indicate the state of the application's actions. For example, the mouse pointer shape changes to indicate when and where special actions can occur. Chapter 2 describes mouse pointer shapes in detail. Other ways to provide the user feedback are described in the following subsections.

6.3.2.1 Showing Progress

If an action takes a long time to complete, the user may mistake the delay to mean that the system or the application stopped working. For actions that take a long time to complete, your application should indicate that there will be a delay with a WorkingDialog. If your application can track the progress of long actions, it should try to update the WorkingDialog with the progress of the action.

6.3.2.2 Providing Warnings

Certain actions can cause destructive results, such as closing an application before saving changes in the current file. Applications should not disallow such destructive actions; instead, they should warn the user of the consequences with a WarningDialog. The WarningDialog must allow the *
user to cancel the destructive action. Note that too many WarningDialogs can be disruptive to the user's main task. WarningDialogs should be reserved for truly destructive actions. For destructive actions that can easily be recovered, applications should provide undo actions to reverse them; for example, the **Undo** element of the **Edit** Pulldown Menu.

6.3.2.3 Providing Help

Even in the most intuitive application, the purpose of a component or the way to do a task can be hard to figure out for a new user. Your application should provide a help mechanism for all of its aspects. Sections 6.2.1.5 and 6.2.1.5.3 describe the most common base for a help mechanism, the **Help** Pulldown Menu on the MenuBar. Context-sensitive help should also be available by using **<Help>**.

6.3.3 Allowing User Flexibility

Good user-application interaction should also allow user flexibility. No matter how well your application is designed, some users will not like parts of it. They will want to change some elements of it; for example, from simple elements like the colors and fonts to complicated elements like the default values. You should allow users to adjust elements of your applications because it increases their sense of control over the applications. You should consider the following attributes of your applications for user customization:

- Application parameters
- Colors
- Fonts
- Default values
- Key bindings
- Labels
- Messages
- Help information

The exact list of attributes you should allow the user to customize depends on your application.

6.4 Component Design

For consistency with other applications, you should always try to use existing components for your application tasks, but there are cases where new components are needed. In designing new components, you should follow the same rules as application designers follow. You should think of components as small applications. They perform a task, present information to the user, and take information from the user. New components must *
follow the guidelines for designing applications.

The first step to designing a new component is to compare its features with those of the other components. If the new component has a feature that is the same as another component, the mechanisms for using the feature, layout, key bindings, graphics, and so on, should be the same in the new component. You should also try to match the appearance style of components on your system. Most OSF/Motif compliant systems use a 3-dimensional beveled presentation style. Appearance is not specified as a matter of component style in this guide; however, any new components will assimilate better with existing components if they are designed to conform to the implied appearance style for the system on which they will be used.

Chapter 7
Window Manager Design Principles

A window manager is a specialized application. In designing a window *
manager, you must follow the same principles as for any other application. *
A window manager must also follow the style guidelines for input, *
navigation, selection, and activation models as set forth in Chapters 2 *
through 5.

There are a few elements of user interface design that are specific to
window managers. This chapter discusses the following elements:

- Configurability
- Window support
- Window decorations
- Window navigation
- Icons

7.1 Configurability

This chapter describes only those elements of window manager design that help create a consistent user interface. A window manager can supply a mechanism that allows the user to configure the window manager. The window manager can make any element user-configurable, including key bindings, Menu contents, default window decorations, or any other rules and elements defined in this guide. Any window manager that supplies a ∗ configuration mechanism must also include support for toggling between the ∗ current user configuration and the default configuration as mandated by this ∗ guide. The configuration toggle key press, **<Alt> <Shift> <Ctrl> <!>**, must ∗ initiate a configuration toggle. When the user issues a request to toggle the configuration, the window manager should request user verification before proceeding.

7.2 Window Support

Users communicate with applications by using windows. A window is an area of the screen (usually rectangular) that provides the user with the functional means to communicate with an application and through which an application can communicate with the user.

A typical environment has several applications in operation simultaneously. Each application typically has a main or primary window that displays data and in which the user carries on primary interaction with the application. Applications can have additional windows to communicate context-specific interactions with the user of the application. These additional windows are called secondary windows, or transient windows. DialogBoxes are often used to create secondary windows. Figure 7-1 illustrates a typical OSF/Motif environment.

Figure 7–1. A Typical OSF/Motif User Environment

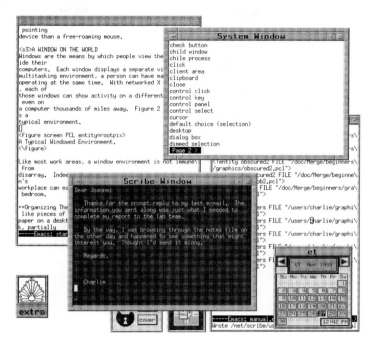

While each application can be made up of many windows, each window is one of only three basic types:

- A primary window, the main application window

- A secondary window, a window that provides secondary and transient interaction with the user

- A Menu window, a temporary window for displaying a Menu of choices for the user

A window manager must support multiple applications, each with one or more primary windows. The window manager must also recognize and support secondary windows. Also, it must associate each secondary window with a primary window or another secondary window. *

7–3

7.2.1 Primary Window

A primary window is the window from which all the other windows used by
an application are generated. The window manager must support one or   *
more primary windows for each windowing application. When an
application has multiple primary windows, the window manager should
treat each primary window as if it were an independent application.

When a primary window is iconized (minimized), the window and all of its   *
associated secondary windows must be removed from the display and   *
replaced with a single icon representing the primary window. Iconizing a   *
window must not automatically suspend any processes of the window.
However, a client can notice that a primary window has been unmapped and
adjust its processing accordingly. When the icon of the window is opened,   *
the primary window and all the current associated secondary windows must   *
be restored. The window manager should try to place the windows in the
same position from which they were iconified.

When a primary window is closed, the window and its icon must be   *
removed from the display. All secondary windows associated with the   *
primary window must also be closed. If the last primary window of an   *
application is closed, the application must also be closed. When an explicit
focus policy is in use, any secondary windows holding a TearOff Menu can
be removed from the display, except when another window of the
application has the focus.

7.2.2 Secondary Windows (Dialog)

Applications use secondary windows to conduct context-specific dialog with
the user. Such context-specific dialogs are usually transitory, and the
secondary windows can be removed when they are no longer needed. When   *
a secondary window is closed, its parent must not be affected, and any   *
secondary windows that are children of it must also be closed.

Secondary windows are always related to a parent window. Sometimes the
parent is a primary window, sometimes another secondary window. Any
window can have any number of secondary window children.

Secondary windows are not constrained to be clipped within their parent   *
window, but they must always appear on top of that parent window in the   *
window hierarchy. In a layered window manager, you can think of a

primary window and its associated secondary windows as occupying one layer in the window hierarchy. Whenever one window is moved in the hierarchy, all of the associated windows must move accordingly. Thus, lowering a window must move that window and all associated windows to the bottom of the window hierarchy. Giving a window the focus must raise that window and all of the associated windows to the top of the hierarchy.

Secondary windows can limit how a user can interact with windows in order to force the order of interaction. A window manager must support the following four types, known as modes, of interaction with secondary windows:

Modeless   Allows interaction with the secondary window and all other windows.

Primary modal   Does not allow interaction with any ancestor of the window.

Application modal   Does not allow interaction with any window created by the same application, even if the application has multiple primary windows.

System modal   Does not allow interaction with any window on the screen. This includes windows from all other applications and any icon box. To indicate a system modal secondary window, the pointer should change shape to a caution pointer whenever it leaves the system modal secondary window.

A window manager must not allow the focus to be given to any window that is not allowed to accept input because of the modality of a DialogBox.

7.2.3 Menu Windows

Menu windows are used to present Menus. They are not specifically created by applications but by the components used to create the application. Menu windows are always related to a parent window. The parent can be either a primary window, secondary window, or another Menu window. A window can only have one Menu window child at a time.

A Menu window is very short lived. It is only available to a client while no
mouse or button actions are being performed elsewhere on the screen. Once   *
interaction starts in another window on the screen, except a child Menu   *
window, the Menu window must be removed.

Some Menus have a special behavior that allows a user to convert them into
a secondary window. These Menus are called TearOff Menus. TearOff
Menus can either be torn off in place or torn off and moved simultaneously.
The window's title should be the name of the Menu entry that was torn off.   *
The window manager must allow TearOff Menu transformations from Menu   *
window to secondary window.

Menu windows are not constrained to be clipped within their parent
window, but they must always appear on top of that parent window in the   *
window hierarchy. The window manager must not supply any window   *
decoration to Menu windows.

7.3 Window Decorations

A window manager can provide windows with a window frame that contains
components called decorations. The window decorations allow user
interaction with the window manager. Along with the frame components, a
window manager contains a client area. The client area is the display area
for an application. Figure 7-2 shows a typical window and its decorations.

Figure 7–2. A Typical OSF/Motif Window Layout

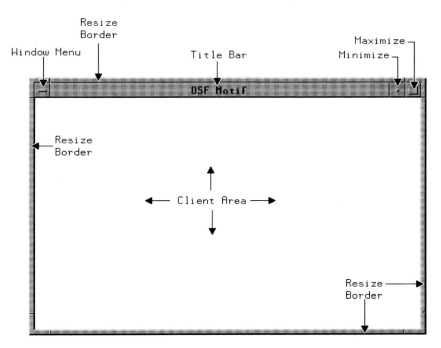

A window manager can support any number of window decorations, but it   *
must support the client area and the window frame. A window manager   *
must support the following window frame components: *

- Title area   *

- Maximize button   *

- Minimize button   *

- Resize border   *

- Window Menu button   *

Each window must have a client area. A window manager must allow each   *
window to choose which combination of decorations to include, except that   *
a window must not have any buttons without a title area. A primary window   *
must by default have all the decorations: window Menu button, maximize   *
button, minimize button, title area, and resize border. A secondary window   *
must by default have a window Menu button and title area.   *

In a secondary window, resize borders and a maximize button can be   *
provided if there is a reason to resize the window.

Clicking **BSelect** on the window frame should give the window focus and
raise the window to the top of the window hierarchy, except when dialog
modality disallows focus to be set in the window.

7.3.1 Client Area

The client area is the portion of the window in which the user performs most
application-level tasks. For example, if the user is working with a graphics
editor or a text editor, the client area contains the figure or document being
edited. The client area is inside the window frame and can be composed of
multiple work areas. Figure 7-2 shows the client area in a typical window.

7.3.2 Title Area

The title area, also called the title bar, supplies a place to identify the
window. If a window includes a title area, it must be a horizontal bar at the   *
top of the window. It must be just above the client area and lie horizontally   *
between the window Menu (or other buttons) on the left and the window   *
control buttons on the right. Figure 7-2 shows the title area in a typical
window.

The title area should contain a short string called the title that labels the
contents of the window. The title must be settable at window startup both   *
by the user and by the application. For applications with a single primary
window, the title should be the name of the application. For applications
with multiple primary windows, the title should indicate the purpose of the
window. The title in secondary windows should indicate the purpose of the
window. The title can also contain other useful information, such as the
machine on which the application is running, the current directory, or
similar relatively static information.

Besides supplying a location for a label, the title area also acts as a position,
or handle, for moving a window. Pressing **BSelect** or **BTransfer** in the title   *
area and dragging the pointer must move the window relative to the moving   *
pointer.

7.3.3 Maximize Button

The maximize button provides mouse users with a shortcut to the **Maximize**
entry in the window Menu. If a window includes a maximize button, it must *
be just above the client area and its right border must align with the right *
border of the client area. Figure 7-2 shows the maximize button in a typical
window. Primary windows should have a maximize button. Secondary
windows generally do not have a maximize button.

The graphic in the maximize button should be a large square or an up arrow.
If the maximize button uses an up arrow as its graphic, a maximized window
should use a double-headed arrow to indicate that it is maximized. If the
maximized button uses a large square as its graphic, a maximized window
can show the graphic in a different state. Activating the maximize button *
must increase the size of the window to the maximum allowable size. As a *
shortcut for mouse users to the **Restore** entry in the window Menu, *
activating the maximize button of a maximized window must restore the *
window to its size and location before being maximized.

7.3.4 Minimize Button

The minimize button provides mouse users with a shortcut to the **Minimize**
entry in the window Menu. If a window includes a minimize button, it must *
be just above the client area and directly to the left of the maximize button.
Figure 7-2 shows the minimize button in a typical window. Primary
windows should have a minimize button. Secondary windows must not *
have a minimize button.

The graphic in the minimize button should be a small square or a down
arrow. Activating the minimize button must iconify the window unless the *
window family contains a system modal DialogBox.

7.3.5 Other Buttons

You can bind additional window manager functions to buttons on the
window frame. Any additional buttons must be placed directly to the left of *
the minimize button or directly to the right of the window Menu button and *
above the client area. Each button action must correspond to a entry in the *
window Menu.

7.3.6 Resize Borders

Applications can suggest the initial size of their windows to the window
manager. Window sizes can vary according to the work performed in them.
At any time, a user should be able to alter the size of most windows. The
Size entry in the window Menu provides a method for the user to alter the
size of windows. The resize borders provide a shortcut for mouse users for
the **Size** entry in the window Menu. Resize borders are not generally
provided on secondary windows.

The resize borders are the outermost components of the window manager
frame. They are made up of two components: the corner handles and the
edge handles. If a window includes resize borders, there must be one corner *
handle in each corner of the window at its extremes, and one edge handle *
between each pair of corner handles. There must be no window components *
outside the boundary formed by the resize borders. Figure 7-2 shows resize
borders in a typical window.

Pressing **BSelect** or **BTransfer** in a corner handle and dragging the pointer *
must change the height and width of the window relative to the moving *
pointer without changing the position of the opposite corner. Pressing *
BSelect or **BTransfer** in a top or bottom edge handle and dragging the *
pointer must change the height of the window relative to the moving pointer *
without changing the width or the position of the opposite edge. Pressing *
BSelect or **BTransfer** in a side edge handle and dragging the pointer must *
change the width of the window relative to the moving pointer without *
changing the height or the position of the opposite edge.

7.3.7 Window Menu

The window Menu, sometimes called the system Menu or control Menu, is used to display the list of window actions. All actions possible for a window should be displayed in the window Menu because keyboard-only users interact with the window manager through this Menu. Because of this, it is rare that a window does not need a window Menu. The window Menu can be configured out by the application or by the user, but it should not be removed by the window manager.

If a window includes a window Menu, the window Menu button must be located just above the client area, the left edge of the button must align with the left edge of the client area, and the button must be just to the left of the title area, unless other buttons are included between the window Menu button and the title area.   *
                                                                                                             *
                                                                                                             *
                                                                                                             *

Double-clicking the window Menu button can be used to close the window, unless focus is disallowed in the window. A user must be able to activate   *
the window Menu button for the window with the focus by using **<Shift>**   *
<Escape> or **<Alt> <Space>**.

Figure 7-3 shows a typical window Menu.

Figure 7–3. The Window Menu Button with Menu Pulled Down

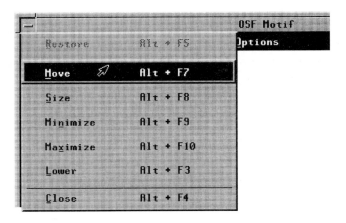

A primary window Menu must have the following entries in the order listed: *

<u>R</u>estore Alt+F5   Restores a minimized or maximized window to the   *
previous size and location of the window. This   *
entry must be deemphasized (grayed out) when the   *

	window is in its normal state. This action must have the mnemonic **R**. If this action has an accelerator, it must be **<Alt> <F5>** if **<F5>** is available.
Move Alt+F7	Moves a window around the workspace. This action must have the mnemonic **M**. If this action has an accelerator, it must be **<Alt> <F7>** if **<F7>** is available.
Size Alt+F8	Changes the height and width of the window in the direction indicated by the pointer. This action must have the mnemonic **S**. If this action has an accelerator, it must be **<Alt> <F8>** if **<F8>** is available.
Mi**n**imize Alt+F9	Changes a window into an icon. This action must have the mnemonic **N**. If this action has an accelerator, it must be **<Alt> <F9>** if **<F9>** is available.
Ma**x**imize Alt+F10	Enlarges a window to its maximum size. This action must have the mnemonic **X**. If this action has an accelerator, it must be **<Alt> <F10>** if **<F10>** is available.
Lower Alt+F3	Moves a window to the bottom of the window hierarchy. This action can be omitted. This action must have the mnemonic **L**. If this action has an accelerator, it must be **<Alt> <F3>** if **<F3>** is available.
Close Alt+F4	Closes a window and removes it from the workspace. This action must have the mnemonic **C**. If this action has an accelerator, it must be **<Alt> <F4>** if **<F4>** is available. Applications should prompt the user to save any unsaved changes when a window is closed.

A secondary window Menu must have the following entries in the order listed: **Move**, **Size**, and **Close**. A secondary window Menu can include **Restore** above **Move**, **Maximize** below **Size**, and **Lower** above **Close**, but the lower option on a secondary window lowers all the windows secondary to that window's primary window.

A secondary window Menu should not include **Restore** if it does not include **Maximize**. A secondary window must not include an entry for **Minimize**.   *

A secondary window resulting from a Menu being torn off must have the   *
following entries in the order listed: **Move, Lower**, and **Close**. It must not   *
include entries for **Restore, Size, Minimize**, or **Maximize**.

Additional Menu items can be added to the window Menus of both primary and secondary windows according to the guidelines for Menus described in Chapter 6.

7.4 Window Navigation

Moving the focus among windows using the keyboard is called window navigation. Because applications should not warp the mouse pointer, a window manager need not support window navigation when the focus policy is in pointer mode. Window managers must support window   *
navigation when the focus policy is in explicit mode.

The window navigation model can be divided into two levels:

1. Moving among window families (among primary windows)

2. Moving within a window family (among secondary windows)

A window family consists of a single primary window and all of its associated secondary windows. A window manager must support moving   *
the keyboard focus among windows in a window family using the **<Alt>**   *
<F6> key. A window manager can support moving the keyboard focus in the opposite direction from **<Alt> <F6>** using the **<Alt> <Shift> <F6>** key.

Moving the focus between window families must be done using **<Alt>**   *
<Tab> and **<Alt> <Shift> <Tab>**. **<Alt> <Shift> <Tab>** should move the focus among the windows in the opposite direction from **<Alt> <Tab>**. If   *
there is no icon box, **<Alt> <Tab>** and **<Alt> <Shift> <Tab>** must move   *
among the icons as well as the windows. When focus moves into a window family, the focus should go to the window in the window family that last had the focus. If no window in the family has ever had the focus, it should go to the most recently opened secondary window.

7.5 Icons

An icon is a stylized representation of an object. A window icon is a minimized representation of a window or window family that can help organize windows and tasks in the display. Iconifying a window is also known as minimizing a window. The window manager must iconify all   *
windows of a window family together. It must not iconify any single   *
window, primary or secondary, from a window family without also   *
iconifying all the other windows in the window family. The iconic representation of a window family should not change any state in the windows, except the visual representation of the window. The application   *
running inside of a window must continue running even when the   *
application is iconified. The application can adjust its own state when it is iconified.

7.5.1 Icon Decoration

An icon is made up of an image and a label. Figure 7-4 shows a typical Motif icon.

Figure 7–4. A Typical OSF/Motif Icon

The image should be surrounded by a border that indicates when the icon has the keyboard focus. The image area can contain text or a bitmap. The label should be located just below the image and its border. The label can also indicate when the icon has the keyboard focus by highlighting with the image area.

The label should contain the same text as the title area of the corresponding primary window, or an abbreviated form of it. When the icon does not have   *
the keyboard focus, the width of the label must be the same as the width of   *
the image area and its border, truncating text if necessary. When the icon has the keyboard focus, the width of the label can expand to display the entire text.

7.5.2 Icon Menu

Clicking **BSelect** in an icon must give the icon the keyboard focus and post   *
the icon Menu. The icon Menu must be the same Menu as the window   *
Menu for the associated primary window. **Size** should not be available from the icon Menu. Navigating to the icon must also give the icon the keyboard   *
focus and should post the icon Menu.

Double-clicking **BSelect** anywhere in the icon must restore the window   *
family, just as the icon Menu item **Restore** does. If the window is currently   *
minimized, but its previous state was maximized, double-clicking **BSelect**   *
returns it to the maximized state. Selecting **Maximize** from the icon Menu   *
always maximizes the corresponding window. If the window is minimized,   *
Minimize must not be available in the icon Menu; otherwise, selecting it   *
minimizes the window family. Pressing **BSelect** or **BTransfer** anywhere in   *
the icon and dragging the mouse pointer must move the icon to track the   *
pointer, just as the icon Menu item **Move** does.

If the window manager has been customized by the user so that the icon   *
Menu does not pop up when the icon gets the focus, **<Shift> <Escape>**,   *
<Alt> <Space>, **<Menu>**, and **BMenu** must pop up the icon Menu.

7.5.3 Icon Box

An icon box is a specialized window that acts as a storage location for icons. An icon box acts like a typical window in the sense that it has a window frame and frame components. The client area of an icon box must   *
have an area for holding icons and can have horizontal and vertical scroll   *
bars for moving around the icon area. Figure 7-5 shows a typical icon box.

Figure 7–5. A Typical OSF/Motif Icon Box

The icon box must have all the same components as any other primary   *
window. Like other windows it can be sized, moved, minimized,
maximized, restored, and lowered. However, the window manager must not   *
allow the icon box to be closed. The system Menu action **Close** must be   *
replaced with the system Menu action **Pack Icons** in an icon box. Double-   *
clicking **BSelect** in the icon box system Menu must only open the icon box   *
system Menu. It must not close the icon box. **Pack Icons** arranges the icons
as close as possible together in the visible icon area if possible. **Pack Icons**   *
must have the mnemonic **P**. If **Pack Icons** has an accelerator, it should be
<Alt> <F12> if **<F12>** is available. When the input focus is in the icon box,   *
<Shift> <Escape> or **<Alt> <Space>** must pop up the icon box system   *
Menu if the Menu is unposted. If the Menu is already posted, **<Shift>**   *
<Escape> or **<Alt> <Space>** must unpost the Menu.

The icon box can contain an icon for each window family, even if it is
active. The icon for minimized window families must be the same as the   *
icon would be outside of the icon box. The icon for an active window
family should be similar to the minimized icon, deemphasized somehow.

Clicking **BSelect** in an icon must give the icon keyboard focus and post the   *
icon Menu. The icon Menu must be the same Menu as the window Menu   *
for the associated primary window. If the icon represents an active window   *
family, **Restore** and **Size** must not be available from the icon Menu. If the   *
icon represents a minimized window family, **Size** must not be available   *
from the icon Menu. If the window manager is customized so that the icon   *
with the focus does not have its window Menu automatically posted,   *
BMenu or **<Menu>** must post its Menu.

Double-clicking **BSelect** anywhere in an icon that represents a minimized   *
window family must restore the window family, just as the icon Menu item   *
Restore does. Double-clicking **BSelect** anywhere in an icon that represents   *
an active window family must raise the window family to the top of the   *
window hierarchy. If the window is currently minimized, but its previous   *
state was maximized, double-clicking **BSelect** returns it to the maximized   *
state. Selecting **Maximize** from the icon Menu always maximizes the   *
corresponding window. If the window is minimized, **Minimize** must not be   *
available in the icon Menu; otherwise, selecting it minimizes the window   *
family. Pressing **BSelect** or **BTransfer** anywhere in the icon and dragging   *
the mouse pointer must move the icon within the icon area to track the   *
pointer, just as the icon Menu item **Move** does.

The directional keys <↓>, <↑>, <→>, and <←> must navigate among the   *
icons in the icon box. Icon navigation must behave as described in the   *
following text. Note that <↓> and <→> do not need to traverse icons in the
same order.

<↓>   In a left-to-right language environment, this key must move the   *
location cursor through the icons in the icon box, starting at the   *
upper-left icon and ending at the lower-right icon, then wrapping   *
back up to the upper left. In a right-to-left language environment,
the location cursor can move, starting at the upper right and
moving to the lower left.

<←>   This key must move the location cursor through the icons in the   *
opposite direction of <→>.

<→>   In a left-to-right language environment, this key must move the   *
location cursor through the icons in the icon box, starting at the   *
upper-left icon and ending at the lower-right icon, then wrapping   *
back up to the upper left. In a right-to-left language environment,
the location cursor can move, starting at the upper right and
moving to the lower left.

<↑>   This key must move the location cursor through the icons in the   *
opposite direction of <↓>.

Chapter 8

Designing for International Markets

This chapter provides basic guidelines for producing applications for international markets. Internationalization is the process of generalizing programs or systems so that they can handle a variety of languages, character sets, and national customs. Localization is the process of providing language-specific or country-specific information or support for programs.

In general, internationalization issues are handled by tools available to programmers on their system. For example, the ANSI C standard (ANS X3.159-1989) and POSIX 1003.1 have defined internationalization in terms of locale. The locale can then be set as part of the user's environment, allowing the program to access locale-specific information, such as data formats, collating sequences, and system messages, from system-specific or application-specific databases. You should use any internationalization tools available on your system to support internationalization in your application.

Following are some of the issues that need to be addressed in an internationalized application. In most cases, these issues are addressed by the internationalization tools available on your system. They are provided here primarily to increase your awareness of issues that can affect your programming. In a few cases, you may need to adjust your program to allow for size and layout changes of data in different locales.

- Internationalized text input
- Collating sequences
- Country-specific data formats
- Icons, symbols, and pointer shapes
- Scanning direction
- Designing modularized software
- Translating screen text

8.1 Internationalized Text Input

Ideally, text is input from a keyboard that can directly produce all the characters needed for that language. It is sometimes the case, however, that text input requires a pre-edit step, whereby text is typed into a pre-edit area using a set of characters, later converted to another set of characters, and passed to the application. An input method is used to convert keyboard input to an encoding suitable for a Text control.

Fortunately, application developers do not need to worry about the input method as long as the Text controls in the application support the display and input of text in the writing system supported by the underlying system. Furthermore, defining how keyboard actions convert into characters suitable for text input and the display is the responsibility of the underlying system.

Designers of Text controls should create Text controls that support display and input of text in any writing system supported by the underlying system. Text controls can also support input and display of multiple writing systems.

System designers need to create input methods that address the following issues of internationalized text input:

- Locating the pre-edit area
- Displaying status
- Converting pre-edit characters to final characters

The following subsections describe these issues and provide some guidelines for addressing them, but there is currently too much variation in systems, and the field is too new for this guide to make many firm recommendations about these issues.

8.1.1 Locating the Pre-Edit Area

The trend over time is for pre-edit areas to move closer to the location of the final text. Ideally, pre-edit should occur in place in the Text control being edited (known as an on-the-spot input method). This is technically difficult to do without fully integrating the Text control with the input method. In the absence of an on-the-spot input method, systems should use an over-the-spot input method. An over-the-spot input method places the pre-edit area above but separate from the Text control. In the absence of on-the-spot or over-the-spot input methods, systems can create input methods where the pre-edit area is separate on the display from the Text control that it sends input to. These models are know as off-the-spot input methods. In these input methods, a single pre-edit area can apply to a single Text control, a group of Text controls, an entire application window, or the whole screen. An input method where a single pre-edit area is responsible for all the Text controls on a screen is known as a root window input method.

Systems should support in-place or per-window input methods. They can support per-control, per-group, or per-screen input methods.

When using an off-the-spot input method, converted text obviously goes to the Text control with the input focus. The pre-edit area itself does not get the input focus. It only acts as an intermediary for the Text control. The contents of the pre-edit area prior to conversion can be maintained separately for each Text control; that is, when moving the focus from one Text control to another, the unconverted text from the pre-edit area can be maintained in the first Text control and any existing unconverted pre-edit text for the second Text control can be restored to the pre-edit area.

8.1.2 Displaying Status

After a block of text is input to the pre-edit area, the user performs some action, usually a key sequence, that causes the system to convert the pre-edit text into the final characters and pass it to Text control. Using an in-place input method, it is important to show the user which text is pre-edit text and which text has already been converted; that is, the system should give the user some idea of the status of input. In an in-place input method, this status is usually provided by some visual effect such as a font or color difference.

Using any input method including an in-place input method, the method can include an additional off-the-spot status area that displays input method status information such as input and output text formats.

8.1.3 Converting Pre-Edit Characters to Final Characters

When the user requests that the pre-edit text be converted to the final text format, the system may still not have enough information to unambiguously convert the text. In this case, the next step of the conversion depends on the system, the pre-edit format, and the final text format. The conversion can either fail, prompt for more pre-edit text, or present a list of possible choices and let the user pick one. An input method can present conversion choices to the user in a number of ways including the following:

- Listing the choices in a DialogBox

- Presenting the choices in an Option Menu

- Presenting the choices in a Popup Menu

- Allowing the user to cycle through choices using key sequences

8.2 Collating Sequences

To produce an alphanumeric list, printable characters are sorted according to a collating sequence. Printable characters include letters possibly with accents, numbers, punctuation characters, and other symbols such as an * (asterisk) or & (ampersand). The collating sequence defines the value and position of a character relative to the other characters.

Many applications make frequent use of collating sequences to produce alphanumeric lists. Examples of alphanumeric lists include the following:

- A directory listing of filenames

- The output from a sorting utility

- An index produced by a text-processing application

- The lists produced by a database application, such as lists of names or addresses

8.3 Country-Specific Data Formats

Country-specific data formats include the following:

- Thousands separators
- Decimal separators (or, radix characters)
- Grouping separators
- Positive and negative values
- Currency
- Date formats
- Time formats
- Time zones
- Telephone numbers
- Proper names and addresses

8.3.1 Thousands Separators

The comma, period, space, and apostrophe are examples of valid separators for units of thousands as shown in the following examples:

1 234 567
1.234.567
1'234'567
1,234,567

8.3.2 Decimal Separators

The period, comma, and the center dot are examples of valid separators for decimal fractions as shown in the following examples:

5,324
5.324
5 324
5·324

8.3.3 Grouping Separators

Grouping may not be restricted to thousands separators as shown in the following examples:

400,001.00
40,0001,00

8.3.4 Positive and Negative Values

Various countries indicate positive and negative values differently. The symbols + (plus) and - (minus) can appear either before or after the number. Negative numbers can be enclosed in parentheses in applications such as a spreadsheet.

8.3.5 Currency

Currency formats differ among various countries. The comma, period, and colon are examples of valid separators for currency. There can be one or no space between the currency symbol and the amount. The currency symbol can be up to four characters.

The following example shows valid currency values:

Sch3.50
SFr. 5.-
3.50FIM
25 c
3F50
760 Ptas
Esc. 3.50
kr. 3,50

8.3.6 Date Formats

Most countries use the Gregorian calendar, but some do not. Dates can be formatted differently based on the locale. Separators can be different in different locales or left out altogether. The hyphen, comma, period, space, and slash are all examples of valid separators for the day, month, and year. In numeric date formats, the month and day fields can be reversed, and, in some cases, the year field can come first. For example, the 4th of August 1992 can be written as either 4/8/92 or 8/4/92 depending on locale. In addition, users in other countries sometimes place the year first, so June 11, 1992 could be 920611 or 921106.

8.3.7 Time Formats

Time formats can change based on locale. The colon, period, and space are examples of valid separators for hours, minutes, and seconds. The letter **h** can separate hours and minutes. There is both 12-hour or 24-hour notation. For 12-hour notation, a.m. or p.m. can appear after the time, separated by a space.

The following example shows a number of valid time formats:

1830
18:30
04 56
08h15
11.45 a.m.
11.45 p.m.
13:07:31.30
13:07:31

8.3.8 Telephone Numbers

Telephone numbers can contain blanks, commas, hyphens, periods, and brackets as valid separators, for example. Telephone numbers can be displayed in local, national, and international formats. Local formats vary widely. National formats can have an area code in parentheses, while the international format can drop the parentheses but add a + (plus sign) at the beginning of the number to indicate the country code. The following examples show valid telephone number formats:

(038) 473589
+44 (038) 473549
617.555.2199
(617) 555-2199
1 (617) 555-5525
(1) 617 555 5525
911
1-800-ORDERME

8.3.9 Proper Names and Addresses

Addresses can vary from two to six lines long and can include any character used in the locale's character set. The post code (zip code) can be in various positions in the address and can include alphabetic characters and separators as well as numbers.

8.4 Icons, Symbols, and Pointer Shapes

It may not always be possible to design an icon, pointer shape, or other graphical symbol that adequately represents the same object or function in different countries. Culture is inherent even in seemingly universal symbols. For example, sending and receiving mail is a commonly understood function, but representing that function with an icon of a mail box can be inappropriate because the appearance of mail boxes varies widely among countries. Therefore, an envelope may be a more appropriate icon. You should make sure that graphical symbols are localizable.

When used correctly, graphical symbols offer the following advantages:

- They are language independent and do not need to be translated. In some cases, you may not be able to avoid changing an icon or symbol for a culture that is vastly different. However, design icons and symbols with the entire user population in mind so that you can try to avoid redesigning.

- They can be used instead of computer terms that have no national-language equivalent.

- They may have more impact when used with text as warnings than the text alone.

Here are a few guidelines to follow when creating icons, symbols, or pointer shapes:

- Use an already existing international icon, if possible.

- Make your icons, symbols, or pointer shapes represent basic, concrete concepts. The more abstract the icon, the more explanatory documentation is needed.

- Check your icons and symbols for conflicts with existing icons or symbols for that function.

- Do not incorporate text in icons because the text will need to be translated. Translated text often expands and might no longer fit the icon.

- Test and retest your symbols and icons in context with real users.

8.5 Scanning Direction

Readers of Western languages scan from left to right across the page (or display screen) and from top to bottom. In other languages, particularly Eastern ones such as Hebrew and Arabic, this is not the case; readers scan from right to left. The scanning direction of the country can have an impact on the location of components in DialogBoxes, the order of selections in Menus, and other areas.

If your application will be used in environments other than those that scan from left to right, remember that the the scanning direction should match the input direction.

8.6 Designing Modularized Software

Modularizing software allows for easier localization; that is, a properly modularized application requires that fewer files be modified to localize the application. Guidelines for designing modularized software are as follows:

- Create separate modules for text, code, and input/output components that need to be changed to accommodate different markets.

- Separate all user interface text from the code that presents it.

- Use standard (registered) data formats, such as ISO and IEEE.

- Use standard processing algorithms for all processing, storage, and interchange.

In general, you should modularize your application so that elements that need to be translated to different languages are in separate files, and that those files are the only files that will need changes for localization. Furthermore, you should have a different set of language-dependent text files for each locale that are read in at run time using the internationalization tools available on your system.

8.7 Translating Screen Text

Well-written screen text makes an application easier for users to understand. It also makes translation easier.

Use the following guidelines to write screen text for translation:

- Write brief and simple sentences; they are easy to understand and translate.

- Write affirmative statements; they are easier to understand than negative statements. For example, use "Would you like to continue?" rather than "Wouldn't you like to continue?"

- Use active voice; it is easier for both application users and application translators to understand. For example, use "Press the Help button." rather than "The Help button should be pressed."

- Use prepositions to clarify the relationship of nouns; avoid stringing three or more nouns together.

- Use simple vocabulary; avoid using jargon unless it is a part of your audience's working vocabulary.

- Allow space for text expansion. Text translated from English is likely to expand 30% to 50%, or even more.

Chapter 9

Controls, Groups, and Models Reference Pages

This chapter presents detailed information about components, user interface models, and concepts in reference format. Each topic starts on a new page and is organized alphabetically. Details on user interface models and concepts are provided in the earlier chapters of this guide. The model and concepts reference pages are provided here only as a quick reference to information provided earlier and are not complete in every detail. Therefore, they should not be used as the definitive source for information about user interface models and concepts. This chapter includes the following model and concepts reference pages:

Accelerators	Focus	Navigation
Activation	Framing Groups	Pointer Shapes
Basic Controls	Help Menu	Popup Menus
Basic Groups	Icon Menu	Primary Selection
Default Activation	IconBox	Quick Transfer
Drag and Drop	Icons	Selection
Edit Menu	Input Devices	Window Menu
Field Controls	Layout Groups	
File Menu	Mnemonics	

The reference pages for components are provided for designers to use when implementing the components described in this guide or when creating new components.

Remember, when designing new components, you should follow the same rules that application designers follow. As such, you should be familiar with all the chapters of this guide, not just this reference-page section. New   * components must follow the guidelines for designing applications. This chapter contains the following control and group reference pages:

Canvas	List	Scale
CascadeButton	MainWindow	ScrollBar
CheckButton	MenuBar	ScrolledWindow
CommandBox	Menus	SelectionBox
CommandDialog	MessageDialog	SelectionDialog
Composition	OptionButton	Separator
DialogBox	PanedWindow	TearOffButton
ErrorDialog	Panel	Text
FileSelectionBox	PromptDialog	ToggleButton
FileSelectionDialog	PushButton	WarningDialog
Frame	QuestionDialog	WorkingDialog
InformationDialog	RadioButton	Label

When designing a new component, compare its features with those of other components. If the new component has a feature that is the same as another   * component, the mechanisms for using the feature, layout, key bindings,   * graphics, and so on, must be similar to the existing component.

Each component reference page may contain the following information about the component:

Description A description of the use and appearance of each component, group, or model.

Illustration An illustration of a typical component. The illustrations in this guide use the OSF/Motif reference appearance with 3-dimensional beveled edges. Although it is important to be consistent in the placement of the elements in a component, the appearance, or rendering, of the component is not an issue of *OSF/Motif Style Guide* compliance.

Navigation A description of the methods for navigating within a component.

Other Operations A description of other operations available within the component.

Common Bindings A list of the virtual keys used by this component and the common substitutions for each virtual key.

Related Information A list of sections and related reference pages in this *OSF/Motif Style Guide* with additional information.

Accelerators

Description

An accelerator is a key or key combination that invokes the action of some component without the location cursor being on the component when the accelerator is pressed. Accelerators are most commonly used to activate Menu items without first posting the Menu. You should provide accelerators primarily as a matter of utility, not for design conformity.

If the button with the accelerator is within a primary or secondary window, or within a Pulldown Menu system from its MenuBar, it must be activatable whenever the input focus is in the window or the MenuBar system. If the button with the accelerator is within a Popup Menu system, it must be activatable whenever the focus is in the Popup Menu system or the component with the Popup Menu.   *
\
*
\
*
\
*
\
*

Applications can provide accelerators for any button component. Implementations must support accelerators in PushButtons and ToggleButtons that are in Menus. If a button has an accelerator, the accelerator must be shown following the label of the button.   *
\
*
\
*

Activation

Description

This reference page only provides a short description of the various types of activation. Chapter 5 describes each type in detail.

Basic Activation

The basic activation model mimics real-life button activation in that pressing on a button activates it. Clicking **BSelect** on the button must activate the button. **<Select>** or **<Space>** on a button with the focus must activate the button. **<Enter>** or **<Return>** on an activatable Menu entry with the focus must activate the entry. In explicit mode, clicking **<Ctrl> BSelect** on a traversable component should move the focus to it. In activatable components, it should have no other effect. In collections, it can change the cursored element or the selection as described in Section 4.1.

Accelerators

An accelerator is a key or key combination that invokes the action of some component without the location cursor on the component when the accelerator is pressed. Accelerators are most commonly used to activate Menu items without first posting the Menu.

Mnemonics

A mnemonic is a single character that can be associated with any component that contains a text label. When the location cursor is on a component within a Menu, a MenuBar, or the same field as a component with a mnemonic, typing the mnemonic character must move the location cursor to the component and activate it. If a mnemonic is used for an OptionButton, for a CascadeButton in a MenuBar, or a PushButton that is not in a basic group (that is, not in a Panel, a Menu, or a MenuBar), pressing **<Alt>** and the mnemonic anywhere in the window or its Menus must move the cursor to the component with that mnemonic and must activate it.

TearOff Activation

Some Menus have TearOffButtons as their first elements. A TearOffButton is like a PushButton with the special interaction of converting a Menu into a DialogBox; that is, tearing off the Menu from its CascadeButton. TearOffButtons must follow the *
basic activation model. TearOffButtons have a second activation mechanism. Once a Menu with a TearOffButton is *
posted, pressing **BTransfer** in the TearOffButton must start a *
tear-off action. As long as **BTransfer** is held, a representation *
of the Menu must follow the movements of the pointer. *
Releasing **BTransfer** must end the tear-off action by unposting *
the Menu system, creating a new window at the current pointer *
location with the contents of the Menu, and in explicit pointer *
mode give focus to the new window.

Help Activation

Pressing **<Help>** on a component must invoke any context- *
sensitive help for the component or its nearest ancestor with *
context-sensitive help available. Within DialogBoxes, context-sensitive help should provide help information on the DialogBox as a whole. **<Shift> <Help>** should invoke the context-sensitive help mode if it is available.

Popup Menu Activation

If the pointer is in an element with an inactive Popup Menu and *
the context of the element allows a Popup Menu to be *
displayed, **BMenu Press** must post (activate) the Menu in a *
spring-loaded manner, and clicking **BMenu** must post (activate) *
the Menu.

Default Activation

In a DialogBox, pressing **<Enter>** or **<Return>** (except in *
Text), or double-clicking **BSelect** must activate the default *
PushButton in the DialogBox. If the double-click is in a *
component used for making selections or choices, such as List *
or RadioBox, the element under the pointer must be selected or *
should be chosen before the default PushButton is activated.

Expert Activation

Some elements, usually PushButtons and ToggleButtons, can have expert actions associated with them. **BSelect Click 2** * must activate any expert action for the element. Expert action should only be available in a Panel, and the expert action of all the buttons should be similar. The expert action should include the regular action of the component in a more global manner.

Cancel Activation

<Cancel> is available in most context to stop the current interaction, including canceling drag and drop operations, unposting TearOff Menus, canceling DialogBoxes, unposting Menu systems, and canceling scrolling operations.

Related Information

See Chapter 5 for more information about the activation model.

Basic Controls

Description

Basic controls are components that only take simple input. They are distinct from field controls in that they are usually elements of navigation fields rather than fields themselves. Basic controls must have no internal $*$ navigation. The following text describes the basic controls:

Separator Draws a separating line within windows, between Menu items, and between Panes of a PanedWindow. A Separator allows no application interaction.

Label Displays static text and images. A Label presents application information to users.

PushButton A button used to activate an operation. A PushButton contains a Label that indicates the operation of the button. The Label can contain text or an image.

CascadeButton A button used to display a Pulldown Menu. A CascadeButton contains a Label that indicates the Menu displayed. CascadeButtons can also contain an arrow graphic after the Label to distinguish it from PushButtons and to indicate the direction of the cascading Menu.

OptionButton A button used to display an Option Menu. An Option Menu allows for a one-of-many selection. An OptionButton contains a Label that indicates the current state of the Option Menu, and a bar graphic to distinguish it from a PushButton.

ToggleButton A button with two states: on and off. A ToggleButton contains a Label that indicates the state of the ToggleButton when it is set. Normally, preceding the Label is a graphic indicator of the state of the ToggleButton.

CheckButton   A ToggleButton in a group of ToggleButtons where any number of the ToggleButtons can be on at a time. The graphic indicator for a CheckButton is usually a filled square to indicate the on state or an empty square to indicate the off state.

RadioButton   A ToggleButton in a group of ToggleButtons where only one of the ToggleButtons can be on at a time. The graphic indicator for a RadioButton is usually a filled diamond or circle to indicate the on state or an empty diamond or circle to indicate the off state.

TearOffButton   A button used for tearing off a Menu to create a dialog representation of the Menu contents. A TearOffButton tears off a Menu in place when activated, or is dragged to tear off and move in one action. A TearOffButton usually contains a dashed line graphic representing perforations.

A single-line Text control can be configured to act like a basic control.

Navigation

Basic controls must have no internal navigation.   *

Other Operations

Activatable basic controls follow the basic activation model described in Section 5.1.

Related Information

For more information, see the reference pages for each basic control.

Basic Groups

Description

Basic groups of controls are used to organize groups of basic controls. The following text describes the basic groups:

Panel Organizes a collection of basic controls in a horizontal, vertical, or 2-dimensional layout. A Panel is usually composed of just one type of control.

Menu Organizes a collection of buttons, labels, and separators in a horizontal, vertical, or 2-dimensional layout within a separate Menu window. There are three types of Menus: Pulldown, Popup, and Option. A Menu is only available while it is popped up or pulled down.

MenuBar Organizes a collection of CascadeButtons in a horizontal layout at the top of a MainWindow.

Navigation

The <↓>, <←>, <→>, and <↑> direction keys must navigate within a basic *
group according to the navigation model described in Chapter 3.

Related Information

For more information, see the reference pages for each basic group.

Canvas

Description

A Canvas is used to present and edit graphics.

Navigation

Canvas navigation is unspecified.

Other Operations

Most Canvas operations are unspecified. A description of the specified Canvas operations follows:

<Help>   Must provide any available help for the Canvas.   *

CascadeButton

Description

A CascadeButton should be used to post a Pulldown Menu. This component   *
must be composed of a button, with either a text or graphics Label.
Following the Label, this component should also include an arrow graphic,
pointing in the direction that the Menu will be posted to distinguish it from a
PushButton. The graphic is usually not shown in a MenuBar.

Illustration

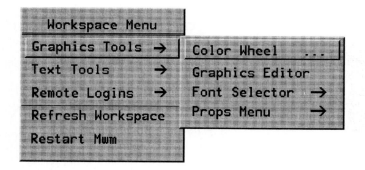

Navigation

A CascadeButton must have no internal navigation.   *

Other Operations

CascadeButtons follow the Menu activation model described in Section 3.3. The following text describes the other operations of this component:

<Help>   Must provide any available help for the CascadeButton.   *

Related Information

For more information, see the reference pages for Menus.

CheckButton

Description

A CheckButton should be used to set options in the application. A CheckButton is a special case of a ToggleButton. Any number of CheckButtons can be set at the same time.

This component must be composed of a text or graphic Label, and a graphic   *
that indicates the state of the CheckButton. The graphic indicator for a CheckButton is usually a filled square to indicate the on state or an empty square to indicate the off state. On color systems, the on state color can be distinct from general application colors to visually distinguish the on state.

Illustration

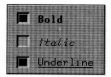

Navigation

CheckButtons must have no internal navigation.   *

Other Operations

The following text describes the CheckButton operations:

BSelect Press

Must arm the CheckButton. If the CheckButton was previously *
unset, it must show the CheckButton in the set state. If the *
CheckButton was previously set, it must show the CheckButton *
in the unset state.

BSelect Release

If the release happens in the same CheckButton that the press *
occurred in: *

- If the CheckButton was previously unset, it must be set. *

- If the CheckButton was previously set, it must be unset. *

In all cases the CheckButton must be disarmed, and, if the *
CheckButton is in a Menu, the Menu must be unposted.

BSelect Release 2

If the CheckButton was previously unset, it should be set. If the
CheckButton was previously set, it should be unset. If the
CheckButton is in a window, the default action of the window
should be activated.

<Enter> or **<Return>**

If the CheckButton is in a window with a default action, the *
default action must be activated. If the CheckButton is in a *
Menu: *

- If the CheckButton was previously unset, it must be set. *

- If the CheckButton was previously set, it must be unset. *

- In both cases, the CheckButton must be disarmed, and the *
  Menu must be unposted. *

<Select> or **<Space>**

If the CheckButton was previously unset, it must be set. If the *
CheckButton was previously set, it must be unset. In both *
cases, the CheckButton must be disarmed, and, if the *
CheckButton is in a Menu, the Menu must be unposted.

<Help>   Must provide any available help for the CheckButton.   *

Related Information

For more information, see the reference pages for RadioButton and ToggleButton.

CommandBox

Description

A CommandBox is a special-purpose composite component for command
entry that provides a built-in command history mechanism. The   *
CommandBox must be composed of a Text component with a command line   *
prompt for command input, and a List component above the Text component   *
for a command history area. The List must use either the single or browse   *
selection model. When a List element is selected, its contents must be   *
placed in the Text area. The default action of the CommandBox must be to   *
pass the command in the Text area to the application for execution and to   *
add the command to the end of the List. The List component can be
scrollable.

The List navigation actions <↑>, <↓>, <Ctrl> <Begin>, and <Ctrl> <End>   *
must be available from the Text component for moving the cursored element   *
within the List and thus changing the contents of the Text. The List
navigation actions <PageUp> and <PageDown> should also be available
from the Text component for moving the cursored element within the List.

Illustration

Related Information

For more information, see the reference page for CommandDialog.

CommandDialog

Description

A CommandDialog should be used to enter commands for processing. It should not interrupt the user's interaction with the application. It should include a CommandBox.

Illustration

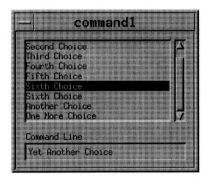

Related Information

For more information, see the reference page for DialogBox.

Composition

Description

The Composition group should be used to organize components in an arbitrary layout. The layout style can be either arbitrary, in even rows and columns, or so that the position of components is relative to the Composition component and the components it contains. This component is composed of an area for organizing components.

Navigation

This group must follow the navigation model as described in Chapter 3.   *

Related Information

For more information, see the reference pages for each layout group.

Default Activation

Description

Any window can have a default action, although default actions are most frequently used in DialogBoxes. A DialogBox should have a default action associated with it. The default action in a window can change depending upon which component has the focus. The current default action should correspond to the action of some PushButton, called the current default PushButton of the window.

The current default PushButton must be highlighted in some way, usually by   *
displaying a border around it. When the focus is on a PushButton, its action   *
must be the default action, and the PushButton must show default   *
highlighting. If the default action in a window varies, some PushButton   *
must always have default highlighting, except when there is no current   *
default action.

In a DialogBox, default PushButtons should be in the bottom area of PushButtons of the DialogBox. However, if a particular default action is associated with a cluster of controls in a window, the corresponding default PushButton can be located adjacent to the cluster.

When an explicit focus policy is in use, and the focus is outside the window, default highlighting should be placed on the PushButton whose action corresponds to the default action that would result from moving the focus to the window by using keyboard navigation among windows.

The default action of a DialogBox is activated according to the following rules:

- If the focus is in a window, **<Enter>** and **<Ctrl> <Return>** must invoke   *
  the default action, and, if the focus is in a component in a window other   *
  than multiline Text, **<Return>** must invoke the default action. These   *
  actions must have no other effect on the component with the focus,   *
  unless the default action has some effect.

- In list-like and graphics-like collections, when the location cursor is not on an activatable element, **BSelect Click 2** should act like **BSelect Click**, followed by invocation of the default action.

- When the focus is on a ToggleButton not used for expert activation, **BSelect Click 2** should activate the ToggleButton and then perform the default action.

Except in the middle of a button motion operation, **<Cancel>** anywhere in a   *
DialogBox must be equivalent to activating the **Cancel** PushButton in the   *
DialogBox.

Related Information

See Chapter 5 for general information about the activation model and default activation.

DialogBox

Description

A DialogBox should be used to group components in a window secondary to the main tasks of the application. Although a DialogBox can contain any components, a simple DialogBox is composed of a Label and PushButtons for supplying a response to the DialogBox. The OSF/Motif toolkit provides a number of ready-designed DialogBoxes for common uses: CommandDialog, FileSelectionDialog, MessageDialog, PromptDialog, and SelectionDialog. There are also a number of different types of MessageDialogs: ErrorDialog, InformationDialog, QuestionDialog, WorkingDialog, and WarningDialog. The illustration on this reference page shows a typical DialogBox.

DialogBox PushButtons should use the following common labels and actions. The actions are in the approximate sequence in which they should appear in DialogBoxes.

Yes   Must indicate an affirmative response to a question posed in the   * DialogBox and then close the window. While **Yes** is not an active-voice label, it implies a positive response to a question in a QuestionDialog or a WarningDialog. Only use **Yes** if it is a clear answer to the question.

No   Must indicate a negative response to a question posed in the   * DialogBox and then close the window. While **No** is not an active-voice label, it implies a negative response to a question in a QuestionDialog. Only use **No** if it is a clear answer to the question.

OK   Must cause the application to apply any changes and perform   * related actions specified by components in the DialogBox, and   * then dismiss the DialogBox. While **OK** is not an active-voice label, its usage is too common to change.

Close   Should cause the current DialogBox to be closed without performing any of the actions specified by components in the DialogBox. This action is usually only available in DialogBoxes that provide status information such as a Working DialogBox. This label can also be used if the actions in the DialogBox cannot be reversed, in which case this label replaces **Cancel** after the first irreversible action is performed.

Apply   Must apply any changes and perform the related actions specified   *
by the components in the DialogBox.

Retry   Must cause the task in progress to be attempted again. This action   *
is commonly found in message boxes that report an error.

Stop   Must end the task in progress at the next possible breaking point.   *
This action is commonly found in a Working DialogBox.

Pause   Must cause the task in progress to be paused. This action is   *
commonly found in a Working DialogBox and should be used in   *
combination with **Resume**.

Resume   Must cause a previously paused task to resume. This action is   *
commonly found in a Working DialogBox and should be used in   *
combination with **Pause**.

Reset   Must cancel any user changes that have not been applied to the   *
application. It must also reset the status of the DialogBox to the   *
state since the last time the DialogBox action was applied or to   *
the initial state of the DialogBox.

Cancel   Must close the DialogBox without performing any DialogBox   *
actions not yet applied to the application. Pressing **<Cancel>**   *
anywhere in the DialogBox, except during a cancelable drag   *
operation, must perform the action of this button.

Help   Must provide any help for the DialogBox.   *

You should arrange PushButton actions in DialogBoxes like other PushButtons, according to order and frequency of use. The common action PushButtons should be ordered as presented in the previous list. Positive responses to the DialogBox should be presented first, followed by negative responses and canceling responses. **Help** should always be the last action on the right.

Illustration

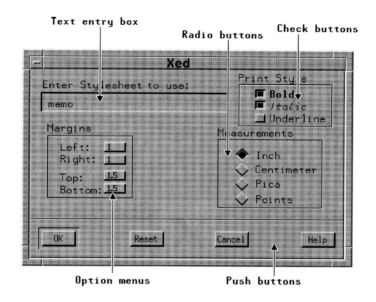

Navigation

A DialogBox must follow the navigation model described in Chapter 3. *

Related Information

For more information, see the reference pages for CommandDialog, ErrorDialog, FileSelectionDialog, InformationDialog, MessageDialog, PromptDialog, QuestionDialog, SelectionDialog, WarningDialog, and WorkingDialog.

Drag and Drop

Description

Drag and drop provides a quick and simple model for transferring data within and between applications. A drag and drop interaction is accomplished in four steps:

1. The user selects elements to drag and grabs them with the pointer, or grabs an unselected element.

2. The user drags elements to the drop location.

3. The user drops the elements on the drop location.

4. The component dropped on processes the drop action.

Pressing **Transfer** in a draggable element and moving the pointer must start *
a drag and drop interaction. If a drag is initiated in an unselected region and *
the pointer is over two possible draggable elements, the drag must occur on *
the highest draggable element in the stacking order. This also implies that
in nested draggable elements the drag occurs from the smallest draggable
element under the pointer.

When **BSelect** is used for dragging operations, its use must supersede the *
use of **BSelect Motion** in the selection models described in Section 4.1.

Any successful drag and drop transfer from a read-only component should *
by default result in a copy of the data, but it can result in a link. Transfers
from writable components can by default result in a copy, a link, or a move. *
<Shift> BTransfer Release must force a move operation if possible; *
otherwise, the operation must fail. **<Ctrl> BTransfer Release** must force a *
copy operation if possible; otherwise, the operation must fail. **<Ctrl>** *
<Shift> BTransfer Release must force a link operation if possible; *
otherwise, the operation must fail.

If a system provides drag and drop help, pressing **<Help>** during a drag and
drop operation should allow the posting of a DialogBox with the help
information and the possible choices for continuing the drag and drop
operation. Pressing **<Cancel>** during a drag operation must cancel the *

current drag operation and return the system to the state prior to the start of *
the drag operation.

Releasing **BTransfer** must end a drag and drop operation. When a user *
releases **BTransfer**, the drop operation must occur at the location of the *
hotspot of the drag icon pointer. The drop must occur into the highest drop *
site in the stacking order. This also implies that in a group of nested drop
sites the drop occurs into the smallest drop site under the pointer.

Related Information

See Section 4.3 for more information on the drag and drop model, and for
information on quick transfer and the selection models.

Edit Menu

Description

The common **Edit** Menu contents are described as follows. Note that you should only include those functions actually supported by your application. The **Edit** Menu can contain a TearOffButton. The illustration on this reference page shows an **Edit** Menu.

Undo Alt+Backspace
> Must reverse the most recently executed action. To provide a *
> visual cue to the user, the **Undo** selection title should be
> dynamically modified to indicate what is being undone. For
> example, if the most recently executed action was a paste, the
> action name would be **Undo paste**. Your application should be
> able to undo all of the actions in the **Edit** Menu. This action must *
> have the mnemonic **U**.

Cut Shift+Del
> Must remove the selected portion of data from the client area to *
> the clipboard. This action must choose the component to act on *
> by following the rules in Section 4.2.2 for operations that act on *
> selections. This action must have the mnemonic **T**.

Copy Ctrl+Ins
> Must copy the selected portion of data to the clipboard without *
> removing the original data from the client area. This action must *
> choose the component to act on by following the rules in Section *
> 4.2.2 for operations that act on selections. This action must have *
> the mnemonic **C**.

Copy Link
> Must copy a link of the selected portion of data to the clipboard *
> without removing the original data from the client area. This *
> action must choose the component to act on by following the rules *
> in Section 4.2.2 for operations that act on selections. This action *
> must have the mnemonic **K**.

Paste   Shift+Ins

Must paste the contents of the clipboard into a client area. This   *
action must choose the component to act on by following the rules   *
in Section 4.2.2 for operations that do not act on selections. This   *
action must have the mnemonic **P**.

Paste Link

Must paste a link of the data represented by the contents of the   *
clipboard into a client area. This action must choose the   *
component to act on by following the rules in Section 4.2.2 for   *
operations that do not act on selections. This action must have   *
the mnemonic **L**.

Clear   Must remove a selected portion of data from the client area   *
without copying it to the clipboard. The remaining data is not
compressed to fill the space that was occupied by the cleared data.   *
This action must choose the component to act on by following the   *
rules in Section 4.2.2 for operations that act on selections. This   *
action must have the mnemonic **E**.

Delete   Must remove a selected portion of data from the client area   *
without copying it to the clipboard. This action must choose the   *
component to act on by following the rules in Section 4.2.2 for   *
operations that act on selections. This action must have the   *
mnemonic **D**.

Select All   Ctrl+/

Must make the primary selection consist of all the elements in a   *
component of the client area. This action must choose the   *
component to act on by following the rules in Section 4.2.2 for   *
operations that do not act on selections. If the action uses an
accelerator, it should be **<Ctrl> </>**.

Deselect All   Ctrl+

Must remove from the primary selection all the elements in a   *
component of the client area. This action must choose the   *
component to act on by following the rules in Section 4.2.2 for   *
operations that do not act on selections. If the action uses an
accelerator, it should be **<Ctrl> <\>**.

Select Pasted
> Must make the primary selection consist of the last element or *
> elements pasted into a component of the client area. This action *
> must choose the component to act on by following the rules in *
> Section 4.2.2 for operations that do not act on selections.

Reselect   Alt+Insert
> Must make the primary selection consist of the last selected *
> element or elements in a component of the client area. This *
> action must choose the component to act on by following the rules *
> in Section 4.2.2 for operations that do not act on selections. The *
> action must be available only in components that do not support *
> persistent selections and only when the current selection is empty.
> If the action uses an accelerator, it should be **<Alt> <Insert>**.

Promote   Alt+Insert
> Must promote to the primary selection the current selection of a *
> component of the client area. This action must choose the *
> component to act on by following the rules in Section 4.2.2 for *
> operations that act on selections. This action must only be *
> available for components that support persistent selections. If the
> action uses an accelerator, it should be **<Alt> <Insert>**.

You should include Menu items in the order described. If you add new
Menu items, you should insert them near similar elements.

If you use accelerators for **Undo**, **Cut**, **Copy**, and **Paste**, you must use either *
one or both of the models presented in the following two tables.

Table 9–1. Edit Menu Accelerators, Model 1

Edit Menu Item	Accelerator
Undo	<Alt> <BackSpace>
Cut	<Shift> <Delete>
Copy	<Ctrl> <Insert>
Paste	<Shift> <Insert>

Table 9–2. Edit Menu Accelerators, Model 2

Edit Menu Item	Accelerator
Undo	<Ctrl> <Z>
Cut	<Ctrl> <X>
Copy	<Ctrl> <C>
Paste	<Ctrl> <V>

In addition, if your keyboard has **<Undo>**, **<Cut>**, **<Copy>**, and **<Paste>** keys, these should be supported as accelerators for the corresponding Menu items as well.

Illustration

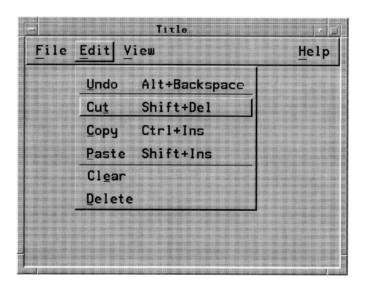

Related Information

See Chapter 6 for more information on the MenuBar system and for general information about Menu design.

ErrorDialog

Description

An ErrorDialog should be used to convey a message about a user error. It should stop user interaction with the application until it is dismissed. It should include an error symbol, a message, and one of the following button arrangements:

OK Cancel
OK Cancel Help

Illustration

Related Information

For more information, see the reference page for DialogBox.

Field Controls

Description

Field controls are components that use internal navigation controls. Field controls should be navigation fields. The following text describes the field controls:

Sash Used to set the boundary between two components. A Sash is usually a small square on the boundary between two components. The separated components are called Panes, and a group of Panes, Separators, and Sashes is called a PanedWindow.

Scale Used to set or display a value in a range. A Scale is usually composed of a slider, moving within an element that indicates the size of the range, and a Label that indicates the current value. The position of the slider indicates the value relative to the range. The slider is moved directly by using the mouse pointer or by using the arrow keys. A Scale can also have buttons with arrow graphics for moving the slider with the mouse.

ScrollBar Used to scroll the visible area of a component. A ScrollBar is usually composed of a slider, moving within an element that indicates the full size of the component, and buttons with arrow graphics for moving the slider with the mouse. The slider indicates the relative position and size of the visible area of the component. The slider is moved directly by using the mouse pointer or by using the arrow keys.

List Used for selecting elements from a list of elements. A List can allow multiple items to be selected or can be constrained to allow only one item to be selected at a time. A List is usually composed of a vertical list of items. A List can also have both horizontal and vertical ScrollBars for scrolling the visible portion of the list of items.

Text	Used for displaying, entering, and modifying text. There are single-line and multiple-line variants. Multiline Text can have both horizontal and vertical ScrollBars for scrolling the visible portion of the text area.
Canvas	Used for displaying, entering, and modifying graphics. A Canvas can have both horizontal and vertical ScrollBars for scrolling the visible portion of the drawing area.

Navigation

Field controls have navigation that is specific to the component. See the reference pages for each field control for information about its navigation.

Other Operations

Field controls have operations that are specific to the component. See the reference pages for each field control for information about its operations.

Related Information

For more information, see the reference pages for each field control.

File Menu

Description

The common **File** Menu contents are described as follows. Note that you should only include those functions actually supported by your application. If the label **File** is not appropriate to the context of your application, you can choose a different, more appropriate label. The **File** Menu can contain a TearOffButton. The illustration on this reference page shows a **File** Menu.

New Must create a new file. The **New** operation must clear existing *
data from the client area. If completion of the operation will *
obliterate current changes to the file, you must display a *
DialogBox, asking the user about saving changes. This action *
must have the mnemonic **N**.

Open . . . Must open an existing file. The **Open** operation must prompt *
the user for the name of the file with a DialogBox. The title
bar should be updated with the name of the newly opened file. *
If completion of the operation will obliterate current changes *
to the file, you must display a DialogBox, asking the user *
about saving changes. This DialogBox should be displayed
after the user selects a new file. This action must have the *
mnemonic **O**.

Save Must save the currently opened file without removing the *
existing contents of the client area. If the currently opened file *
has no name, **Save** must prompt for a filename with a *
DialogBox. This action must have the mnemonic **S**.

Save As . . . Must save the currently opened file under a new name without *
removing the existing contents of the client area. The **Save As** *
operation must prompt for the name of the file with a *
DialogBox. If the user tries to save the new file under an *
existing name, **Save As** must alert the user with a DialogBox *
of a possible loss of data. This action must have the *
mnemonic **A**.

Print   Must schedule a file for printing. If your application requires   *
                  specific printing information before printing, the operation   *
                  must first request that information with a DialogBox, and the   *
                  entry title must be followed by an ellipsis. Printing
                  information can also be specified for the application in the
                  Options Menu. This action must have the mnemonic **P**.   *

Close   Can be supplied in applications that have multiple
                  independent primary windows. This action must not be   *
                  supplied in applications with a single primary window or   *
                  multiple dependent primary windows. This action must only   *
                  close the current primary window and its associated secondary   *
                  windows; that is, the window family. This action must have   *
                  the mnemonic **C**. You can include this action even though it is
                  similar to the **Close** action in the window Menu. This ensures
                  that users have a way to close the primary window even if they
                  are not running a compliant window manager. Applications
                  should prompt the user to save any unsaved changes if the
                  action would cause loss of data.

Exit   Must end the current application and all windows associated   *
                  with it. This action is equivalent to closing all primary
                  windows of the application. If completion of the operation   *
                  will obliterate current changes to the file, you must display a   *
                  DialogBox, asking the user about saving changes. This action   *
                  must have the mnemonic **X**. You should include this action
                  even though it is similar to the **Close** action in the window
                  Menu. This ensures that users have a way to end the
                  application even if they are not running a compliant window
                  manager. Applications should prompt the user to save any
                  unsaved changes if the action would cause loss of data. If your
                  application does not have a **File** Menu, put **Exit** at the end of
                  the first Pulldown Menu.

Illustration

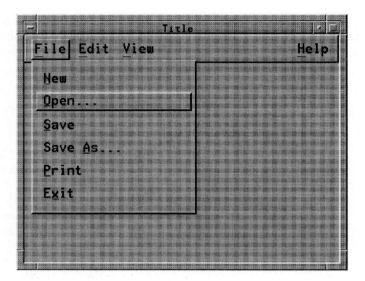

Related Information

See Chapter 6 for more information on the MenuBar system and for general information about Menu design.

FileSelectionBox

Description

A FileSelectionBox is a special-purpose composite component for file selection. It can be used to traverse through directories, view the files and subdirectories in them, and then select files. The FileSelectionBox must be composed of at least the following components:

- A Text component for displaying and editing a directory mask used to select the files to be displayed. The directory mask must be a string specifying the base directory to be examined and a search pattern.

- A List component for displaying filenames. The file list should display all files and subdirectories in the base directory that match the search pattern. The List must use either the single or browse selection model.

- A List component for displaying subdirectories. The directory list should display the subdirectories of the base directory, as well as the base directory itself and its parent directory. The List must use either the single or browse selection model.

- A Text component for displaying and editing a filename.

- A group of PushButtons, labeled **OK**, **Filter**, **Cancel**, and **Help**. If the FileSelectionBox is used to perform a specific action to the selected files, **OK** can be replaced by a label describing the action to be done.

- Additional elements can be added by an application.

The user must be able to select a new directory to examine by scrolling through the list of directories and selecting the desired directory or by editing the directory mask. Selecting a new directory from the directory list must not change the search pattern. A user must be able to select a new search pattern by editing the directory mask.

The List navigation actions <↑>, <↓>, **<Ctrl> <Begin>**, and **<Ctrl> <End>** must be available from the Text components for moving the cursored element within each List and thus changing the contents of the Text. The List navigation actions **<PageUp>** and **<PageDown>** should also be available from the Text components for moving the cursored element within

each List. The contents of the directory Text must correspond to the *
contents of the directory List, and the contents of the filename Text must *
correspond to the contents of the filename List.

The user must be able to select a file by scrolling through the list of *
filenames and selecting the desired file or by entering the filename directly *
into the Text component. Selecting a file from the list causes that filename
to appear in the file selection Text component.

The user can select a new file as many times as desired. The application *
must not be notified until one of the following events occurs: *

- The user activates the **OK** PushButton. *

- The user presses **<Enter>** or **<Return>** while the filename Text *
  component has the keyboard focus. *

- The user presses **<Enter>** or **<Return>** while the location cursor is on *
  an item in the file List. *

- The user double-clicks **BSelect** on an item in the file List. *

The FileSelectionBox must initiate a directory and file search when any of *
the following occurs: *

- The FileSelectionBox is initialized. *

- The user activates the **Filter** PushButton. *

- The user double-clicks or presses **<Enter>** or **<Return>** on an item in *
  the directory List. *

- The user presses **<Enter>** or **<Return>** while the directory mask Text *
  edit area has the keyboard focus. *

Illustration

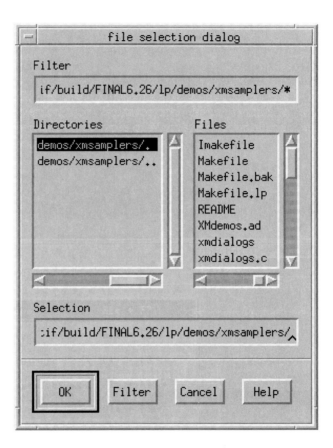

Related Information

For more information, see the reference page for FileSelectionDialog.

FileSelectionDialog

Description

A FileSelectionDialog should be used to enter the name of a file for processing. It should not interrupt the user's interaction with the application. It should include a FileSelectionBox.

Illustration

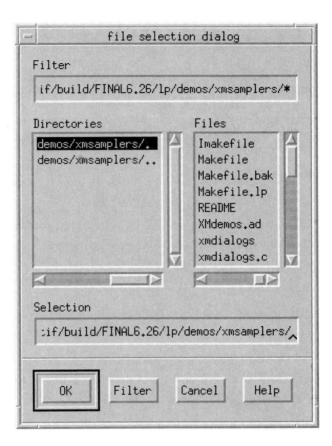

Related Information

For more information, see the reference page for DialogBox.

Focus

Description

The keyboard focus model is defined by a focus policy. A focus policy is a specific mechanism for moving the focus among windows and components.   *
The implicit and explicit focus policies must be supported.

In the implicit focus policy, also called the pointer, real-estate driven, or point-to-type policy, the keyboard focus moves to the window or component into which a user moves the mouse pointer. No explicit action is performed to set the keyboard focus in the implicit focus model. Keyboard events are sent to the window or component that the mouse pointer is in, more specifically to the component that the mouse pointer is in. In implicit mode, the keyboard focus tracks the mouse pointer. Because of this, there is no way to move the keyboard focus from the keyboard using implicit mode. In this focus policy, the location cursor for keyboard events does not need to be shown; however, the application can show it.

The explicit focus policy requires the user to explicitly select which window or component receives the keyboard focus. In explicit focus mode at the window level, a user moves the keyboard focus to a window by pressing **BSelect** while the mouse pointer is over the window. Simply moving the mouse pointer over a window does not give the window the keyboard focus. Because of this, explicit mode is often called click-to-type. In explicit mode within a window, a user generally moves the keyboard focus to a specific component within a window by pressing **BSelect** over the component. Pressing **BSelect** must not move focus to a component that is   *
not traversable or does not accept input. Pressing **BSelect** in a component that is used only to change the visible portion of another component, such as a ScrollBar or Sash, should act on that component but should not move focus to it. In this focus policy, the location of keyboard focus must be   *
shown by a location cursor.

Related Information

See Chapter 2 for more information about the focus model.

Frame

Description

A Frame should be used to frame other components. It simply provides a decorative border.

Other Operations

This component can indicate the input focus.

Framing Groups

Description

Framing groups are used to frame groups of components as the following text describes:

Frame   Draws framing decorations around a component.

ScrolledWindow   Frames a component and adds ScrollBars for scrolling the visible area of the component.

MainWindow   Organizes the contents of a primary window. A MainWindow frames the client area and can optionally include ScrollBars, a MenuBar, a command area, and a message area.

Navigation

These groups must follow the navigation model as described in Chapter 3.   *

Related Information

For more information, see the reference pages for each framing group.

Help Menu

Description

There are two acceptable models for the contents of the **Help** Menu. The *OSF/Motif Style Guide* allows either model.

The common Menu contents for this model are described in the following text. Note that you should only include those functions actually supported by your application. The **Help** Menu can contain a TearOffButton. The illustration on this reference page shows this first model of a **Help** Menu.

On Context   Shift+Help

Must initiate context-sensitive help by changing the *
shape of the pointer to the question pointer described in *
Section 2.2.2. When the user moves the pointer to the *
component help is wanted on and presses **BSelect**, any *
available context-sensitive help for the component must *
be presented, and the pointer reverts from the question *
pointer. This action must have the mnemonic **C**. If the
action uses an accelerator, it should be **<Shift>**
<Help>.

On Help

Must provide information on how to use the *
application's help facility. This action must have the *
mnemonic **H**.

On Window

Must provide general information about the window *
from which help was requested. This action must have *
the mnemonic **W**.

On Keys

Must provide information about the application's use of *
function keys, mnemonics, and keyboard accelerators. *
This action must have the mnemonic **K**.

Index

Must provide an index for all help information in the *
application. This action must have the mnemonic **I**.
The index can provide search capabilities.

Tutorial Must provide access to the application's tutorial. This *
action must have the mnemonic **T**.

On Version Must provide the name and version of the application. *
This action must have the mnemonic **V**. It can provide
other information as well.

The common Menu contents in the second model are described in the
following text. Note that you should only include those functions actually
supported by your application. The **Help** Menu can contain a
TearOffButton.

Context-Sensitive Help   **Shift+Help**

Must initiate context-sensitive help by changing the *
shape of the pointer to the question pointer described in *
Section 2.2.2. When the user moves the pointer to the *
component help is wanted on and presses **BSelect**, any *
available context-sensitive help for the component must *
be presented, and the pointer reverts from the question *
pointer. This action should be followed by a separator. *
This action must have the mnemonic **C**. If the action
uses an accelerator, it should be **<Shift> <Help>**.

Overview Must provide general information about the application *
window from which help was requested. This action *
must have the mnemonic **O**.

Index Must provide an index for all help information in the *
application. This action must have the mnemonic **I**.
The index can provide search capabilities.

Keyboard Must provide information about the application's use of *
function keys, mnemonics, and keyboard accelerators. *
This action must have the mnemonic **K**.

Tutorial Must provide access to the application's tutorial. This *
action must have the mnemonic **T**.

Using Help Must provide information on how to use the *
application's help facility. This action must have the *
mnemonic **H**.

Product Information

Must provide the name and version of the application.   *
This action must have the mnemonic **P**. It can provide
other information as well.

Applications should place additional **Help** Menu items between **Index** and
Using Help.

Help is usually provided in DialogBoxes but can also appear in the message
area. You should include Menu items in the order described. If you add
new Menu items, you should insert them near similar elements.

Illustration

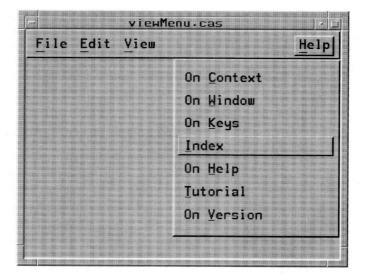

Related Information

See Chapter 6 for more information on the MenuBar system and for general information about Menu design.

Icon Menu

Description

Clicking **BSelect** in an icon must give the icon the keyboard focus and post   *
the icon Menu. The icon Menu must be the same Menu as the window   *
Menu for the associated primary window. **Size** should not be available from
the icon Menu. Navigating to the icon must also give the icon the keyboard   *
focus and should post the icon Menu.

Double-clicking **BSelect** anywhere in the icon must restore the window   *
family, just as the icon Menu item **Restore** does. If the window is currently   *
minimized, but its previous state was maximized, double-clicking **BSelect**   *
returns it to the maximized state. Selecting **Maximize** from the icon Menu   *
always maximizes the corresponding window. If the window is minimized,   *
Minimize must not be available in the icon Menu; otherwise, selecting it   *
minimizes the window family. Pressing **BSelect** or **BTransfer** anywhere in   *
the icon and dragging the mouse pointer must move the icon to track the   *
pointer, just as the icon Menu item **Move** does.

If the window manager has been customized by the user so that the icon   *
Menu does not pop up when the icon gets the focus, **<Shift> <Escape>**,   *
<Alt> <Space>, **<Menu>**, and **BMenu** must pop up the icon Menu.

Related Information

See Chapter 7 for more information on the icon Menu and the window
manager in general. See Chapter 6 for information about Menu design.

IconBox

Description

An icon box is a specialized window that acts as a storage location for icons. An icon box acts like a typical window in the sense that it has a window frame and frame components. The client area of an icon box must   *
have an area for holding icons and can have horizontal and vertical scroll   *
bars for moving around the icon area.

The icon box must have all the same components as any other primary   *
window. Like other windows it can be sized, moved, minimized,
maximized, restored, and lowered. However, the window manager must not   *
allow the icon box to be closed. The system Menu action **Close** must be   *
replaced with the system Menu action **Pack Icons** in an icon box. Double-   *
clicking **BSelect** in the icon box system Menu must only open the icon box   *
system Menu. It must not close the icon box. **Pack Icons** arranges the icons
as close as possible together in the visible icon area if possible. **Pack Icons**   *
must have the mnemonic **P**. If **Pack Icons** has an accelerator, it should be
<Alt> <F12> if **<F12>** is available. When the input focus is in the icon box,   *
<Shift> <Escape> or **<Alt> <Space>** must pop up the icon box system   *
Menu if the Menu is unposted. If the Menu is already posted, **<Shift>**   *
<Escape> or **<Alt> <Space>** must unpost the Menu.

The icon box can contain an icon for each window family, even if it is
active. The icon for minimized window families must be the same as the   *
icon would be outside of the icon box. The icon for an active window
family should be similar to the minimized icon, deemphasized somehow.

Clicking **BSelect** in an icon must give the icon keyboard focus and post the   *
icon Menu. The icon Menu must be the same Menu as the window Menu   *
for the associated primary window. If the icon represents an active window   *
family, **Restore** and **Size** must not be available from the icon Menu. If the   *
icon represents a minimized window family, **Size** must not be available   *
from the icon Menu. If the window manager is customized so that the icon   *
with the focus does not have its window Menu automatically posted,   *
BMenu or **<Menu>** must post its Menu.

Double-clicking **BSelect** anywhere in an icon that represents a minimized *
window family must restore the window family, just as the icon Menu item *
Restore does. Double-clicking **BSelect** anywhere in an icon that represents *
an active window family must raise the window family to the top of the *
window hierarchy. If the window is currently minimized, but its previous *
state was maximized, double-clicking **BSelect** returns it to the maximized *
state. Selecting **Maximize** from the icon Menu always maximizes the *
corresponding window. If the window is minimized, **Minimize** must not be *
available in the icon Menu; otherwise, selecting it minimizes the window *
family. Pressing **BSelect** or **BTransfer** anywhere in the icon and dragging *
the mouse pointer must move the icon within the icon area to track the *
pointer, just as the icon Menu item **Move** does.

The <↓>, <↑>, <→>, and <←> directional keys must navigate among the *
icons in the icon box. Icon navigation must behave as described in the *
following text. Note that <↓> and <→> do not need to traverse icons in the
same order.

<↓>   In a left-to-right language environment, this key must move the *
        location cursor through the icons in the icon box, starting at the *
        upper-left icon and ending at the lower-right icon, then wrapping *
        back up to the upper left. In a right-to-left language environment,
        the location cursor can move, starting at the upper right and
        moving to the lower left.

<←>   This key must move the location cursor through the icons in the *
        opposite direction of <→>.

<→>   In a left-to-right language environment, this key must move the *
        location cursor through the icons in the icon box, starting at the *
        upper-left icon and ending at the lower-right icon, then wrapping *
        back up to the upper left. In a right-to-left language environment,
        the location cursor can move, starting at the upper right and
        moving to the lower left.

<↑>   This key must move the location cursor through the icons in the *
        opposite direction of <↓>.

Illustration

Related Information

See Chapter 7 for more information about icons and the window manager.

Icons

Description

An icon is a stylized representation of an object. A window icon is a minimized representation of a window or window family that can help organize windows and tasks in the display. Iconifying a window is also known as minimizing a window. The window manager must iconify all   * windows of window family together. It must not iconify any single window,   * primary or secondary, from a window family without also iconifying all the   * other windows in the window family. The iconic representation of a window family should not change any state in the windows, except the visual representation of the window. The application running inside of a   * window must continue running even when the application is iconified. The application can adjust its own state when it is iconified.

An icon is made up of an image and a label. The illustration on this reference page shows a typical Motif icon.

The image should be surrounded by a border that indicates when the icon has the keyboard focus. The image area can contain text or a bitmap. The label should be located just below the image and its border. The label can also indicate when the icon has the keyboard focus by highlighting with the image area.

The label should contain the same text as the title area of the corresponding primary window, or an abbreviated form of it. When the icon does not have   * the keyboard focus, the width of the label must be the same as the width of   * the image area and its border, truncating text if necessary. When the icon has the keyboard focus, the width of the label can expand to display the entire text.

Clicking **BSelect** in an icon must give the icon keyboard focus and should   * post the icon Menu. Navigating to the icon must also give the icon the   * keyboard focus and should post the icon Menu.

Double-clicking **BSelect** anywhere in the icon must restore the window   * family, just as the icon Menu item **Restore** does. If the window is currently   * minimized, but its previous state was maximized, double-clicking **BSelect**   *

returns it to the maximized state. Selecting **Maximize** from the icon Menu   *
always maximizes the corresponding window. If the window is minimized,   *
Minimize must not be available in the icon Menu; otherwise, selecting it   *
minimizes the window family. Pressing **BSelect** or **BTransfer** anywhere in   *
the icon and dragging the mouse pointer must move the icon to track the   *
pointer, just as the icon Menu item **Move** does.

If the window manager has been customized by the user so that the icon   *
Menu does not pop up when the icon gets the focus, **<Shift> <Escape>**,   *
<Alt> <Space>, **<Menu>**, and **BMenu** must pop up the icon Menu.

Illustration

Related Information

See Chapter 7 for more information about icons and the window manager.

InformationDialog

Description

An InformationDialog should be used to convey information to the user. It *
must not interrupt the user's interaction with the application. It should
include an information symbol, a message, and one of the following button
arrangements:

OK
OK Help

Illustration

Related Information

For more information, see the reference page for DialogBox.

Input Devices

Description

The most typical pointing device is a mouse, although a graphics tablet, track ball, joystick, and other tools also work as pointing devices. You can use any pointing device in place of a mouse. This guide assumes that a mouse, or any pointing device, has the following three buttons. Chapter 2 describes the button bindings for pointing devices that do not have three buttons.

BSelect   Used for selection, activation, and setting the location cursor.   *
This button must be the leftmost button, except for left-handed   *
users where it can be the rightmost button.

BTransfer Used for moving and copying elements. This button must be   *
the middle mouse button, unless dragging is integrated with   *
selection. Details about the effects of integrating **BTransfer**
with **BSelect** are described in Chapter 4.

BMenu   Used for popping up Menus. This button must be the rightmost   *
button, except for left-handed users where it can be the leftmost   *
button.

Since not all keyboards are the same, it is difficult to give style guidelines that are correct for every manufacturer's keyboard. To solve this problem, this guide describes keys using a model keyboard mechanism. Wherever keyboard input is specified, the keys are indicated by the engraving they have on the OSF/Motif model keyboard. The model keyboard does not correspond directly to any existing keyboard; rather, it assumes a keyboard with an ideal set of keys.

In addition to the standard letter, number, and character keys, the OSF/Motif model keyboard is composed of the following special keys:

- The special printing characters **</>**, **<\>**, and **<!>**

- The standard modifier keys **<Ctrl>**, **<Alt>**, and **<Shift>**

- Ten function keys **<F1>** through **<F10>**

- The arrow keys <↓>, <←>, <→>, and <↑>
- **<BackSpace>**
- **<Cancel>**
- **<Delete>**
- **<End>**
- **<Escape>**
- **<Help>**
- **<Home>**
- **<Insert>**
- **<Menu>**
- **<PageDown>**
- **<PageUp>**
- **<Return>**
- **<Space>**
- **<Tab>**

The OSF/Motif model keyboard also contains the following optional keys, which although useful, either are not necessary or can be replaced by combinations of other keys:

- **<CapsLock>**
- **<Copy>**
- **<Cut>**
- **<Enter>**
- **<ModeSwitch>**
- **<NumLock>**
- **<PageLeft>**
- **<PageRight>**
- **<Paste>**

- **\<ScrollLock\>**

- **\<Select\>**

- **\<Undo\>**

Throughout this guide, behavior is described in terms of model keyboard keys. When a behavior takes advantage of an optional key from the model keyboard, it is also described in terms of the required special keys. Each of   *
the nonoptional keys described on the OSF/Motif model keyboard must be   *
available either as specified or by using other keys or key combinations if   *
the specified key is unavailable.

Related Information

See Chapter 2 for a more information about input devices.

Label

Description

A Label should be used to display text or graphics that label other
components. This component must be composed of an area for displaying a   *
text or graphics label.

Illustration

Navigation

A Label must have no internal navigation.   *

Layout Groups

Description

Layout groups are used for organizing components into groups as described in the following text:

Composition Organizes a collection of components, including groups, in an arbitrary layout.

PanedWindow A linear grouping of components and Sashes. Sashes are used to set the boundary between two components. The separated components are called Panes and can contain any components.

Navigation

Layout groups must follow the navigation model as described in Chapter 3. *

Related Information

For more information, see the reference pages for each layout group.

List

Description

A List should be used to present a list of elements for selection. The List elements can be selected using either the single selection model, the browse selection model, the multiple selection model, or the discontiguous selection model. This component must be composed of an area for presenting a list of text or graphics elements. It can optionally have vertical and horizontal ScrollBars, which show different views of the List elements.

The location cursor in a List should differentiate between normal mode and add mode. The location cursor should be a solid box in normal mode and a dashed box in add mode.

*

Illustration

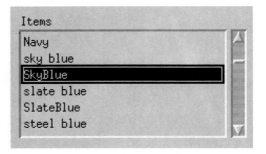

Navigation

The following text describes the navigation actions of this component:

<Ctrl> <Begin>   Must move the location cursor to the first item in the List.   *

<Ctrl> <End>   Must move the location cursor to the last item in the List.   *

<↑>   Must move the location cursor to the previous item in the   *
List.

<↓>   Must move the location cursor to the next item in the List.   *

<PageDown>   In a scrollable List, must move the location cursor to the   *
item one page down in the List.

<PageUp>   In a scrollable List, must move the location cursor to the   *
item one page up in the List.

Other Operations

The following text describes the operations of this component:

BSelect Click 2   Must select the current List item and cause any default   *
action for the window to occur.

<Begin>   In a scrollable List, must move the horizontal scroll   *
region so that the leftmost edge of the List is visible.

<End>   In a scrollable List, must move the horizontal scroll   *
region so that the rightmost edge of the List is visible.

<←>   In a scrollable List, must scroll the List one character to   *
the left.

<PageLeft> or **<Ctrl> <PageUp>**
In a scrollable List, must scroll the List one page to the   *
left.

<→>   In a scrollable List, must scroll the List one character to   *
the right.

<PageRight> or **<Ctrl> <PageDown>**
In a scrollable List, must scroll the List one page to the   *
right.

<Help>   Must provide any available help for the List.   *

Related Information

For more information on List element selection, see the description of the selection models in Chapter 4. For more information about the ScrollBars, see the reference page for ScrollBar.

MainWindow

Description

A MainWindow should be used to organize the contents of a primary window. A MainWindow must frame the client area and can optionally include ScrollBars, a MenuBar, a command area, and a message area. *

Illustration

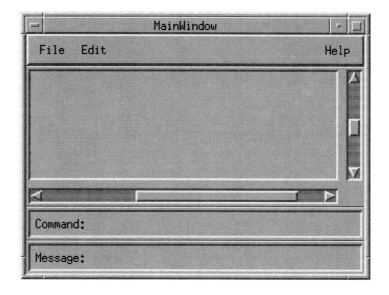

Navigation

A MainWindow must follow the navigation model described in Chapter 3.   *

Related Information

For more information about the components of the MainWindow, see the reference pages for MenuBar, ScrollBar, and Text.

MenuBar

Description

A MenuBar is a basic group that organizes the most common features of an application. The MenuBar must be a horizontal bar at the top edge of the application just below the title area of the window frame. The MenuBar contains a list of Menu topics in CascadeButtons with Pulldown Menus connected to them. A MenuBar must contain only CascadeButtons, because other buttons inhibit Menu browsing. Each Menu topic should have a single-letter mnemonic indicated by underlining.

The following Pulldown Menus provide general functions common to most applications. Remember that these Menu guidelines, like all the guidelines in this *OSF/Motif Style Guide*, apply only in a left-to-right language environment in an English-language locale. You need to make the appropriate changes for other locales.

File   The **File** Menu should contain components for performing actions on the files, such as opening, saving, closing, and printing. It should also contain components for performing actions on the application as a whole, such as quitting. If the Label **File** is not appropriate to the context of your application, you can choose a different, more appropriate Label. The **File** Menu should have a mnemonic of **F**.

Selected   The **Selected** Menu should contain components for performing actions on the objects represented by the current selection of the application, such as opening or printing a selected item. This Menu is often similar to the **File** Menu, except that it acts on the objects denoted by the current selection. For example, in a directory browser, **Open** in the **File** Menu could (using a DialogBox) prompt the user for the name of a directory to open for browsing, while **Open** in the **Selected** Menu opens the file whose icon is currently selected in the browser. The **Selected** Menu should not contain editing functions normally found in the **Edit** Menu. The **Selected** Menu should have a mnemonic of **S**.

Edit   The **Edit** Menu should contain components for performing actions on the current data of the application, such as an undo action or making global substitutions in a block of text. It should also include components for interacting with the system clipboard, such as cut, copy, and paste. The **Edit** Menu should have a mnemonic of **E**.

View   The **View** Menu should contain components for changing the user's view on the data. Components in the **View** Menu should not actually change the data. The exact contents of the **View** Menu are application specific but can include components that change the appearance of the data, the amount of data that is displayed, or the order in which the data is displayed. The **View** Menu should have a mnemonic of **V**.

Options   The **Options** Menu should contain components for a user to customize the application. The exact contents of the **Options** Menu are application specific. The **Options** Menu should have a mnemonic of **O**.

Help   The **Help** Menu should contain components that provide user help facilities. The components in the **Help** Menu usually bring up a DialogBox with help information. Every application should have a **Help** Menu. The **Help** Menu should have a mnemonic of **H**.

While we recommend that you include the common Menus in the MenuBar of your application, your choice of Menu titles and items depends on the nature of your application. If your application requires it, you should design more relevant titles and selections, but do not change the meanings of items used in the common Menus.

If any of the common Menus are present, they must be arranged in the *
following order with respect to each other, ranging from left to right across *
the MenuBar in a left-to-right language environment: *

    File Menu *
    Selected Menu *
    Edit Menu *
    View Menu *
    Options Menu *
    Help Menu *

You can omit any of these Menus if they are not relevant to the application. You can also intersperse other, application-specific, Menus among these Menus. However, if a **File** Menu is present, it must be the first Menu and *
must be placed at the far left of the MenuBar. If a **Help** Menu is present, it *
must be the last Menu and must be placed at the far right of the MenuBar.

The recommended contents of the **File**, **Edit**, and **Help** Menus are described on their own reference pages. The contents of the **View** and **Options** Menus are application specific and are not specified here. Each of these common Menus can contain a TearOffButton.

Illustration

Navigation

The MenuBar follows the navigation model described in Chapter 3.

Other Operations

The following text describes the operations of this component:

<Help>   Must provide any available help for the current CascadeButton.   *

Related Information

For information about the suggested contents of these Menus, see the reference pages for File Menu, Edit Menu, and Help Menu.

Menus

Description

Menus should be used to organize a collection of basic controls in a horizontal, vertical, or 2-dimensional layout within a separate Menu window. There are three types of Menus: Pulldown, Popup, and Option. A Menu is only available while it is posted.

Illustration

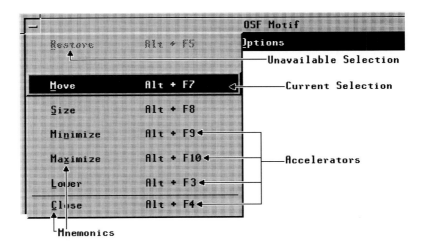

Navigation

Menus follow the navigation model described in Chapter 3.

Other Operations

The following text describes the operations of this component:

\<Help\>   Must provide any available help for the Menu.   *

Related Information

For more information, see the reference pages for CascadeButton, OptionButton, and MenuBar.

MessageDialogs

Description

MessageDialogs should be used to convey a message to the user. They must *
not interrupt the user's interaction with the application. They should
include a message and one of the following button arrangements:

OK
OK Help
OK Cancel
OK Cancel Help
Yes No
Yes No Help
Yes No Cancel
Yes No Cancel Help
Cancel
Cancel Help
Retry Cancel
Retry Cancel Help

There are a number of different types of MessageDialogs: ErrorDialog,
InformationDialog, QuestionDialog, WorkingDialog, and WarningDialog.

Related Information

For more information, see the reference pages for DialogBox, ErrorDialog,
InformationDialog, QuestionDialog, WorkingDialog, and WarningDialog.

Mnemonics

Description

A mnemonic is a single character that can be associated with any
component that contains a text label. The label must contain the character, *
and the character must be underlined within the label. The mnemonic
should be the first character of the label. If a label does not naturally *
contain the character of the mnemonic, the mnemonic must be placed in *
parentheses following the label. Labels can also be sequentially numbered,
and the number can serve as the mnemonic. Labels that are duplicated
within an application should be given the same mnemonic. Mnemonics *
must be case insensitive for activation. Either an uppercase or lowercase
letter can be underlined in the label.

When the location cursor is within a Menu, or a MenuBar, typing the *
mnemonic character of a component within that Menu or MenuBar must *
move the location cursor to the component and activate it. If a mnemonic is *
used for an OptionButton or for a CascadeButton in a MenuBar, pressing *
<Alt> and the mnemonic anywhere in the window or its Menus must move *
the cursor to the component with that mnemonic and must activate it.

Collections can also support mnemonics associated with its elements. *
Pressing a mnemonic key while the collection has the keyboard focus must *
be equivalent to moving the location cursor to the element and pressing *
<Select> or **<Space>**.

Navigation

Description

Using a mouse, navigation is a simple matter of moving the mouse pointer. *
Using the keyboard, the following component navigation actions must be *
available:

<Tab> or **<Ctrl> <Tab>**

> **<Tab>** (if not used for internal navigation) and **<Ctrl>** *
> **<Tab>** must move the location cursor forward through *
> fields. If the next field is a control, **<Tab>** (if not used for *
> internal navigation) and **<Ctrl> <Tab>** must move the *
> location cursor to that control. If the next field is a group, *
> **<Tab>** (if not used for internal navigation) and **<Ctrl>** *
> **<Tab>** must move the location cursor to a traversable *
> component within the group. If the field contains a button
> that currently shows default highlighting, the location
> cursor should be placed on that button; otherwise, the first
> control in the field (the top-leftmost one in a left-to-right
> language environment) should get focus. If the next field *
> contains no traversable components, **<Tab>** (if not used *
> for internal navigation) and **<Ctrl> <Tab>** must skip the *
> field.

<Shift> <Tab> or **<Ctrl> <Shift> <Tab>**

> **<Shift> <Tab>** (if not used for internal navigation) and *
> **<Ctrl> <Shift> <Tab>** must move the location cursor *
> backward through fields in the order opposite to that of *
> **<Tab>** (if not used for internal navigation) and **<Ctrl>** *
> **<Tab>**.

<↓>

> When used for component navigation within a field, in a *
> left-to-right language environment, **<↓>** must move the *
> location cursor through all traversable controls in the *
> field, starting at the upper left and ending at the lower *
> right, then wrapping to the upper left. If the controls are *
> aligned in a matrix-like arrangement, **<↓>** must first *

traverse one column from top to bottom, then traverse the *
column to its right, and so on. In a right-to-left language *
environment, <↓> must move the location cursor through *
all traversable controls, starting at the upper right and *
ending at the lower left.

This key can also be used for internal purposes within a
component.

<↑>   When used for component navigation within a field, <↑> *
must move the location cursor through all traversable *
components or elements in the order opposite to that of *
<↓>.

This key can also be used for internal purposes within a
component.

<—→>   When used for component navigation within a field, in a *
left-to-right language environment, <—→> must move the *
location cursor through all traversable controls in the *
field, starting at the upper left and ending at the lower *
right, then wrapping to the upper left. If the controls are *
aligned in a matrix-like arrangement, <—→> must first *
traverse one row from left to right, then traverse the row *
below it, and so on. In a right-to-left language *
environment, <—→> must move the location cursor through *
all traversable controls, starting at the lower left and *
ending at the upper right.

This key can also be used for internal purposes within a
component.

<←—>   When used for component navigation within a field, <←—> *
must move the location cursor through all traversable *
components or elements in the order opposite to that of *
<—→>.

This key can also be used for internal purposes within a
component.

<Ctrl> <↓>   This key can be used for component navigation within a field, following the same rules as <↓>. It can also be used for internal purposes within a component. When <↓> causes a change that is based on some unit, **<Ctrl> <↓>** can cause a change based on a larger unit.

<Ctrl> <↑>   This key can be used for component navigation within a field, following the same rules as <↑>. It can also be used for internal purposes within a component. When <↑> causes a change that is based on some unit, **<Ctrl> <↑>** can cause a change based on a larger unit.

<Ctrl> <→>   This key can be used for component navigation within a field, following the same rules as <→>. It can also be used for internal purposes within a component. When <→> causes a change that is based on some unit, **<Ctrl>** <→> can cause a change based on a larger unit.

<Ctrl> <←>   This key can be used for component navigation within a field, following the same rules as <←>. It can also be used for internal purposes within a component. When <←> causes a change that is based on some unit, **<Ctrl>** <←> can cause a change based on a larger unit.

<Begin>   If a control uses <→> and <←> for internal navigation, **<Begin>** must behave as follows: *

In a left-to-right language environment, this action must move the location cursor to the leftmost edge of the data or the leftmost element. In a right-to-left language environment, this action must move the location cursor to the rightmost edge of the data or the rightmost element. *

In a group that is a field, this key can move the location cursor to an appropriate control within the group.

<End>   If a control uses <→> and <←> for internal navigation, **<End>** must behave as follows: *

In a left-to-right language environment, this action must move the location cursor to the rightmost edge of the data or the rightmost element. In a right-to-left language environment, this action must move the location cursor to the leftmost edge of the data or the leftmost element. *

In a group that is a field, this key can move the location cursor to an appropriate control within the group.

<Ctrl> <Begin> If a control uses <↑> and <↓> for internal navigation, *
<Ctrl> <Begin> must move the location cursor to one of *
the following: *

- The first element *

- The topmost edge of the data *

- In a left-to-right language environment, the topmost *
  left edge of the data; in a right-to-left language *
  environment, the topmost right edge of the data *

In a group that is a field, this key can move the location cursor to an appropriate control within the group.

<Ctrl> <End> If a control uses <↑> and <↓> for internal navigation, *
<Ctrl> <End> must move the location cursor to one of *
the following: *

- The last element *

- The bottommost edge of the data *

- In a left-to-right language environment, the *
  bottommost right edge of the data; in a right-to-left *
  language environment, the bottommost left edge of *
  the data *

In a group that is a field, this key can move the location cursor to an appropriate control within the group.

<PageDown> In a vertically scrollable component, **<PageDown>** must *
scroll the visible region down by one page increment.

<PageUp> In a vertically scrollable component, **<PageUp>** must *
scroll the visible region up by one page increment.

<PageRight> or **<Ctrl> <PageDown>**

In a horizontally scrollable component, **<PageRight>** or *
<Ctrl> <PageDown> must scroll the visible region to the *
right by one page increment.

\<PageLeft\> or \<Ctrl\> \<PageUp\>

In a horizontally scrollable component, **\<PageLeft\>** or   *
\<Ctrl\> \<PageUp\> must scroll the visible region to the   *
left by one page increment.

\<F10\>

If the MenuBar is inactive, **\<F10\>** must traverse to the   *
MenuBar system. The location cursor must be placed on   *
the first traversable CascadeButton in the MenuBar. If   *
there are no traversable CascadeButtons in the MenuBar,   *
\<F10\> must do nothing. If the MenuBar system is active,
\<F10\> should unpost all Menus in the MenuBar system.   *
If **\<F10\>** is used to unpost all Menus in the MenuBar   *
system and if the focus policy is explicit, the location   *
cursor must be moved back to the component that had it   *
before the Menu system was posted. **\<Shift\> \<Menu\>**   *
must replace **\<F10\>** if **\<F10\>** is not available.

\<Menu\>

If the keyboard focus is on an element with an inactive   *
Popup Menu and the context of the element allows a   *
Popup Menu to be displayed, **\<Menu\>** must post   *
(activate) the Popup Menu. The location cursor must be   *
placed on the default item of the Menu, or the first   *
traversable item if there is no default item. Note that the
availability of the Popup Menu can depend on the
location of the cursor within the element, the contents of
the element, or the selection state of the element. If there
are no traversable items in the Popup Menu, it is up to the
system and the application whether to post the Menu or
not.

If there is an active Popup Menu, **\<Menu\>** should unpost
all Menus in the Popup Menu system. If **\<Menu\>** is used   *
to unpost all Menus in the Popup Menu system and if the   *
focus policy is explicit, the location cursor must be   *
moved back to the component that had it before the Menu   *
system was posted. **\<Shift\> \<F10\>** must replace   *
\<Menu\> if **\<Menu\>** is not available.

\<Alt\> \<F6\>

Must move the focus to the next window in the window   *
family.

<Alt> <Shift> <F6>
> Can move the focus to the previous window in the window family.

<Alt> <Tab>   Must move the focus to the last window that had the input   *
> focus in the next window family in the window hierarchy.

<Alt> <Shift> <Tab>
> Can move the focus to the previous window that had the input focus in the next window family in the window hierarchy.

Related Information

See Chapter 3 for more information about internal window navigation. See Chapter 7 for more information about navigation among windows.

OptionButton

Description

An OptionButton should be used to post an Option Menu.

This component must be composed of a button, with either a text or graphics   *
Label. Following the Label, this component should also include a bar
graphic to distinguish it from a PushButton. The Label must be the last   *
selection made from the OptionButton.

Illustration

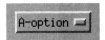

Navigation

An OptionButton must have no internal navigation.   *

Other Operations

The following text describes the operations of this component:

BSelect Press

Must post the associated Option Menu.   *

BSelect Release

If the release is within the same OptionButton as the press:

- If the associated Option Menu was posted at the time of the press, it should be unposted.

- If the associated Option Menu was not posted at the time of *
  the press, it must be posted.

If the release is outside of the OptionButton, the associated *
Option Menu must be unposted.

<Select> or <Space>

Must post the associated Option Menu.   *

<Cancel>

Must unpost the last posted Menu in the Menu system without *
changing the value of the OptionButton.

<Help>   Must provide any available help for the OptionButton.   *

Related Information

For more information, see the reference page for Menus.

PanedWindow

Description

A PanedWindow should be used to group components into Panes separated by Sashes and Separators for adjusting the relative size of each Pane. This component must be composed of any number of groups of components, called Panes, each separated by a Sash and a Separator. The Panes, Sashes, and Separators must be grouped linearly, either horizontally or vertically. A Sash must be composed of a handle on the Separator between two Panes for adjusting the position of the Separator, and therefore the size of the Panes next to it.

As a Sash is moved, the Pane in the direction of the Sash movement must get smaller and the other Pane must get larger by an equal amount. If a Pane is adjusted to its minimum size, adjustment should continue with the next Pane in the direction of the Sash movement.

Illustration

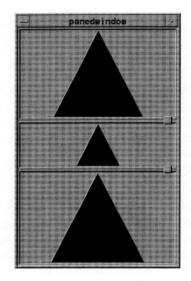

Navigation

This component must follow the navigation model described in Chapter 3.   *

Related Information

For information about activating a Sash, see the reference page for Sash.

Panel

Description

A Panel group should be used to organize a collection of basic controls in a horizontal, vertical, or 2-dimensional layout. This component is usually composed of just one type of basic control. This component is composed of an area for organizing basic controls.

Illustration

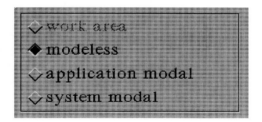

Navigation

The <↓>, <←>, <→>, and <↑> direction keys must navigate among   *
components in the Panel according to the navigation model described in   *
Chapter 3.

Pointer Shapes

Description

You should not create new mouse pointer shapes for functions that already have mouse pointer shapes associated with them, except for localization; however, you can create new mouse pointer shapes for functions not already associated with a pointer shape. You should not use a predefined shape to symbolize a function it was not designed to represent.

A list of the defined pointer shapes follows, along with their usage and hotspots. The hotspot of a pointer is the actual position on the pointer that tracks the movements of the mouse. As the pointer changes from one shape   * to another, the location of the hotspot must not move on the screen. The hotspot is the precise location on the pointer where mouse actions occur.

The upper-left pointing arrow pointer is a general-purpose pointer. It is used in most window areas for single-object selection and activation. The hotspot for the arrow pointer should be in the point of the arrow.

You can optionally use an I-beam pointer in any Text component. It is used to change the location of the text insertion cursor and to perform actions on text. If the I-beam is used, it can be hidden during the time between any keyboard action and a mouse movement. This helps the user distinguish the I-beam pointer from the text insertion cursor, which can also be an I-beam. The hotspot for the I-beam pointer should be on the vertical bar of the I-beam about one-third up from the bottom.

The X pointer can indicate when the pointer is outside of any application area. The hotspot for the X pointer should be where the lines intersect.

The resize pointers indicate positions for area resize, and they remain during a resize operation. The direction of the arrow in the pointer indicates the direction of increasing size. The horizontal and vertical pointers indicate resize in either the horizontal or vertical direction. The diagonal pointers indicate resize in both the horizontal and vertical directions simultaneously. The hotspot for the resizing pointers should be on the elbow or the line at the position pointed to by the arrow.

 The hourglass pointer, a working pointer, indicates that an action is in progress in the area, and that the pointer has no effect in the area. While the hourglass pointer is active, all mouse button and keyboard events are ignored in the area. The hotspot for the hourglass pointer should be located at the center of the hourglass, although it should not be used for activation. The hourglass pointer can be used interchangeably with the watch pointer.

The watch pointer, a working pointer, indicates that an action is in progress in the area, and that the pointer has no effect in the area. While the watch pointer is active, all mouse button and keyboard events are ignored in the area. The hotspot for the watch pointer should be located at the top of the watch, although it should not be used for activation. The watch pointer can be used interchangeably with the hourglass pointer.

The 4-directional arrow pointer indicates a move operation is in progress, or a resize operation before the resize direction has been determined. During a move operation, the object, or an outline of the object should move to track the location of the pointer. During a resize operation, the pointer is used to indicate a direction for resizing. The 4-directional arrow pointer should change to the appropriate resize arrow when the resize direction is determined, either by crossing an object boundary with the pointer or by pressing a keyboard direction key. The hotspot for the 4-directional arrow pointer should be at the spot where the arrows intersect.

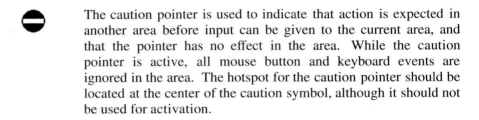

The sighting pointer is used to make fine position selections. For example, in a drawing program it can be used to indicate a pixel to fill or the connecting points of lines. The hotspot for the sighting pointer should be at the spot where the lines intersect.

The caution pointer is used to indicate that action is expected in another area before input can be given to the current area, and that the pointer has no effect in the area. While the caution pointer is active, all mouse button and keyboard events are ignored in the area. The hotspot for the caution pointer should be located at the center of the caution symbol, although it should not be used for activation.

The question pointer is used to request an input position or component from the user. This is often used to input an object for interactive help. The user requests interactive help, then the question pointer is displayed to allow the user to indicate what position or component help is requested for. The hotspot for the question pointer should be at the bottom of the question mark.

You can optionally use an arrow pointing to the upper-right corner to indicate a pending Menu action. This shape indicates that a Menu is popped up or pulled down and waiting for a Menu item to be activated or the Menu to be removed. The hotspot for this arrow pointer should be in the point of the arrow.

Related Information

See Chapter 2 for information on the input device model and designing new pointer shapes.

Popup Menus

Description

The common Popup Menu contents are described as follows. Note that you should only include those functions actually supported by your application. The illustration on this reference page shows a Popup Menu.

Properties

Must display a properties DialogBox that the user can use to   *
set the properties of the component. If the Menu is popped up over a selection, it can display the properties of the selection. If the Menu is popped up over an unselected item, it can display the properties of that item. If the Menu is popped up over the background, it should display the properties of the collection, except over a part of the background considered to be in the selection. This action should have the mnemonic **S**.

Undo   Alt+Backspace

Must reverse the most recently executed action. To provide a   *
visual cue to the user, the **Undo** selection title should be dynamically modified to indicate what is being undone. For example, if the most recently executed action was a paste, the action name would be **Undo paste**. This action should have the mnemonic **U**. This action should have the same accelerator as the corresponding entry in the **Edit** Menu.

Primary Move   Alt+Shift+Delete

Must move the contents of the primary selection to the   *
component. This action must only be used in an editable   *
component. If the action uses an accelerator, it should be **<Alt> <Shift> <Delete>**, **<Alt> <Ctrl> <X>**, or both. In addition, if the keyboard has a **<Cut>** key, this action should support **<Alt> <Cut>** as an accelerator. If more than one format can be moved from the primary selection, **Primary Copy** can cascade a Menu of possible transfer formats, in which case it should not have an accelerator.

Primary Copy   Alt+Ctrl+Insert

Must copy the contents of the primary selection to the *
component. This action must only be used in an editable *
component. If the action uses an accelerator, it should be
<Alt> <Ctrl> <Insert>, **<Alt> <Ctrl> <C>**, or both. In
addition, if the keyboard has a **<Copy>** key, this action should
support **<Alt> <Copy>** as an accelerator. If more than one
format can be copied from the primary selection, **Primary
Copy** can cascade a Menu of possible transfer formats, in
which case it should not have an accelerator.

Primary Link

Must place a link to the primary selection in the component. *
This action must only be used in an editable component. If the
link can be viewed in more than one way, **Primary Link** can
cascade a Menu of possible viewing representations.

Cut

Must cut elements to the clipboard and can mark them for use *
in a subsequent **Paste Link** operation. If the Menu is popped *
up in a selection, the entire selection must be cut. If the Menu
is popped up over an unselected element, just that element
should be cut. If the Menu is popped up in the background, the
entire collection can be cut. This action should have the
mnemonic **T**.

Copy

Must copy elements to the clipboard and can mark them for *
use in a subsequent **Paste Link** operation. If the Menu is *
popped up in a selection, the entire selection must be copied.
If the Menu is popped up over an unselected element, just that
element should be copied. If the Menu is popped up in the
background, the entire collection can be copied. This action
should have the mnemonic **C**.

Copy Link

Must copy a link of elements to the clipboard and can mark *
them for use in a subsequent **Paste Link** operation. If the *
Menu is popped up in a selection, a link to the entire selection *
must be copied. If the Menu is popped up over an unselected
element, a link to just that element should be copied. If the
Menu is popped up in the background, a link to the entire
collection can be copied. This action should have the
mnemonic **K**.

P̲aste   Shift+Insert

Must paste the contents of the clipboard to the component. *
This action must only be used in an editable component. This
action should have the mnemonic **P**. This action should have
the same accelerator as the corresponding entry in the **Edit**
Menu.

Paste L̲ink

Must paste a link of the contents of the clipboard to the *
component. This action must only be used in an editable *
component. This action should have the mnemonic **L**.

Cl̲ear   Must remove a selected portion of data from the client area *
without copying it to the clipboard. If the Menu is popped up *
in a selection, it must delete the selection. If the Menu is
popped up over an unselected element, it should delete that
element. If the Menu is popped up over the background,
except over a part of the background considered to be in the
selection, it can delete all the elements. The remaining data is
not compressed to fill the space that was occupied by the
cleared data. This action should have the mnemonic **E**.

D̲elete   Must remove a selected portion of data from the client area *
without copying it to the clipboard. If the Menu is popped up *
in a selection, it must delete the selection. If the Menu is
popped up over an unselected element, it should delete that
element. If the Menu is popped up over the background,
except over a part of the background considered to be in the
selection, it can delete all the elements. This action should
have the mnemonic **D**.

Select All   Ctrl+/

Must make the primary selection consist of all the elements in *
the collection with the Popup Menu. If the action uses an
accelerator, it should be **<Ctrl> </>**.

Deselect All   Ctrl+

Must deselect the current selection in the collection with the *
Popup Menu. If the action uses an accelerator, it should be
<Ctrl> <\>.

Select Pasted

> Must make the primary selection consist of the last element or   *
> elements pasted into the collection with the Popup Menu.

Reselect Alt+Insert

> Must make the primary selection consist of the last selected   *
> element or elements in the component with the Popup Menu.   *
> The action must be available only in components that do not   *
> support persistent selections and only when the current   *
> selection is empty. If the action uses an accelerator, it should
> be **<Alt> <Insert>**.

Promote Alt+Insert

> Must promote the current selection to the primary selection.   *
> This action must only be available in components that support   *
> persistent selections. If the action uses an accelerator, it
> should be **<Alt> <Insert>**.

Appropriate words, such as **Selection** or words denoting the type of a single element of the collection as a whole, should be added to a Label to specify which elements are affected. For example, if a Popup Menu contains the entry **Copy Selection**, the current selection is copied to the clipboard regardless of where in the collection the Menu is popped up.

A Popup Menu item should only have an accelerator if the result of typing the accelerator would be equivalent to popping up the Menu by typing **<Menu>**, and then selecting the Menu item. If **Cut Selection** is included in a Popup Menu, it should use the same accelerators as **Cut** in the **Edit** Menu. If **Copy Selection** is included in a Popup Menu, it should use the same accelerators as **Copy** in the **Edit** Menu.

Related Information

See Chapter 6 for more information on Popup Menus and for general information about Menu design.

Primary Selection

Description

Each collection maintains its own selection. A selection need not contain any elements, in which case it is said to be an empty selection. At any time, there is one selection called the primary selection, which is the last selection explicitly started by the user.

Clicking **BSelect** or **<Ctrl> BSelect** only moves the primary selection to a collection when it results in making a selection that is not empty. When **<Shift> BSelect** is clicked, an implementation can move the primary selection to the component even if the resulting selection is empty. *
Dragging **BSelect**, **<Shift> BSelect**, or **<Ctrl> BSelect** must move the *
primary selection to the component if a button release during the pointer *
motion could have potentially selected any element.

A selection is said to be persistent if it is highlighted even when it is not the primary selection.

Persistent

There are two variants of persistent selections: persistent always, in which the current selection is always highlighted, and persistent on focus, in which the current selection is only highlighted when it is the primary selection or when the collection has the keyboard focus. In either case, stronger highlighting should be used when the current selection is also the primary selection. When focus is in the collection, **<Alt> <Insert>** can be used to promote the current selection to the primary selection.

Nonpersistent

The collection only highlights a primary selection. When the primary selection is lost to another collection, the current selection is set to empty. When focus is in the collection, and it does not have the primary selection, **<Alt> <Insert>** can be used to restore the previous selection and make it the primary selection.

Collections that are never editable (such as noneditable Lists) should always use persistent selections. Collections that are editable can either use persistent or nonpersistent selections.

Primary transfer can be invoked by clicking **BTransfer** or through standard keyboard bindings. There are three primary transfer operations:

Primary Copy

In an editable collection, **BTransfer Click**, **<Ctrl> BTransfer Click**, *
<Alt> <Copy>, and **<Alt> <Ctrl> <Insert>** must copy the primary *
selection to the insertion position, as defined in Section 4.3. (Note *
that the insertion position is usually different for mouse and keyboard *
operations.)

Primary Move

In an editable collection, **<Shift> BTransfer Click**, **<Alt> <Cut>**, *
and **<Alt> <Shift> <Delete>** must move the primary selection to the *
insertion position, as defined in Section 4.3. (Note that the insertion *
position is usually different for mouse and keyboard operations.)

Primary Link

In an editable collection, **<Ctrl> <Shift> BTransfer Click** must *
place a link to the primary selection at the insertion position, as *
defined in Section 4.3.

Related Information

See Sections 4.2 and 4.3 for more information about the primary selection.

PromptDialog

Description

A PrompDialog should be used to prompt the user for input. It can interrupt the user's interaction with the application. It should include a message, a text input area, and one of the following button arrangements:

OK Cancel
OK Cancel Help
OK Apply Cancel
OK Apply Cancel Help
OK Apply Reset Cancel
OK Apply Reset Cancel Help

Illustration

Related Information

For more information, see the reference page for DialogBox.

PushButton

Description

A PushButton should be used to start an operation. A PushButton must   *
contain either a text or graphic Label that indicates the operation of the   *
button.

Illustration

Navigation

A PushButton must have no internal navigation.   *

Other Operations

The following text describes the operations of this component:

BSelect Press
Must arm the PushButton.   *

BSelect Release
If the release is within the same PushButton as the press,   *
BSelect Release must disarm the PushButton and activate it. If   *
the release is outside of the PushButton, **BSelect Release** must   *
disarm the PushButton without activating it.

<Enter> or <Return>
> If the PushButton is in a window with a default action, the   *
> PushButton must be activated. If the PushButton is in a Menu,   *
> this action must activate the PushButton and unpost the Menu.

<Select> or <Space>
> Must activate the PushButton. If the PushButton is in a Menu,   *
> the Menu must be unposted.

<Help>   Must provide any available help for the PushButton.   *

QuestionDialog

Description

A QuestionDialog should be used to get a user response to a question. It should interrupt the user's interaction with the application. It should include a question symbol, a message, and one of the following button arrangements:

Yes No
Yes No Help

It is possible that both the **Yes** and **No** actions of a Question DialogBox will perform an action. If this is the case, the Question DialogBox should use one of the following button arrangements:

Yes No Cancel
Yes No Cancel Help

Illustration

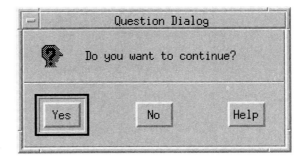

Related Information

For more information, see the reference page for DialogBox.

Quick Transfer

Description

Quick transfer is used to make a temporary (or secondary) selection and then immediately copy, move, or link that selection to the insertion position of the destination component. Quick transfer is implemented using **<Alt> BTransfer Motion**, with the standard modifiers used to force the various transfer operations.

Text components must support quick transfer.   *

There are three quick transfer operations:

Quick Copy

If a component supports quick transfer, **<Alt> BTransfer Motion** or *
<Alt> <Ctrl> BTransfer Motion must temporarily select elements in *
the specified range and, on release, must copy them to the insertion *
position of the destination component.

Quick Cut

If a component supports quick transfer, **<Alt> <Shift> BTransfer** *
Motion must temporarily select elements in the specified range and, *
on release, must move them to the insertion position of the destination *
component.

Quick Link

If a component supports quick transfer, **<Alt> <Ctrl> <Shift>** *
BTransfer Motion must temporarily select elements in the specified *
range and, on release, must place a link to them at the insertion *
position of the destination component.

The range of the temporary selection must be determined by using exactly *
the same model used when **BSelect Motion** determines the range of a *
primary selection.

Related Information

See Section 4.3 for more information about quick transfer.

RadioButton

Description

A RadioButton should be used to select one option from a number of options. A RadioButton is a special case of a ToggleButton. Only one RadioButton can be set at a time. This component must be composed of a *
text or graphic label, and a graphic that indicates the state of the *
RadioButton. The graphic indicator for a RadioButton is usually a filled diamond or circle to indicate the on state or an empty diamond or circle to indicate the off state. On color systems, the on state color can be distinct from general application colors to visually distinguish the on state.

Illustration

Navigation

RadioButtons must have no internal navigation.   *

Other Operations

The following text describes the operations of this component:

BSelect Press

Must arm the RadioButton. If the RadioButton was previously   *
unset, it must show the RadioButton in the set state.

BSelect Release

If the release happens in the same RadioButton that the press   *
occurred in and if the RadioButton was previously unset, it must   *
be set, and any other RadioButton in the same Panel that was   *
previously set must be unset. The RadioButton must be   *
disarmed, and, if the RadioButton is in a Menu, the Menu must   *
be unposted.

BSelect Release 2

If the RadioButton was previously unset, it should be set, and
any other RadioButton in the same Panel that was previously set
should be unset. If the RadioButton is in a window, the default
action of the window should be activated.

<Enter> or <Return>

If the RadioButton is in a window with a default action, the   *
default action must be activated. If the RadioButton is in a   *
Menu: *

- If the RadioButton was previously unset, it must be set, and   *
  any other RadioButton in the same Panel that was   *
  previously set must be unset.   *

- The RadioButton must be disarmed, and the Menu must be   *
  unposted.   *

\<Select> or **\<Space>**
    If the RadioButton was previously unset, it must be set, and any   *
other RadioButton in the same Panel that was previously set   *
must be unset. The RadioButton must be disarmed, and, if the   *
RadioButton is in a Menu, the Menu must be unposted.

\<Help>   Must provide any available help for the RadioButton.   *

Related Information

For more information, see the reference pages for CheckButton and ToggleButton.

Sash

Description

A Sash should be used to adjust the border between groups of components in a PanedWindow. A Sash must be composed of a handle on the Separator *
between two Panes for adjusting the position of the Separator, and therefore *
the size of the Panes next to it.

As a Sash is moved, the Pane in the direction of the Sash movement must *
get smaller and the other Pane must get larger by an equal amount. If a Pane is adjusted to its minimum size, adjustment should continue with the next Pane in the direction of the Sash movement. The PanedWindow can optionally support movement of the Pane in the initial direction of mouse movement with the modifier **<Shift>** on button events, rather than resizing the Pane.

Illustration

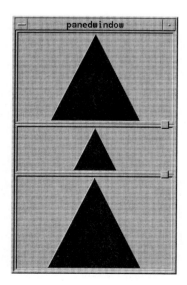

Navigation

A Sash must have no internal navigation.   *

Other Operations

The following text describes the operations of this component:

BSelect or **BTransfer Motion**
Must cause the Sash to track the movement of the pointer. In a   *
vertically oriented PanedWindow, the Sash must track the   *
vertical position of the pointer. In a horizontally oriented   *
PanedWindow, the Sash must track the horizontal position of   *
the pointer.

BSelect or **BTransfer Motion**
Can cause the Pane in the initial direction of movement to track
the movement of the pointer. In a vertically oriented   *
PanedWindow, the Pane must track the vertical position of the   *
pointer. In a horizontally oriented PanedWindow, the Pane   *
must track the horizontal position of the pointer.

<↑> and <↓>
For a Sash that can move vertically, must cause the Sash to   *
move in the specified direction one increment.

<→> and <←>
For a Sash that can move horizontally, must cause the Sash to   *
move in the specified direction one increment.

<Shift> <↑> and **<Shift> <↓>**
For a Sash that can move vertically, can cause the Pane in the
initial direction to move one increment in the specified
direction.

<Shift> <→> and **<Shift> <←>**
For a Sash that can move horizontally, can cause the Pane in the
initial direction to move one increment in the specified
direction.

<Ctrl> <↑> and <Ctrl> <↓>

> For a Sash that can move vertically, must cause the Sash to   *
> move in the specified direction one large increment.

<Ctrl> <→> and <Ctrl> <←>

> For a Sash that can move horizontally, must cause the Sash to   *
> move in the specified direction one large increment.

<Ctrl> <Shift> <↑> and <Ctrl> <Shift> <↓>

> For a Sash that can move vertically, can cause the Pane in the
> initial direction to move one large increment in the specified
> direction.

<Ctrl> <Shift> <→> and <Ctrl> <Shift> <←>

> For a Sash that can move horizontally, can cause the Pane in the
> initial direction to move one large increment in the specified
> direction.

<Help>   Must provide any available help for the Sash.   *

Related Information

For more information, see the reference page for PanedWindow.

Scale

Description

A Scale should be used to select a value from a range. This component should be composed of a slider, moving within an element that indicates the size of the range, called the trough, and a Label that indicates the current value. The position of the slider indicates the value relative to the range. A Scale can also have buttons with arrow graphics for moving the slider.

Illustration

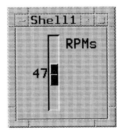

Other Operations

The following text describes the operations of this component:

BSelect Press

In an arrow button, this action must move the slider one   *
increment in the direction of the side of the slider on which the   *
button was pressed, and autorepeat until the button is released.

In the trough, if the Scale has tick marks, **BSelect Press** must   *
move the slider one major tick mark in the direction of the side   *
of the slider on which the trough was pressed, and autorepeat   *

until the button is released. It can stop when the slider reaches
the position of the pointer. If the Scale does not have tick   *
marks, **BSelect Press** in the trough must move the slider one   *
large increment in the direction of the side of the slider on   *
which the trough was pressed, and autorepeat until the button is   *
released. It can stop when the slider reaches the position of the
pointer.

BSelect Motion

If the button is pressed in the slider, must cause the slider to   *
track the position of the pointer. In a vertical Scale, the slider   *
must track the vertical position of the pointer. In a horizontal   *
Scale, the slider must track the horizontal position of the   *
pointer.

\<Ctrl\> BSelect Press

In the slider trough or an arrow button, this action should move
the slider to the end of the Scale on which the button was
pressed.

BTransfer Press

In the trough, this action should directly position the slider to
the position of the button press.

BTransfer Motion

If the button is pressed in the slider or the trough, must directly   *
position the slider to the point of the button press and then cause   *
the slider to track the position of the pointer. In a vertical   *
Scale, the slider must track the vertical position of the pointer.   *
In a horizontal Scale, the slider must track the horizontal   *
position of the pointer.

\<Cancel\> If a mouse-based sliding action is in progress, **\<Cancel\>** must   *
cancel the sliding action and return the slider to its position   *
prior to the start of the sliding operation.

\<↓\> For vertical Scales, this action must move the slider one   *
increment down.

\<↑\> For vertical Scales, this action must move the slider one   *
increment up.

\<←\> For horizontal Scales, this action must move the slider one   *
increment left.

<→>   For horizontal Scales, this action must move the slider one   *
increment right.

<Ctrl> <↓>

For vertical Scales, this action must move the slider one large   *
increment down.

<Ctrl> <↑>

For vertical Scales, this action must move the slider one large   *
increment up.

<Ctrl> <←>

For horizontal Scales, this action must move the slider one large   *
increment left.

<Ctrl> <→>

For horizontal Scales, this action must move the slider one large   *
increment right.

<Begin> or <Ctrl> <Begin>

Must move the slider to the minimum value.   *

<End> or <Ctrl> <End>

Must move the slider to the maximum value.   *

<Help>   Must provide any available help for the Scale.   *

ScrollBar

Description

A ScrollBar should be used to scroll the visible area of another component. A ScrollBar should be composed of a slider, moving within an element that indicates the full size of the scrolled component, and two buttons with arrow graphics for moving the slider. The slider indicates the relative position and size of the visible area of the scrolled component.

Illustration

Other Operations

The following text describes the operations of this component:

BSelect Press

In an arrow button, this action must move the slider one increment in the direction of the side of the slider on which the button was pressed, and autorepeat until the button is released. *

In the trough, this action must move the slider one page in the direction of the side of the slider on which the trough was pressed, and autorepeat until the button is released. It can stop when the slider reaches the position of the pointer. *

BSelect Motion

If the button is pressed in the slider, must cause the slider to *
track the position of the pointer. In a vertical ScrollBar, the *
slider must track the vertical position of the pointer. In a *
horizontal ScrollBar, the slider must track the horizontal *
position of the pointer.

<Ctrl> BSelect Press

In the slider trough or an arrow button, this action should move
the slider to the end of the ScrollBar on which the button was
pressed.

<Shift> BSelect Press

Can scroll the view so that the cursor within that view is
positioned at the edge of the view region on the side of the
ScrollBar on which the button was pressed.

BTransfer Press

In the trough, this action can directly position the slider to the
position of the button press.

BTransfer Motion

If the button is pressed in the slider or the trough, must directly *
position the slider to the point of the button press and then cause *
the slider to track the position of the pointer. In a vertical *
ScrollBar, the slider must track the vertical position of the *
pointer. In a horizontal ScrollBar, the slider must track the *
horizontal position of the pointer.

<Cancel>   If a mouse-based scrolling action is in progress, **<Cancel>** must *
cancel the scrolling action and return the slider to its position *
prior to the start of the scrolling operation.

<↓>   For vertical ScrollBars, this action must move the slider one *
increment down.

<↑>   For vertical ScrollBars, this action must move the slider one *
increment up.

<←>   For horizontal ScrollBars, this action must move the slider one *
increment left.

<—→>   For horizontal ScrollBars, this action must move the slider one   *
increment right.

<Ctrl> <↓>

For vertical ScrollBars, this action must move the slider one   *
large increment down.

<Ctrl> <↑>

For vertical ScrollBars, this action must move the slider one   *
large increment up.

<Ctrl> <←>

For horizontal ScrollBars, this action must move the slider one   *
large increment left.

<Ctrl> <—→>

For horizontal ScrollBars, this action must move the slider one   *
large increment right.

<PageDown>

For vertical ScrollBars, this action must move the slider one   *
page down.

<PageUp> For vertical ScrollBars, this action must move the slider one   *
page up.

<PageLeft> or **<Ctrl> <PageUp>**

For horizontal ScrollBars, this action must move the slider one   *
page left.

<PageRight> or **<Ctrl> <PageDown>**

For horizontal ScrollBars, this action must move the slider one   *
page right.

<Begin> or **<Ctrl> <Begin>**

Must move the slider to the minimum value.   *

<End> or **<Ctrl> <End>**

Must move the slider to the maximum value.   *

<Help>   Must provide any available help for the ScrollBar.   *

ScrolledWindow

Description

A ScrolledWindow should be used to frame other components and to provide ScrollBars as necessary to scroll the visible area of the framed components. When the area framed by the ScrolledWindow is completely displayed, the ScrollBars need not be displayed. When the area provided in   *
the ScrolledWindow is too small to display the entire component area, the   *
ScrollBars must be displayed and must then allow scrolling of the visible   *
area.

Illustration

Navigation

A ScrolledWindow must follow the navigation model that is described in   *
Chapter 3.

Related Information

For information about the activation of the ScrollBars, see the reference
page for ScrollBar. For more information about navigation within general
scrollable components, see Section 3.4.

Selection

Description

The selection model determines how elements are selected from a group of elements. OSF/Motif compliant systems must support the five different *
selection models. The five selection models are as follows:

Single Selection   *

Used to select a single element in a collection. Clicking **BSelect** on a deselected element selects it and deselects the previously selected element in the collection. Single selection is described in Section 4.1.1.   *

Browse Selection   *

Used to allow browsing through single selection collections. Browse selection is also used to select a single element of a collection. Browse selection works just like single selection, but additionally allows the user to browse through the elements by dragging **BSelect** through the elements in the collection. Browse select highlights each element as it is traversed, and gives the application an opportunity to provide information about each element as it is highlighted. Releasing **BSelect** on an element selects it and deselects the previously selected element. Browse selection is described in Section 4.1.2.   *

Multiple Selection   *

Used to select or deselect multiple elements of a collection. Clicking **BSelect** on an unselected element adds that element to the current selection. Clicking **BSelect** on a selected element removes that element from the current selection. Multiple selection is described in Section 4.1.3.

Range Selection   *
Used to select a contiguous range of elements in a collection. Clicking **BSelect** on an element selects the single element and deselects any previous selection. **BSelect Motion** over a range of elements selects all the elements within the range and deselects any previous selection. Range selection is described in Section 4.1.4.   *

Discontiguous Selection   *
Used for selecting multiple discontiguous ranges of elements in a collection. Clicking or dragging **BSelect** operates the same as for range selection. Discontiguous selection also allows **<Ctrl> BSelect** to be used to add new selection ranges to or remove selection ranges from the selection. Discontiguous selection is described in Section 4.1.5.

Related Information

See Chapter 4 for more information about the selection models.

SelectionBox

Description

A SelectionBox is a special-purpose composite component for making selections from a list of choices. The SelectionBox must be composed of at *
least a Text component for the selected alternative and a List component *
above the Text component for presenting the alternatives. Both the List and Text components should have a Label above them. The List component can be scrollable. The SelectionBox should also include one of the following button arrangements:

OK Cancel Help
OK Cancel Apply Help

The List must use either the single or browse selection model. Selecting an *
element from the list must place the selected element in the Text *
component. Entering an item name into the Text component should make that element visible in the List component. The List navigation actions *
<↑>, <↓>, <Ctrl> <Begin>, and <Ctrl> <End> must be available from the *
Text component for moving the cursored element within the List and thus *
changing the contents of the Text. The List navigation actions **<PageUp>** and **<PageDown>** should also be available from the Text component for moving the cursored element within the List.

Illustration

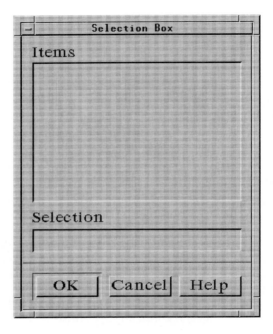

Related Information

For more information, see the reference page for SelectionDialog.

SelectionDialog

Description

A SelectionDialog should be used to allow a user to make a selection from a list of choices. It can interrupt the user's interaction with the application. It should contain a SelectionBox.

Illustration

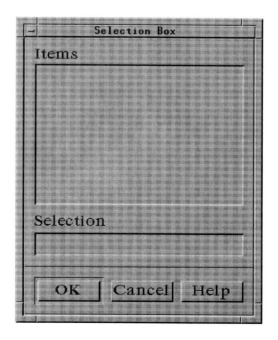

Related Information

For more information, see the reference page for DialogBox.

Separator

Description

A Separator should be used to separate elements of the application. It should be composed of a vertical or horizontal line.

Illustration

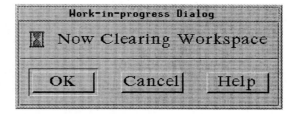

Navigation

A Separator must have no internal navigation.   *

TearOffButton

Description

A TearOffButton should be used to tear off a Menu to create a dialog representation of the Menu contents. A TearOffButton tears off a Menu in place when activated, or it is dragged to tear off and move in one action. * This component must be composed of a button with a graphic that indicates * the tear-off action. The graphic should be a dashed line representing perforations.

Illustration

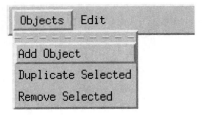

Navigation

A TearOffButton must have no internal navigation.   *

Other Operations

The following text describes the operations of this component:

BSelect Press
> Must arm the TearOffButton.   *

BSelect Release
> If the release is within the same TearOffButton as the press,   *
> **BSelect Release** must disarm the TearOffButton and activate it.   *
> If the release is outside of the TearOffButton, **BSelect Release**   *
> must disarm the TearOffButton without activating it.

BTransfer Press
> Must activate the TearOffButton and cause the newly torn off   *
> Menu or its representation to start to track the position of the   *
> pointer.

BTransfer Motion
> Must cause the newly torn off Menu or its representation to   *
> track the position of the pointer.

BTransfer Release
> Must cause the newly torn off Menu or its representation to stop   *
> tracking the position of the pointer and become a torn off Menu.

<Enter> or <Return>
> Must activate the TearOffButton.   *

<Select> or <Space>
> Must activate the TearOffButton.   *

<Help>   Must provide any available help for the TearOffButton.   *

Related Information

See Chapter 6 for more information on TearOff Menus and for general information about Menu design.

Text

Description

A Text component should be used to display and enter text. A Text *
component must be composed of an area for displaying and entering text.
The text can be either a single line or multiple lines. Text must support the *
range selection model as described in Chapter 4 and can support the
discontiguous selection model.

Illustration

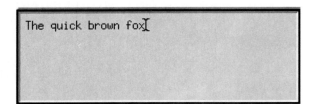

Navigation

The following text describes the navigation actions of this component:

<↑>   In multiline Text components, <↑> must move the location *
cursor up one line. In single-line Text components, <↑> must *
navigate upward to the previous component if the Text *
component is designed to act like a basic control.

<↓>   In multiline Text components, <↓> must move the location *
cursor down one line. In single-line Text components, <↓> *
must navigate downward to the next component if the Text *
component is designed to act like a basic control.

<←>   Must move the location cursor left one character.   *

<→>   Must move the location cursor right one character.   *

<PageUp> In multiline Text components, **<PageUp>** must move the   *
location cursor up one page.

<PageDown>
In multiline Text components, **<PageDown>** must move the   *
location cursor down one page.

<PageLeft> or **<Ctrl> <PageUp>**
Must move the location cursor left one page.   *

<PageRight> or **<Ctrl> <PageDown>**
Must move the location cursor right one page.   *

<Ctrl> <→>
In a Text component used generally to hold multiple words,   *
must move the location cursor to the right by a word. That is,   *
<Ctrl> <→> must place the location cursor before the first   *
character that is not a space, tab, or newline character after the   *
next space, tab, or newline character. In short single-line Text
controls, **<Ctrl> <→>** can navigate rightward to the next
component if the Text is designed to act like a basic control.

<Ctrl> <←>
In a Text component used generally to hold multiple words,   *
must move the location cursor to the left by a word. That is,   *
<Ctrl> <←> must place the location cursor after the first space,   *
tab, or newline character preceding the first previous character   *
that is not a space, tab, or newline. In short single-line Text
controls, **<Ctrl> <←>** can navigate leftward to the next
component if the Text is designed to act like a basic control.

<Ctrl> <↓>
In multiline Text components, **<Ctrl> <↓>** can optionally move
the location cursor to the beginning of the next paragraph.

<Ctrl> <↑>
In multiline Text components, **<Ctrl> <↑>** can optionally move
the location cursor to the beginning of the previous paragraph.

<Begin>
> In a Text component used generally to hold multiple words,   *
> must move the location cursor to the beginning of the line.

<End>   In a Text component used generally to hold multiple words,   *
> must move the location cursor to the end of the line.

<Ctrl> <Begin>
> In multiline Text components, **<Ctrl> <Begin>** must move the   *
> location cursor to the beginning of the file.

<Ctrl> <End>
> In multiline Text components, **<Ctrl> <End>** must move the   *
> location cursor to the end of the file.

Other Operations

The following text describes the operations of this component:

<Space> or <Shift> <Space>
> Must insert a space. Modifying these with **<Ctrl>** must evoke   *
> its normal selection function.

<Return>   In multiline Text components, **<Return>** must insert a carriage   *
> return.

<Ctrl> <Return> and <Enter>
> Must invoke the default action.   *

<Tab> and <Shift> <Tab>
> In multiline Text, **<Tab>** must be used for tabbing (either   *
> inserting a tab or moving to the next tab stop). In single-line   *
> Text, **<Tab>** must be used either for tabbing or to move to the   *
> next field. If **<Tab>** is used for tabbing and the location cursor
> is at the end of the text, **<Tab>** can optionally move to the next
> field.

<Shift> <Tab> must be used to move to the previous field if *
<Tab> is used to move to the next field. Otherwise, <Shift>
<Tab> should be used for tabbing backward. If <Shift> <Tab>
is used for tabbing backward and the location cursor is at the
beginning of the text, <Shift> <Tab> can optionally move to
the previous field.

Modifying <Tab> or <Shift> <Tab> with <Ctrl> must evoke *
the same field navigation function as <Tab> or <Shift> <Tab>.

<BackSpace>

When the selection is empty or when the component is in add *
mode with the cursor disjoint from the selection, <BackSpace> *
must delete one character backward. Otherwise, <BackSpace> *
must delete the selection.

<Delete> When the selection is empty or when the component is in add *
mode with the cursor disjoint from the selection, <Delete> must *
delete one character forward. Otherwise, <Delete> must delete *
the selection.

<Ctrl> <Delete>

When the selection is empty or when the component is in add
mode with the cursor disjoint from the selection, <Ctrl>
<Delete> can delete the character following the location cursor
to the end of the line. Otherwise, <Ctrl> <Delete> can delete
the selection.

<Insert> If the Text component supports replace mode, must toggle *
between insert mode and replace mode.

By default, Text components must start in insert mode, where *
the location cursor is between two characters. In insert mode, *
typing a character must insert the character at the position of *
the location cursor. Text components can also implement
replace mode, where the location cursor is on a character. In *
replace mode, typing a character must replace the current *
character with that newly entered character and move the *
location cursor to the next character, selecting it. Many of the
requirements for a text-like collection in this guide assume that
the collection is in insert mode and do not apply in replace
mode.

BSelect Click 2+

Selects text a block at a time. A double-click must select text a   *
word at a time. A triple-click can optionally select text a line or
sentence at a time. Larger numbers of clicks can optionally
select increasingly larger blocks of text.

BSelect Motion 2+

Can drag out a new selection by blocks as described for **BSelect
Click 2+**.

<Shift> BSelect Click 2+

Can extend the selection to a block boundary as described for
BSelect Click 2+.

<Shift> BSelect Motion 2+

Can extend the selection by blocks as described for **BSelect
Click 2+**.

<Ctrl> BSelect Click 2+

If the Text component supports discontiguous selection, this can
extend the discontiguous selection by blocks as described for
BSelect Click 2+.

<Ctrl> BSelect Motion 2+

If the Text component supports discontiguous selection, this can
drag out the discontiguous selection by blocks as described for
BSelect Click 2+.

<Help>   Must provide any available help for the Text control.   *

Related Information

For more information on Text selection, see the description of the selection
models in Chapter 4.

ToggleButton

Description

A ToggleButton should be used to select options in an application. When the choice is one of many, the ToggleButton is called a RadioButton. When the choice is any of many, the ToggleButton is called a CheckButton. The   *
ToggleButton must be composed of a text or graphic label, and it can contain a graphic that indicates the state of the ToggleButton. The graphic should precede the label and should have two distinctive states that indicate the set and unset states of the ToggleButton.

Illustration

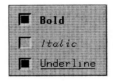

Navigation

ToggleButtons must have no internal navigation.   *

Related Information

For a description of the activation of the two types of ToggleButtons, see the reference pages for CheckButton and RadioButton.

WarningDialog

Description

A WarningDialog should be used to alert the user to a possible danger. It should interrupt the user's interaction with the application. It should contain a warning symbol, a message, and one of the following button arrangements:

Yes No
Yes No Help
OK Cancel
OK Cancel Help

Illustration

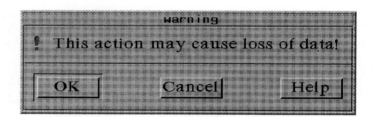

Related Information

For more information, see the reference page for DialogBox.

Window Menu

Description

The window Menu, sometimes called the system Menu, is used to display the list of window actions. All actions possible for a window should be displayed in the window Menu, since keyboard-only users interact with the window manager through this Menu.

The window Menu button must be located in the upper-left corner of the window. Double-clicking the window Menu button must close the window. * Pressing **<Shift> <Escape>** or **<Alt> <Space>** must activate the window * Menu button for the window with the focus. The illustration on this reference page shows a posted window Menu.

A primary window Menu must have the following selections in the order * listed: *

Restore   Alt+F5   Restores a minimized or maximized window to the * previous size and location of the window. This * selection must be deemphasized (grayed out) when * the window is in its normal state. This action must * have the mnemonic **R**. If this action has an * accelerator, it must be **<Alt> <F5>** if **<F5>** is * available. *

Move   Alt+F7   Moves a window around the workspace. This action * must have the mnemonic **M**. If this action has an * accelerator, it must be **<Alt> <F7>** if **<F7>** is * available. *

Size   Alt+F8   Changes the height and width of the window in the * direction indicated by the pointer. This action must * have the mnemonic **S**. If this action has an * accelerator, it must be **<Alt> <F8>** if **<F8>** is * available. *

Mi<u>n</u>imize	**Alt+F9**	Changes a window into an icon. This action must have the mnemonic **N**. If this action has an accelerator, it must be **<Alt> <F9>** if **<F9>** is available.	* * * *
Ma<u>x</u>imize	**Alt+F10**	Enlarges a window to its maximum size. This action must have the mnemonic **X**. If this action has an accelerator, it must be **<Alt> <F10>** if **<F10>** is available.	* * * *
<u>L</u>ower	**Alt+F3**	Moves a window to the bottom of the window hierarchy. This action can be omitted. This action must have the mnemonic **L**. If this action has an accelerator, it must be **<Alt> <F3>** if **<F3>** is available.	* * * * *
<u>C</u>lose	**Alt+F4**	Closes a window and removes it from the workspace. This action must have the mnemonic **C**. If this action has an accelerator, it must be **<Alt> <F4>** if **<F4>** is available.	* * * *

A secondary window Menu must have the following selections in the order *
listed: **Move**, **Size**, and **Close**. A secondary window Menu can include
Restore above **Move**, **Maximize** below **Size**, and **Lower** above **Close**, but
the lower option on a secondary window lowers all the windows secondary
to that window's primary window. A secondary window Menu should not
include **Restore** if it does not include **Maximize**. A secondary window *
must not include an entry for **Minimize**.

A secondary window resulting from a Menu being torn off must have the *
following entries in the order listed: **Move**, **Lower**, and **Close**. It must not *
include entries for **Restore**, **Size**, **Minimize**, or **Maximize**.

Illustration

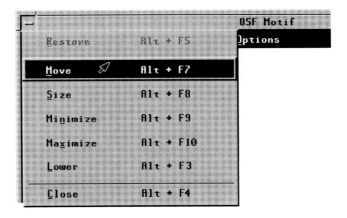

Related Information

See Chapter 7 for more information on the window Menu and the window manager in general. See Chapter 6 for information about Menu design.

WorkingDialog

Description

A WorkingDialog should be used to show work in progress and give the user an opportunity to cancel the operation. It should not interrupt the user's interaction with the application. It should contain a working symbol, a message, and one of the following button arrangements:

OK Cancel
OK Cancel Help

Illustration

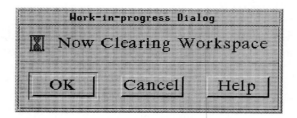

Related Information

For more information, see the reference page for DialogBox.

Appendix A

OSF/Motif Widgets and Components Correspondence

This appendix shows how actual OSF/Motif widgets correspond to the components described in this guide. Gadgets, which are essentially performance-oriented versions of widgets, are not listed in this appendix but correspond closely to their widget counterparts.

Table A–1. Component to Widget Correspondence

Components	Motif Widgets
Basic Controls:	
Separator	**XmSeparator**
Label	**XmLabel**
PushButton	**XmPushButton**
	XmArrowButton
	XmDrawnButton
ToggleButton	**XmToggleButton**
	It can also be simulated by **XmPushButton** and **XmDrawnButton**
CheckButton	**XmToggleButton** with **XmNindicatorType** set to **XmN_OF_MANY**

Components	Motif Widgets
RadioButton	**XmToggleButton** with **XmNindicatorType** set to **XmONE_OF_MANY**
CascadeButton	**XmCascadeButton**
OptionButton	An **XmCascadeButton** within an **XmRowColumn** with **XmNrowColumnType** set to **XmMENU_OPTION**
Field Controls:	
ScrollBar	**XmScrollBar**
Scale	**XmScale**
Sash	Private element of **XmPanedWindow**
Text	**XmText** and **XmTextField**
Canvas	**XmDrawingArea** (without children), **XmDrawnButton**
List	**XmList**
Basic Groups:	
Panel	**XmRowColumn** with **XmNrowColumnType** set to **XmWORK_AREA** and composed of basic controls
Menu	**XmRowColumn** with **XmNrowColumnType** set to **XmMENU_PULLDOWN** or **XmMENU_POPUP**
MenuBar	**XmRowColumn** with **XmNrowColumnType** set to **XmMENU_BAR**
Layout Groups:	
Composite	**XmBulletinBoard**, **XmDrawingArea** (with children), **XmForm**, **XmRowColumn** when **XmNrowColumnType** is set to **XmWORK_AREA** and it is not a basic group
PanedWindow	**XmPanedWindow**
Framing Groups:	
Frame	**XmFrame**
ScrolledWindow	**XmScrolledWindow**
MainWindow	**XmMainWindow**

A–2

Components	Motif Widgets
DialogBoxes:	
CommandDialog	**XmCommand**
ErrorDialog	**XmMessageBox**
FileSelectionDialog	**XmFileSelectionBox**
InformationDialog	**XmMessageBox**
MessageDialog	**XmMessageBox**
PromptDialog	**XmSelectionBox**
QuestionDialog	**XmMessageBox**
SelectionDialog	**XmSelectionBox**
WarningDialog	**XmMessageBox**
WorkingDialog	**XmMessageBox**

Appendix B

OSF/Motif Level One Certification Checklist

The *OSF/Motif Level One Certification Checklist* (Revision 1.2) provides the list of requirements for OSF/Motif application-level certification. In order for your application to be certified *OSF/Motif Style Guide* compliant, it must behave according to these requirements. You certify your own application by comparing its behavior with that specified in the Checklist. For each Checklist item, check **Yes** only if your application performs exactly as described for that item. If you have not implemented a specified type of behavior in any manner anywhere in your application, you may mark **N/A** (not applicable) for the items pertaining to that behavior.

The Checklist describes keys using a model keyboard mechanism. Wherever keyboard input is specified, the keys are indicated by the engravings that they have on the OSF/Motif model keyboard. Mouse buttons are described using a virtual button mechanism to better describe behavior independent from the number of buttons on the mouse. For more information on the model keyboard and virtual button mechanisms, consult the Preface and Section 2.2.1 of this guide.

By default, this Checklist assumes that your application is being designed for a left-to-right language environment in an English-language locale. Some sections of the Checklist may require appropriate changes for other locales.

As you compare the behavior of your application to the requirements in the Checklist, we recommend that you follow along in the *OSF/Motif Style Guide* (Revision 1.2). For each Checklist item, corresponding section numbers in the guide have been provided for your convenience. Each item in the Checklist is also followed by a brief explanation and/or justification. If you do not understand a particular item, refer to the appropriate section in the guide and check the glossary in the guide for any terms that are unclear.

B.1 Preface

Yes   N/A   No

——   ——   ——   **1-1:**   Each of the nonoptional keys described on the OSF/Motif model keyboard is available either as specified or by using other keys or key combinations if the specified key is unavailable (Preface).

The model keyboard does not correspond directly to any existing keyboard; rather, it assumes a keyboard with an ideal set of keys. However, to ensure consistency across applications, the nonoptional keys or substitutes for them must always be available.

B.2 Input Models

B.2.1 The Keyboard Focus Model

Yes   N/A   No

——   ——   ——   **2-1:**   Only one window at a time has the keyboard focus. The window that has the focus is highlighted. Within the window that has the keyboard focus, only one component at a time has the focus (Section 2.1).

The keyboard focus determines which component on the screen receives keyboard events. This rule prevents confusion about which window and component have the focus.

— — — **2-2:** When your application uses an explicit focus policy, pressing **BSelect** does not move focus to a component that is not traversable or does not accept input (Section 2.1.2).

*An explicit focus policy requires the user to explicitly select which window or component receives the keyboard focus. Generally, the user gives the focus to a window or component by pressing **BSelect** over it. However, this policy must not allow the user to give focus to a component that is not traversable or does not accept input.*

— — — **2-3:** When your application uses an explicit focus policy, the component with the keyboard focus is highlighted by a location cursor (Section 2.1.2).

The user needs to know the location of the keyboard focus to be able to control an application.

B.2.2 The Input Device Model

Yes   N/A   No

— — — **2-4:** Your application supports methods of interaction for keyboard-only users. All features of your application are available from the keyboard (Section 2.2).

Some users may not have access to a pointing device. These users need to be able to access the full functionality of the application from the keyboard. Additionally, advanced users will be able to use the keyboard to perform some tasks more quickly than with a pointing device.

— — — **2-5:** Your application uses the following bindings for mouse buttons (Section 2.2.1):

- **BSelect**, used for selection, activation, and setting the location cursor, is the leftmost button, except for left-handed users, where it can be the rightmost button.

- **BTransfer**, used for moving and copying elements, is the middle mouse button, unless dragging is integrated with selection or the mouse has fewer than three buttons.

- **BMenu**, used for popping up Menus, is the rightmost button, except for left-handed users, where is can be the leftmost button, or unless the mouse has fewer than three buttons. If the mouse has one button, **BMenu** is bound to **<Alt> BSelect**.

These bindings ensure a consistent interface for using standard mouse-based operations across applications.

— — — **2-6:** Your application does not warp the pointer unless you have given the user a means of disabling the behavior (Section 2.2.4).

The pointer position is intended only as input to applications, not as an output mechanism. An application **warps** *the pointer when it changes the pointer's position. This practice is confusing to users and reduces their sense of control over an application. Warping the pointer can also cause problems for users of absolute location pointing devices.*

B.3 Navigation

B.3.1 Mouse-Based Navigation

Yes   N/A   No

——— ——— ——— **3-1:** When the keyboard focus policy is explicit, pressing **BSelect** on a component moves focus to it, except for components, such as ScrollBars, that are used to adjust the size and location of other elements (Section 3.1).

BSelect *provides a convenient mechanism for using the mouse to move focus when the keyboard focus policy is explicit.*

——— ——— ——— **3-2:** When the pointer is on a Menu, your application uses **BSelect Press** to activate the Menu in a spring-loaded manner (Section 3.1).

A spring-loaded Menu is one that appears when the user presses a mouse button, remains on the screen for as long as the button is pressed, and disappears when the user releases the button. **BSelect**, *the first mouse button, provides a means of activating spring-loaded Menus that is consistent across applications.*

——— ——— ——— **3-3:** When the pointer is in an element with an inactive Popup Menu and the context of the element allows the Popup Menu to be displayed, your application uses **BMenu Press** to activate the Popup Menu in a spring-loaded manner (Section 3.1).

The availability of a Popup Menu can depend on the location of the pointer within an element, the contents of an element, or the selection state of an element. **BMenu**, *the third mouse button, provides a consistent means of activating a spring-loaded Popup Menu.*

— — — **3-4:** If the user takes an action to post a Popup Menu, and a Menu can be posted for both an inner element and an outer element that contains the inner element, the Popup Menu for the internal element is posted (Section 3.1).

This specification ensures that the Popup Menu for an internal element is always accessible.

— — — **3-5:** Once a Popup Menu is posted, **BMenu** behaves just as **BSelect** does for any Menu system (Section 3.1).

*The specified operation of **BMenu** is for manipulating Popup Menus.*

— — — **3-6:** **BSelect** is also available from within posted Popup Menus and behaves just as in any Menu system (Section 3.1).

*Once a Popup Menu is posted, the user can select an element from it using the standard selection mechanism, **BSelect**.*

— — — **3-7:** When a Menu is popped up or pulled down in a posted manner, your application places the location cursor on the Menu's default entry, or on the first entry in the Menu if there is no default entry (Section 3.1).

A posted Menu remains visible until it is explicitly unposted. Placing the location cursor on the default entry allows the user to select the default operation easily. When there is no default entry, placing the location cursor on the first entry yields uniform behavior across applications.

— — — **3-8:** Your application removes a spring-loaded Menu system when the mouse button that activated it is released, except when the button is released on a CascadeButton in the Menu hierarchy (Section 3.1).

The concept of a spring-loaded Menu system requires that the Menu disappear when the mouse button is released.

— — — **3-9:** While a spring-loaded Menu system is popped up or pulled down, moving the pointer within the Menu system moves the location cursor to track the pointer (Section 3.1).

Once a spring-loaded Menu system has appeared on the screen, the user needs to be able to maneuver the location cursor through the Menu system using the mouse.

— — — **3-10:** When a spring-loaded Menu system is popped up or pulled down and the pointer rests on a CascadeButton, the associated Menu is pulled down and becomes traversable. The associated Menu is removed, possibly after a short delay, when the pointer moves to a Menu item outside of the Menu or its CascadeButton (Section 3.1).

The user needs to be able to use the mouse to access all of the associated Menus of a Menu system. This feature allows the user to move quickly to any Menu in a Menu system.

— — — **3-11:** When a spring-loaded Menu system that is part of the MenuBar is pulled down, moving the pointer to any other element on the MenuBar unposts the current Menu system and posts the Pulldown Menu associated with the new element (Section 3.1).

This feature of a spring-loaded Menu system allows the user to browse quickly through all of the Menus attached to a MenuBar.

— — — **3-12:** When a spring-loaded Menu system is popped up or pulled down, and the button that activated the Menu system is released within a component in the Menu system, that component is activated. If the release is on a CascadeButton or an OptionButton, the associated Menu is activated in a posted manner if it was not posted prior to the associated button press (Section 3.1).

Releasing the mouse button that activated a spring-loaded Menu provides a means of activating a Menu element that is consistent across applications.

3-13: When the pointer is in an area with a Popup Menu, your application uses **BMenu Click** to activate the Menu in a posted manner if it was not posted prior to the **BMenu Click** (Section 3.1).

BMenu Click *provides a means of posting a Popup Menu that is consistent across applications.*

3-14: Once a Pulldown or Option Menu is posted, **BSelect Press** in the Menu system causes the Menu to behave as a spring-loaded Menu (Section 3.1).

This feature of a posted Pulldown or Option Menu allows the user to switch easily between using a posted Menu and a spring-loaded Menu.

3-15: If a button press unposts a Menu and that button press is not also passed to the underlying component, subsequent events up to and including the button release are not passed to the underlying component (Section 3.1).

When a button press unposts a Menu, the press can be passed to the underlying component. Whether or not it is passed to the underlying component, the press can have additional effects, such as raising and giving focus to the underlying window. If the press is not passed to the underlying component, events up to and including the release must not be passed to that component.

3-16: Once a Popup Menu is posted, **BSelect Press** or **BMenu Press** in the Menu system causes the Menu to behave as a spring-loaded Menu (Section 3.1).

This feature of a posted Popup Menu allows the user to switch easily between using a posted Menu and a spring-loaded Menu.

B.3.2 Keyboard-Based Navigation

Yes   N/A   No

—   —   —   **3-17:** In a Text component, the text cursor is shown differently when the component does and does not have the keyboard focus (Section 3.2.1).

In a Text component, the text cursor serves as the location cursor and therefore must indicate whether or not the component has keyboard focus.

—   —   —   **3-18:** If a Text component indicates that it has lost the keyboard focus by hiding the text cursor and if the component subsequently regains the focus, the cursor reappears at the same position it had when the component lost focus (Section 3.2.1).

To ensure predictability, it is important that the text cursor not change position when a Text component loses and then regains the keyboard focus.

—   —   —   **3-19:** If a small component, such as a Sash, indicates that it has the keyboard focus by filling, no other meaning is associated with the filled state (Section 3.2.1).

This rule reduces possible confusion about the significance of filling in a small component.

—   —   —   **3-20:** All components are designed and positioned within your application so that adding and removing each component's location cursor do not change the amount of space that the component takes up on the screen (Section 3.2.1).

For visual consistency, the sizes and positions of components should not change when keyboard focus moves from one component to another.

—   —   —   **3-21:** **<Ctrl> <Tab>** moves the location cursor to the next field, and **<Ctrl> <Shift> <Tab>** moves the location cursor to the previous field. Unless **<Tab>** and **<Shift> <Tab>** are used for internal navigation within a field, **<Tab>** also moves the location cursor to the next field, and **<Shift> <Tab>** also moves the location cursor to the previous field (Section 3.2.3).

These keys provide a consistent means of navigating among fields in a window.

—— —— —— **3-22:** **<Tab>** (if not used for internal navigation) and **<Ctrl> <Tab>** move the location cursor forward through fields in a window according to the following rules (Section 3.2.3):

- If the next field is a control, **<Tab>** (if not used for internal navigation) and **<Ctrl> <Tab>** move the location cursor to that control.

- If the next field is a group, **<Tab>** (if not used for internal navigation) and **<Ctrl> <Tab>** move the location cursor to a traversable component within the group.

- If the next field contains no traversable components, **<Tab>** (if not used for internal navigation) and **<Ctrl> <Tab>** skip the field.

These rules ensure the consistent operation of **<Tab>** *(if not used for internal navigation) and* **<Ctrl> <Tab>** *across applications.*

—— —— —— **3-23:** **<Shift> <Tab>** (if not used for internal navigation) and **<Ctrl> <Shift> <Tab>** move the location cursor backward through fields in the order opposite to that of **<Tab>** (if not used for internal navigation) and **<Ctrl> <Tab>** (Section 3.2.3).

These rules result in the uniform operation of **<Shift> <Tab>** *(if not used for internal navigation) and* **<Ctrl> <Shift> <Tab>** *across applications.*

—— —— —— **3-24:** When a window acquires focus, the location cursor is placed on the control that last had focus in the window, providing that all the following conditions are met (Section 3.2.3):

- The window uses an explicit keyboard focus policy.

- The window acquires the focus through keyboard navigation or through a button press other than within the client area of the window.

- The window had the focus at some time in the past.

- The control that last had focus in the window is still traversable.

This rule ensures that when the user returns to a window after navigating away, the focus returns to the component where the user left it.

—— —— —— **3-25:** Field navigation wraps between the first and last fields in the window. (Section 3.2.3).

This feature of field navigation provides the user with a convenient way to move through all of the fields in a window.

—— —— —— **3-26:** When <↓> and <↑> are used for component navigation within a field, they behave according to the following rules (Section 3.2.3):

- In a left-to-right language environment, <↓> moves the location cursor through all traversable controls in the field, starting at the upper left and ending at the lower right, then wrapping to the upper left. If the controls are aligned in a matrix-like arrangement, <↓> first traverses one column from top to bottom, then traverses the column to its right, and so on. In a right-to-left language environment, <↓> moves the location cursor through all traversable controls, starting at the upper right and ending at the lower left.

- <↑> moves the location cursor through all traversable controls in the field in the order opposite to that of <↓>.

These rules ensure a consistent means of navigating among components using the directional keys.

——— ——— ——— **3-27:** When <→> and <←> are used for component navigation within a field, they behave according to the following rules (Section 3.2.3):

- In a left-to-right language environment, <→> moves the location cursor through all traversable controls in the field, starting at the upper left and ending at the lower right, then wrapping to the upper left. If the controls are aligned in a matrix-like arrangement, <→> first traverses one row from left to right, then traverses the row below it, and so on. In a right-to-left language environment, <→> moves the location cursor through all traversable controls, starting at the lower left and ending at the upper right.

- <←> moves the location cursor through all traversable controls in the field in the order opposite to that of <→>.

These rules ensure a consistent means of navigating among components using the directional keys.

——— ——— ——— **3-28:** If a control uses <→> and <←> for internal navigation, **<Begin>** moves the location cursor to the leftmost edge of the data or the leftmost element in a left-to-right language environment. In a right-to-left language environment, **<Begin>** moves the location cursor to the rightmost edge of the data or the rightmost element (Section 3.2.3).

This rule permits convenient navigation to the left or right edge of the data or the left or right element in a control.

——— ——— ——— **3-29:** If a control uses <→> and <←> for internal navigation, **<End>** moves the location cursor to the rightmost edge of the data or the rightmost element in a left-to-right language environment. In a right-to-left language environment, **<End>** moves the location cursor to the leftmost edge of the data or the leftmost element (Section 3.2.3).

This rule permits convenient navigation to the left or right edge of the data or the left or right element in a control.

—— —— —— **3-30:** If a control uses <↑> and <↓> for internal navigation, **<Ctrl> <Begin>** moves the location cursor to one of the following (Section 3.2.3):

- The first element

- The topmost edge of the data

- In a left-to-right language environment, the topmost left edge of the data; in a right-to-left language environment, the topmost right edge of the data

This rule permits convenient navigation to the beginning of the data in a control.

—— —— —— **3-31:** If a control uses <↑> and <↓> for internal navigation, **<Ctrl> <End>** moves the location cursor to one of the following (Section 3.2.3):

- The last element

- The bottommost edge of the data

- In a left-to-right language environment, the bottommost right edge of the data; in a right-to-left language environment, the bottommost left edge of the data

This rule permits convenient navigation to the end of the data in a control.

B.3.3 Menu Traversal

Yes   N/A   No

—— —— —— **3-32:** If the user traverses to a Menu while the keyboard focus policy is implicit, the focus policy temporarily changes to explicit and reverts to implicit whenever the user traverses out of the Menu system (Section 3.3).

Menus must always be traversable, even when the keyboard focus policy is generally implicit.

—— —— —— **3-33:** Your application uses **<F10>** to activate the MenuBar system if it is inactive. The location cursor is placed on the first traversable CascadeButton in the MenuBar. If there are no traversable CascadeButtons, the key does nothing (Section 3.3).

<F10> *provides a consistent means of traversing to the MenuBar using the keyboard.*

—— —— —— **3-34:** When the keyboard focus is in an element with an inactive Popup Menu and the context of the element allows the Popup Menu to be displayed, your application uses **<Menu>** to activate the Popup Menu. The location cursor is placed on the default item of the Menu, or on the first traversable item in the Popup Menu if there is no default item (Section 3.3).

<Menu> *provides a uniform way of activating a Popup Menu from the keyboard.*

—— —— —— **3-35:** When the keyboard focus is in an OptionButton, your application uses **<Select>** or **<Space>** to post the Option Menu. The location cursor is placed on the previously selected item in the Option Menu; or, if the Option Menu has been pulled down for the first time, the location cursor is placed on the default item in the Menu. If there is an active Option Menu, **<Enter>**, **<Return>**, **<Select>**, or **<Space>** selects the current item in the Option Menu, unposts the Menu system, and returns the location cursor to the OptionButton (Section 3.3).

These keys provide a means of posting an Option Menu from the keyboard that is consistent across applications.

—— —— —— **3-36:** Your application uses <↓>, <←>, <→>, and <↑> to traverse through the items in a Menu system (Section 3.3).

The <↓>, <←>, <→>, and <↑> directional keys provide a consistent means of navigating among items in a Menu system.

—— —— —— **3-37:** When a Menu traversal action traverses to the next or previous component in a Menu or MenuBar, the order of traversal and the wrapping behavior are the same as that of the corresponding component navigation action within a field, as described in Section 3.2.3 (Section 3.3).

This specification provides consistency between Menu traversal and component navigation within a field.

—— —— —— **3-38:** If your application uses any 2-dimensional Menus, they do not contain any CascadeButtons (Section 3.3).

CascadeButtons in a 2-dimensional Menu would restrict the user's ability to navigate to all of the elements of the Menu using the keyboard.

—— —— —— **3-39:** When focus is on a component in a Menu or MenuBar system, <↓> behaves in the following way (Section 3.3):

- If the component is in a vertical or 2-dimensional Menu, traverse down to the next traversable component, wrapping within the Menu if necessary.

- If the component is in a MenuBar, and the component with the keyboard focus is a CascadeButton, post its associated Pulldown Menu and traverse to the default entry in the Menu or, if the Menu has no default, to the first traversable entry in the Menu.

This rule results in consistent operation of the directional keys in a Menu or MenuBar system.

—— —— —— **3-40:** When focus is on a component in a Menu or MenuBar system, <↑> behaves in the following way (Section 3.3):

If the component is in a vertical or 2-dimensional Menu, this action traverses up to the previous traversable component, wrapping within the Menu if necessary, and proceeding in the order opposite to that of <↓>.

This rule results in consistent operation of the directional keys in a Menu or MenuBar system.

—— —— —— **3-41:** When focus is on a component in a Menu or MenuBar system, <←> behaves in the following way (Section 3.3):

- If the component is in a MenuBar or 2-dimensional Menu, but not at the left edge, traverse left to the previous traversable component.

- If the component is at the left edge of a MenuBar, wrap within the MenuBar.

- If the component is at the left edge of a vertical or 2-dimensional Menu that is the child of a vertical or 2-dimensional Menu, unpost the current Menu and traverse to the parent CascadeButton.

- If the component is at the left edge of a vertical or 2-dimensional Menu that is the child of a MenuBar, unpost the current Menu and traverse left to the previous traversable entry in the MenuBar. If that entry is a CascadeButton, post its associated Pulldown Menu and traverse to the default entry in the Menu or, if the Menu has no default, to the first traversable entry in the Menu.

This rule results in consistent operation of the directional keys in a Menu or MenuBar system.

—— —— —— **3-42:** When focus is on a component in a Menu or MenuBar system, <→> behaves in the following way (Section 3.3):

- If the component is a CascadeButton in a vertical Menu, post its associated Pulldown

Menu and traverse to the default entry in the Menu or, if the Menu has no default, to the first traversable entry in the Menu.

- If the component is in a MenuBar or 2-dimensional Menu, but not at the right edge, traverse right to the next traversable component.

- If the component is at the right edge of a MenuBar, wrap within the MenuBar.

- If the component is not a CascadeButton and is at the right edge of a vertical or 2-dimensional Menu, and if the current Menu has an ancestor CascadeButton (typically in a MenuBar) from which <↓> posts its associated Pulldown Menu, unpost the Menu system pulled down from the nearest such ancestor CascadeButton and traverse right from that CascadeButton to the next traversable component. If that component is a CascadeButton, post its associated Pulldown Menu and traverse to the default entry in the Menu or, if the Menu has no default, to the first traversable entry in the Menu.

This rule results in consistent operation of the directional keys in a Menu or MenuBar system.

—— —— —— **3-43:** All Menu traversal actions, with the exception of Menu posting, traverse to TearOffButtons in the same way as for other Menu entries (Section 3.3).

Traversal of TearOffButtons needs to be consistent with traversal of other Menu items.

—— —— —— **3-44:** If your application uses **<F10>**, **<Menu>**, or **<Cancel>** to unpost an entire Menu system and an explicit focus policy is in use, the location cursor is moved back to the component that had it before the Menu system was posted (Section 3.3).

Returning the location cursor to the component that had it previously allows the user to resume a task without disruption.

B.3.4 Scrollable Component Navigation

Yes N/A No

—— —— —— **3-45:** Any scrollable components within your application support the appropriate navigation and scrolling operations. Your application uses the page navigation keys **<PageUp>**, **<PageDown>**, **<PageLeft>** or **<Ctrl> <PageUp>**, and **<PageRight>** or **<Ctrl> <PageDown>** for scrolling the visible region by a page increment (Section 3.4).

A user needs to be able to view and access the entire contents of a scrollable component.

—— —— —— **3-46:** When scrolling by a page, your application leaves at least one unit of overlap between the old and new pages (Section 3.4).

The overlap between one page and the next yields visual continuity for the user.

—— —— —— **3-47:** Any keyboard operation that moves the cursor to or in the component, or that inserts, deletes, or modifies items at the cursor location scrolls the component so that the cursor is visible when the operation is complete (Section 3.4).

The user needs to be able to see the results of moving the location cursor or operating on the contents of the scrollable component.

—— —— —— **3-48:** If a mouse-based scrolling action is in progress, **<Cancel>** cancels the scrolling action and returns the scrolling device to its state prior to the start of the scrolling operation (Section 3.4).

<Cancel> *provides a convenient way for the user to cancel a scrolling operation.*

B.4 Selection

B.4.1 Selection Models

Yes   N/A   No

——   ——   ——   **4-1:** Your system supports five selection models: single selection, browse selection, multiple selection, range selection, and discontiguous selection (Section 4.1).

Each collection has one or more appropriate selection models. The model limits the kinds of choices the user can make in the collection. Some collections enforce a selection model, while others allow the user or application to change it.

B.4.1.1 Mouse-Based Single Selection

Yes   N/A   No

——   ——   ——   **4-2:** In a collection that uses single selection, when **BSelect** is clicked in a deselected element, the location cursor moves to that element, that element is selected, and any other selection in the collection is deselected (Section 4.1.1).

Single selection is the simplest selection model, used to select a single element. **BSelect**, *the first mouse button, provides a consistent means of selecting an object within a group using the mouse.*

B.4.1.2 Mouse-Based Browse Selection

Yes   N/A   No

—— —— —— **4-3:** In a collection that uses browse selection, when **BSelect** is released in a selectable element, that element is selected, and any other selection in the collection is deselected. As **BSelect** is dragged through selectable elements, each element under the pointer is selected, and the previously selected element is deselected. The selection remains on the element where **BSelect** is released, and the location cursor is moved there (Section 4.1.2).

Browse selection is used to select a single element. It also allows the user to browse through the collection by dragging **BSelect***.*

B.4.1.3 Mouse-Based Multiple Selection

Yes   N/A   No

—— —— —— **4-4:** In a collection that uses multiple selection, clicking **BSelect** on an unselected element adds that element to the current selection in the collection. Clicking **BSelect** on a selected element removes that element from the current selection in the collection. Clicking **BSelect** on an element moves the location cursor to that element (Section 4.1.3).

Multiple selection allows the user to select or deselect multiple elements of a collection, one at a time, by using **BSelect Click***.*

B.4.1.4 Mouse-Based Range Selection

Yes   N/A   No

——   ——   ——   **4-5:** In a collection that uses range selection, pressing **BSelect** sets an anchor on the element, or at the position where **BSelect** was pressed, and deselects all elements in the collection. The anchor and the current position of the pointer determine the current range. As **BSelect** is dragged through the collection, the current range is highlighted. When **BSelect** is released, the anchor does not move, and all the elements within the current range are selected (Section 4.1.4).

*Range selection allows the user to select multiple contiguous elements of a collection by pressing and dragging **BSelect**.*

——   ——   ——   **4-6:** In a text-like collection that uses range selection, the anchor point is the text pointer position when **BSelect** is pressed, and the current range consists of all elements between the anchor point and the current text pointer position (Section 4.1.4).

In text-like collections, elements are ordered linearly, and a text pointer is always considered to be between elements at a point near the actual pointer position.

——   ——   ——   **4-7:** In a graphics-like or list-like collection that uses a marquee to indicate the range of a range selection, the current range consists of those elements that fall completely within the marquee. If there is an anchor element, the marquee is always made large enough to enclose it completely. Otherwise, an anchor point is used and is the point at which **BSelect** was pressed; the anchor point determines one corner of the marquee. If the collection is not arranged as a list or matrix, the marquee is extended to the pointer position. If the collection is arranged as a list or matrix, the marquee is either extended to completely enclose the element under the pointer or extended to the pointer position. Clicking **BSelect** on a selectable element makes it an anchor element, selects it, and deselects all other elements (Section 4.1.4).

A marquee, or highlighted rectangle, is often used to indicate the range of a selection in graphics-like and list-like collections.

— — — **4-8:** In a collection that uses range selection, when the user presses **<Shift> BSelect**, the anchor remains unchanged, and an extended range for the selection is determined, based on one of the following extension models (Section 4.1.4):

Reselect

The extended range is determined by the anchor and the current pointer position, in exactly the same manner as when the selection was initially made.

Enlarge Only

The selection can only be enlarged. The extended range is determined by the anchor and the current pointer position, but then is enlarged to include the current selection.

Balance Beam

A balance point is defined at the midpoint of the current selection. When the user presses **<Shift> BSelect** on the opposite side of the balance point from the anchor, this model works exactly like the **Reselect** model. When the user presses **<Shift> BSelect** or starts a navigation action modified by **<Shift>** on the same side of the balance point as the anchor, this model moves the anchor to the opposite end of the selection and then works exactly like the **Reselect** model.

When the user releases **BSelect**, the anchor does not move, all the elements within the extended range are selected, and all the elements outside of it are deselected (Section 4.1.4).

<Shift> BSelect *provides a convenient means of extending the range of a selection.*

B.4.1.5 Mouse-Based Discontiguous Selection

Yes   N/A   No

____   ____   ____   **4-9:** In a collection that uses discontiguous selection, the behavior of **BSelect** is exactly the same as in the range selection model. After the user sets the anchor with **BSelect**, **<Shift> BSelect** works exactly as in the range selection model (Section 4.1.5).

Discontiguous selection is an extension of range selection that allows the user to select multiple discontiguous ranges of elements.

____   ____   ____   **4-10:** In a collection that uses discontiguous selection, when the current selection is not empty and the user clicks **<Ctrl> BSelect**, the anchor and location cursor move to that point. If the current selection is not empty and the user clicks **<Ctrl> BSelect** on an element, the selection state of that element is toggled, and that element becomes the anchor element (Section 4.1.5).

*In discontiguous selection, **<Ctrl> BSelect Click** provides a convenient means of moving the anchor and toggling the selection state of the element under the pointer.*

____   ____   ____   **4-11:** In a collection that uses discontiguous selection, **<Ctrl> BSelect Motion** toggles the selection state of a range of elements. The range itself is determined exactly as for **BSelect Motion**.

Releasing **<Ctrl> BSelect** toggles the selection state of the elements in the range according to one of two models (Section 4.1.5):

Anchor Toggle

Toggling is based on an anchor element. If the range is anchored by a point, and is not empty, the anchor element is set to the element within the range that is nearest to the anchor point. Toggling sets the selection state of all elements in the range to the inverse of the initial state of the anchor element.

Full Toggle

The selection state of each element in the extended range is toggled.

In discontiguous selection, **<Ctrl> BSelect** *provides a convenient means of toggling the selection state of elements in a range.*

—— —— —— **4-12:** In a collection that uses discontiguous selection, after **<Ctrl> BSelect** toggles a selection, **<Shift> BSelect** or **<Ctrl> <Shift> BSelect** extends the range of toggled elements. The extended range is determined in exactly the same way as when **<Shift> BSelect** is used to extend a range selection. When the user releases **<Ctrl> <Shift> BSelect** the selection state of elements added to the range is determined by the toggle model in use (either **Anchor Toggle** or **Full Toggle**). If elements are removed from the range, they either revert to their state prior to the last use of **<Ctrl> BSelect** or change to the state opposite that of the elements remaining within the extended range (Section 4.1.5).

<Shift> BSelect *and* **<Ctrl> <Shift> BSelect** *provide a convenient means of extending the range of toggled elements.*

B.4.1.6 Keyboard Selection

Yes   N/A   No

—   —   — **4-13:**   The selection models support keyboard selection modes according to the following rules (Section 4.1.6):

- Single selection supports only add mode.

- Browse selection supports only normal mode.

- Multiple selection supports only add mode.

- Range selection supports normal mode. If it also supports add mode, normal mode is the default.

- Discontiguous selection supports both normal mode and add mode. Normal mode is the default.

Selection must be available from the keyboard. In normal mode, used for making simple contiguous selections from the keyboard, the location cursor is never disjoint from the current selection. In add mode, used for making more complex and possibly disjoint selections, the location cursor can move independent of the current selection.

—   —   — **4-14:**   If a collection supports both normal mode and add mode, **<Shift> <F8>** switches from one mode to the other. Mouse-based selection does not change when the keyboard selection mode changes. In editable components, add mode is a temporary mode that is exited when the user performs an operation on the selection or deselects the selection (Section 4.1.6).

<Shift> <F8> provides a convenient means of switching between normal mode and add mode.

B.4.1.6.1 Keyboard-Based Single Selection

Yes   N/A   No

___   ___   ___ **4-15:** In a collection that uses single selection, the navigation keys move the location cursor independent from the selected element. If the user presses **<Select>** or **<Space>** on an unselected element, the element with the location cursor is selected, and any other selection in the collection is deselected (Section 4.1.6.1).

Single selection supports only add mode. Pressing **<Select>** *or* **<Space>** *is similar to clicking* **BSelect**.

B.4.1.6.2 Keyboard-Based Browse Selection

Yes   N/A   No

___   ___   ___ **4-16:** In a collection that uses browse selection, the navigation keys move the location cursor and select the cursored element, deselecting any other element. If the application has deselected all elements or if the cursor is left disjoint from the selection, **<Select>** or **<Space>** selects the cursored element and deselects any other element (Section 4.1.6.2).

Browse selection supports only normal mode. A navigation operation is similar to dragging **BSelect**.

B.4.1.6.3 Keyboard-Based Multiple Selection

Yes   N/A   No

___   ___   ___ **4-17:** In a collection that uses multiple selection, the navigation keys move the location cursor independent from the current selection. **<Select>** or **<Space>** on an unselected element adds the element to the current selection. **<Select>** or **<Space>** on a selected element removes the element from the current selection (Section 4.1.6.3).

Multiple selection supports only add mode. Pressing **<Select>** *or* **<Space>** *is similar to clicking* **BSelect**.

B.4.1.6.4 Keyboard-Based Range Selection

Yes   N/A   No

___   ___   ___ **4-18:**   In a collection that uses range selection and is in normal mode, the navigation keys move the location cursor and deselect the current selection. If the cursor is on an element, it is selected. The anchor moves with the location cursor.

Text-like collections can use a different model in which the navigation keys leave the anchor at its current location, except that, if the current selection is not empty, it is deselected and the anchor is moved to the location of the cursor prior to navigation (Section 4.1.6.4).

Range selection supports normal mode, and, if the collection also supports add mode, normal mode is the default.

___   ___   ___ **4-19:**   In a collection that uses range selection, whether in normal mode or add mode, **<Select>** or **<Space>** (except in a Text component) moves the anchor to the cursor, deselects the current selection, and, if the cursor is on an element, selects the element. Unless the anchor is on a deselected item, **<Shift> <Select>** or **<Shift> <Space>** (except in Text) extends the selection from the anchor to the cursor, based on the extension model used by **<Shift> BSelect** (**Reselect**, **Enlarge Only**, or **Balance Beam**) (Section 4.1.6.4).

In range selection, pressing **<Select>** *or* **<Space>** *is similar to clicking* **BSelect**, *and pressing* **<Shift> <Select>** *or* **<Shift> <Space>** *extends the range as with* **<Shift> BSelect**.

— — — **4-20:** In a collection that uses range selection and is in normal mode, using **<Shift>** in conjunction with the navigation keys extends the selection, based on the extension model used by **<Shift> BSelect**. If the current selection is empty, the anchor is first moved to the cursor. The cursor is then moved according to the navigation keys, and the selection is extended based on the extension model used by **<Shift> BSelect** (Section 4.1.6.4).

In range selection, shifted navigation extends the selection in a similar manner to dragging **<Shift> BSelect**.

— — — **4-21:** In a collection that uses range selection and is in add mode, the navigation keys move the location cursor but leave the anchor unchanged. Shifted navigation moves the location cursor according to the navigation keys, and the selection is extended based on the extension model used by **<Shift> BSelect** (Section 4.1.6.4).

Shifted navigation in add mode is similar to shifted navigation in normal mode, except that when the selection is empty the anchor does not move to the cursor prior to navigation.

B.4.1.6.5 Keyboard-Based Discontiguous Selection

Yes   N/A   No

— — — **4-22:** In a collection that uses discontiguous selection and is in normal mode, all keyboard operations have the same effect as in the range selection model (Section 4.1.6.5).

Normal mode does not permit multiple discontiguous selections.

—— —— —— **4-23:** In a collection that uses discontiguous selection and is in add mode, **<Select>** or **<Space>** moves the anchor to the location cursor and initiates toggling. If the cursor is on an element, the selection state of that element is toggled, but the selection state of all other elements remains unchanged. **<Shift> <Select>** or **<Shift> <Space>** and shifted navigation operations extend the selection between the anchor and the location cursor, based on the toggle mechanism used by **<Ctrl> BSelect** (**Anchor Toggle** or **Full Toggle**) (Section 4.1.6.5).

Add mode permits use of the keyboard to make multiple discontiguous selections.

B.4.1.7 Canceling a Selection

Yes   N/A   No

—— —— —— **4-24:** Your application uses **<Cancel>** to cancel or undo any incomplete motion operation used for selection. Once the user presses **<Cancel>** to cancel a motion operation, the application ignores subsequent key and button releases until after all buttons and keys are released. **<Cancel>** while extending or toggling leaves the selection state of all elements as they were prior to the button press (Section 4.1.7).

<Cancel> *allows the user to cancel an incomplete selection operation quickly and consistently.*

B.4.1.8 Autoscrolling and Selection

Yes N/A No

— — — **4-25:** If the user drags the pointer out of a scrollable collection during a motion-based selection operation, autoscrolling is used to scroll the collection in the direction of the pointer. If the user presses **<Cancel>** with **BSelect** pressed, the selection operation is canceled as described in Section 4.1.7 (Section 4.1.8).

Autoscrolling provides a convenient means of extending a selection to elements outside the viewport of a scrollable collection.

B.4.1.9 Selecting and Deselecting All Elements

Yes N/A No

— — — **4-26:** In a collection that uses multiple, range, or discontiguous selection, **<Ctrl> </>** selects all the elements in the collection, places the anchor at the beginning of the collection, and leaves the location cursor at its previous position (Section 4.1.9).

<Ctrl> </> provides the user with a convenient means of selecting all of the objects in a collection.

— — — **4-27:** In a collection that is in add mode, **<Ctrl> <\>** deselects all the elements in the collection. In a collection that is in normal mode, **<Ctrl> <\>** deselects all the elements in the collection, except the element with the location cursor if the location cursor is being displayed. In either mode, **<Ctrl> <\>** leaves the location cursor at its current position and moves the anchor to the location cursor (Section 4.1.9).

<Ctrl> <\> allows the user to deselect all of the selected objects quickly and uniformly.

B.4.1.10 Using Mnemonics for Elements

Yes   N/A   No

_____   _____   _____ **4-28:**   If your application supports mnemonics associated with selectable elements, typing a mnemonic while the collection has the keyboard focus is equivalent to moving the location cursor to the element and pressing **<Select>** or **<Space>** (Section 4.1.10).

Mnemonics within a collection of selectable elements provide an additional selection method.

B.4.2 Selection Actions

Yes   N/A   No

_____   _____   _____ **4-29:**   When the keyboard focus policy is explicit, the destination component is the editable component that last had the keyboard focus. When the keyboard focus policy is implicit, the destination component is the editable component that last received mouse button or keyboard input (Section 4.2.1).

The destination component is used to identify the component on which certain operations, primarily data transfer operations, act. There is only one destination component at a time.

_____   _____   _____ **4-30:**   If the keyboard focus is in a component (or a Popup Menu of a component) that supports selections, operations that act on a selection act on the selection in that component (Section 4.2.2).

A selection operation acts on the component that has focus, if that component supports selections.

_____   _____   _____ **4-31:**   If the keyboard focus is in a component (or a Popup Menu of a component) that supports some operation that does not act on a selection, invoking the operation acts on that component (Section 4.2.2).

An operation that does not act on a selection acts on the component that has focus, if that component supports the operation.

4-32: Inserting or pasting elements into a selection, except for a primary transfer operation at the bounds of the primary selection, first deletes the selection if pending delete is enabled (Section 4.2.3).

Pending delete controls the conditions under which the selection is deleted. It is enabled by default.

4-33: In normal mode, inserting or pasting elements disjoint from the selection also deselects the selection, except for primary transfer operations whose source and destination are in the same collection. In add mode, the selection is not deselected (Section 4.2.3).

In add mode, a transfer operation that is disjoint from the selection does not affect the selection.

4-34: In editable list-like and graphics-like collections, **<Delete>** deletes the selected elements (Section 4.2.3).

<Delete> *provides a consistent means of deleting the selection.*

4-35: In editable text-like collections, **<Delete>** and **<BackSpace>** behave as follows:

- If the selection is not empty and the control is in normal mode, the selection is deleted.

- If the selection is not empty, the control is in add mode, and the cursor is not disjoint from the selection, the selection is deleted.

- If the selection is not empty and the control is in add mode, but the cursor is disjoint from the selection, **<Delete>** deletes one character forward, and **<BackSpace>** deletes one character backward.

- If the selection is empty, **<Delete>** deletes one character forward, and **<BackSpace>** deletes one character backward.

In text, **<Delete>** *and* **<BackSpace>** *provide a convenient way to delete the entire selection or single characters.*

B.4.3 Transfer Models

Yes N/A No

___ ___ ___ **4-36:** If the move, copy, or link operation the user requests is not available, the transfer operation fails (Section 4.3).

Three transfer operations are generally available: copy, move, and link. The user requests one of these operations by pressing the buttons or keys appropriate for the type of transfer. In general, for mouse-based operations, the modifier **<Ctrl>** *forces a copy,* **<Shift>** *forces a move, and* **<Ctrl>** **<Shift>** *forces a link. However, any requested transfer operation must fail if that operation is not available.*

___ ___ ___ **4-37:** If a collection does not have a fixed insertion point or keep elements ordered in a specific way, the insertion position for transferred data is determined as follows (Section 4.3):

- For **BTransfer**-based primary and drag transfer operations, the insertion position is the position at which the user releases **BTransfer**.

- In a text-like collection, the insertion position for other transfer operations is the location cursor, and the data is pasted before it.

- In a list-like collection, the insertion position for other transfer operations is the element with the location cursor, and the data is pasted before it.

The insertion position is the position in the destination where transferred data is placed. Some mouse-based transfer operations place data at the pointer position if possible. Other operations, including keyboard-based transfer, generally place the data at the location cursor.

B.4.3.1 Clipboard Transfer

Yes   N/A   No

——   ——   —— **4-38:**   Keyboard-based clipboard selection actions are available in every editable collection in your application (Section 4.3.1).

Clipboard selection actions need to be available from the keyboard.

——   ——   —— **4-39:**   Your application uses **<Cut>** or **<Shift> <Delete>** and the **Cut** entry on the **Edit** Menu to cut the selected elements from an editable component to the clipboard (Section 4.3.1).

<Cut> *or* **<Shift> <Delete>** *and the* **Cut** *entry on the* **Edit** *Menu offer a consistent means of cutting the selection to the clipboard from the keyboard.*

——   ——   —— **4-40:**   Your application uses **<Copy>** or **<Ctrl> <Insert>** and the **Copy** entry on the **Edit** Menu to copy the selected elements to the clipboard (Section 4.3.1).

<Copy> *or* **<Ctrl> <Insert>** *and the* **Copy** *entry on the* **Edit** *Menu offer a consistent means of copying the selection to the clipboard from the keyboard.*

——   ——   —— **4-41:**   Your application uses **<Paste>** or **<Shift> <Insert>** to paste the contents of the clipboard into an editable component (Section 4.3.1).

<Paste> *or* **<Shift> <Insert>** *offers a consistent way of pasting the contents of the clipboard from the keyboard.*

____ ____ ____ **4-42:** If **Paste** or **Paste Link** is invoked using a component's Popup Menu, the data is pasted at the insertion position of the component. However, if the Popup Menu is popped up over a selection, the selection is first deleted, even if pending delete is disabled, and the pasted data replaces it, if possible (Section 4.3.1).

Popping up a Popup Menu over a selection indicates that a **Paste** *or* **Paste Link** *operation should replace the selection.*

____ ____ ____ **4-43:** If **Paste** or **Paste Link** is invoked from the **Edit** Menu or by a keyboard operation, and the insertion position in the target component is not disjoint from a selection, the pasted data replaces the selection contents if pending delete is enabled (Section 4.3.1).

Pending delete determines whether the selection is deleted when the insertion position is not disjoint from the selection and **Paste** *or* **Paste Link** *is invoked from the* **Edit** *Menu or by a keyboard operation.*

B.4.3.2 Primary Transfer

Yes N/A No

____ ____ ____ **4-44:** In an editable collection, **BTransfer Click**, **<Ctrl> BTransfer Click**, **<Alt> <Copy>**, and **<Alt> <Ctrl> <Insert>** copy the primary selection to the insertion position, as defined in Section 4.3. (Note that the insertion position is usually different for mouse and keyboard operations.) (Section 4.3.2)

These operations provide a convenient way for the user to force a copy operation.

____ ____ ____ **4-45:** In an editable collection, **<Shift> BTransfer Click**, **<Alt> <Cut>**, and **<Alt> <Shift> <Delete>** move the primary selection to the insertion position, as defined in Section 4.3. (Note that the insertion position is usually different for mouse and keyboard operations.) (Section 4.3.2)

These operations provide a convenient way for the user to force a move operation.

— — — **4-46:** In an editable collection, **<Ctrl> <Shift> BTransfer Click** places a link to the primary selection at the insertion position, as defined in Section 4.3 (Section 4.3.2).

<Ctrl> <Shift> BTransfer *provides a convenient way for the user to force a link operation.*

— — — **4-47:** A **Primary Move** moves the primary selection as well as the elements selected; that is, the element moved to the destination becomes selected as the primary selection. **Primary Copy** and **Primary Link** do not select transferred data at the destination (Section 4.3.2).

This rule provides the expected treatment of the selection in move, copy, and link operation.

B.4.3.3 Quick Transfer

Yes   N/A   No

— — — **4-48:** All Text components support quick transfer (Section 4.3.3).

Quick transfer is used to make a temporary selection and then immediately move, copy, or link that selection to the insertion position of the destination component. In Text quick transfer provides a convenient way to move, copy, or link text without disturbing the primary selection.

— — — **4-49:** If a component supports quick transfer, **<Alt> BTransfer Motion** or **<Alt> <Ctrl> BTransfer Motion** temporarily selects elements in the specified range and, on release, copies them to the insertion position of the destination component (Section 4.3.3).

These operations provide a convenient way to perform a quick copy.

— — — **4-50:** If a component supports quick transfer, **<Alt> <Shift> BTransfer Motion** temporarily selects elements in the specified range and, on release, moves them to the insertion position of the destination component (Section 4.3.3).

This operation provides a convenient way to perform a quick cut.

— — — **4-51:** If a component supports quick transfer, **<Alt> <Ctrl> <Shift> BTransfer Motion** temporarily selects elements in the specified range and, on release, places a link to them at the insertion position of the destination component (Section 4.3.3).

This operation provides a convenient way to perform a quick link.

— — — **4-52:** Quick transfer does not disturb the primary selection or affect the clipboard, except when the destination of the transfer is within or on the boundaries of the primary selection and pending delete is enabled. In this case, quick transfer deletes the contents of the primary selection, leaving an empty primary selection, before pasting the transferred elements (Section 4.3.3).

Quick transfer is a secondary selection mechanism, so it cannot disrupt the primary selection. When the destination of the transfer is in the primary selection, quick transfer replaces the primary selection with the secondary selection.

— — — **4-53:** With quick transfer, the range of the temporary selection is determined by using the same model as when **BSelect Motion** determines the range of a primary selection (Section 4.3.3).

This rule provides consistency between primary selection and quick transfer operations.

— — — **4-54:** If the user drags the pointer out of a scrollable collection while making the temporary selection, autoscrolling is used to scroll the collection in the direction of the pointer. If the user releases **BTransfer** with the pointer outside of the collection, or if the user presses **<Cancel>** with **BTransfer** pressed, the highlighting is removed and a transfer is not performed (Section 4.3.3).

Autoscrolling provides a convenient means of extending a temporary selection to elements outside the viewport of a scrollable collection.

B.4.3.4 Drag Transfer

Yes   N/A   No

— — — **4-55:** In a collection that supports selection, **<Shift> BTransfer Release** forces a drag move operation. If a move is not possible, the operation fails (Section 4.3.4).

This mechanism offers a convenient way for the user to force a move operation.

— — — **4-56:** In a collection that supports selection, **<Ctrl> BTransfer Release** forces a drag copy operation. If a copy is not possible, the operation fails (Section 4.3.4).

This mechanism offers a convenient way for the user to force a copy operation.

— — — **4-57:** In a collection that supports selection, **<Ctrl> <Shift> BTransfer Release** forces a drag link operation. If a link is not possible, the operation fails (Section 4.3.4).

This mechanism offers a convenient way for the user to force a link operation.

— — — **4-58:** When a drag move operation moves a selection within the same component, the selection moves along with the elements selected (Section 4.3.4).

This mechanism offers a convenient way to move the selection within a component.

— — — **4-59:** In text-like collections, initiating a drag within a selected region drags the entire text selection (Sections 4.3.4 and 4.3.5).

To be consistent, drag and drop actions need to operate on the entire selection.

— — — **4-60:** In list-like and graphics-like collections, initiating a drag on a selected element drags the entire selection (Sections 4.3.4 and 4.3.5).

To be consistent, drag and drop actions need to operate on the entire selection.

— — — **4-61:** In list-like and graphics-like collections, initiating a drag with **BTransfer** on an unselected element drags just that element and leaves the selection unaffected (Section 4.3.4).

Unselected elements can be dragged without affecting the selection.

— — — **4-62:** When a drag is initiated in an unselected region and the pointer is over two possible draggable elements, the drag uses the highest draggable element in the stacking order (Section 4.3.4).

This guideline ensures the consistency of drag operations.

— — — **4-63:** When your application starts a drag operation, the pointer is replaced with a drag icon (Section 4.3.4.1).

A drag icon provides visual feedback that a drag operation is in progress.

— — — **4-64:** All drag icons used by your application include a source indicator (Section 4.3.4.1).

A source indicator gives a visual representation of the elements being dragged.

—— —— —— **4-65:** Pressing **<Cancel>** ends a drag and drop operation by canceling the drag in progress (Section 4.3.4.2).

<Cancel> *provides a consistent way for the user to cancel a drag operation.*

—— —— —— **4-66:** Releasing **BTransfer** ends a drag and drop operation (Section 4.3.4.3).

Releasing **BTransfer** *offers a consistent means of ending a drag operation.*

—— —— —— **4-67:** When **BTransfer** is released, the drop operation ordinarily occurs at the location of the hotspot of the drag icon pointer and into the highest drop site in the stacking order. However, if a drop occurs within a selection and pending delete is enabled, the transferred data replaces the contents of the entire selection (Section 4.3.4.3).

This rule provides consistency in the treatment of mouse-based transfer operations.

—— —— —— **4-68:** After a successful transfer, the data is placed in the drop site, and any transfer icon used by your application is removed (Section 4.3.4.4).

A transfer icon can be used to represent the type of data being transferred during a drop operation. A successful drop operation results in the transfer of data.

—— —— —— **4-69:** After a failed transfer, the data remains at the drag source and is not placed in the drop site. Any transfer icon used by your application is removed (Section 4.3.4.4).

A failed drop operation does not result in the transfer of data.

B.5 Component Activation

B.5.1 Basic Activation

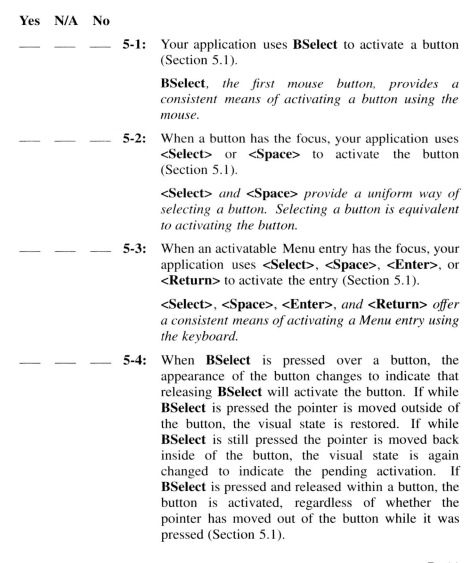

Yes   N/A   No

— — — **5-1:** Your application uses **BSelect** to activate a button (Section 5.1).

BSelect, *the first mouse button, provides a consistent means of activating a button using the mouse.*

— — — **5-2:** When a button has the focus, your application uses **<Select>** or **<Space>** to activate the button (Section 5.1).

<Select> and <Space> provide a uniform way of selecting a button. Selecting a button is equivalent to activating the button.

— — — **5-3:** When an activatable Menu entry has the focus, your application uses **<Select>**, **<Space>**, **<Enter>**, or **<Return>** to activate the entry (Section 5.1).

<Select>, <Space>, <Enter>, and <Return> offer a consistent means of activating a Menu entry using the keyboard.

— — — **5-4:** When **BSelect** is pressed over a button, the appearance of the button changes to indicate that releasing **BSelect** will activate the button. If while **BSelect** is pressed the pointer is moved outside of the button, the visual state is restored. If while **BSelect** is still pressed the pointer is moved back inside of the button, the visual state is again changed to indicate the pending activation. If **BSelect** is pressed and released within a button, the button is activated, regardless of whether the pointer has moved out of the button while it was pressed (Section 5.1).

The visual state of a button offers a cue to the user about whether or not the button will be activated when the mouse button is released.

— — — **5-5:** If a selectable element of a collection is activatable, **BSelect Click**, <Select>, and <Space> (except in Text) select it. **BSelect Click 2** selects and activates it (Section 5.1).

This rule provides for consistent integration of activation and selection in a collection where elements can be both selected and activated.

B.5.2 Accelerators

Yes   N/A   No

— — — **5-6:** If your application uses accelerators, the component with the accelerator displays the accelerator key or key combination following the Label of the component (Section 5.2).

An accelerator is a key or key combination that invokes the action of some component regardless of the position of the location cursor when the accelerator is pressed. So that the user knows that there is an accelerator associated with a component, the accelerator needs to be displayed.

— — — **5-7:** If a button with an accelerator is within a primary or secondary window, or within a Pulldown Menu system from its MenuBar, it is activatable whenever the input focus is in the window or the MenuBar system. If a button with an accelerator is within a Popup Menu system, it is activatable whenever the focus is in the Popup Menu system or the component with the Popup Menu (Section 5.2).

An accelerator must be activatable from the window or component associated with the accelerator.

B.5.3 Mnemonics

Yes   N/A   No

—— —— —— **5-8:**   If your application uses mnemonics, the Label for the component with the mnemonic contains the character that is its mnemonic. If the Label does not naturally contain the character, the mnemonic is placed in parentheses following the Label (Section 5.3).

A mnemonic is a single character that can be associated with any component that contains a text Label. Mnemonics provide a fast way of selecting a component from the keyboard. So that the user knows that there is a mnemonic associated with a selection, the mnemonic is underlined in the Label of the selection by the toolkit. In order for a mnemonic to be underlined, the Label for a selection needs to contain the mnemonic character. Putting the mnemonic in parentheses following the Label provides visual consistency.

—— —— —— **5-9:**   All mnemonics are case insensitive for activation (Section 5.3).

The user must be able to activate a mnemonic by pressing either the lowercase or the uppercase variant of the mnemonic key.

—— —— —— **5-10:**   When the location cursor is within a Menu or a MenuBar, pressing the mnemonic key of a component within that Menu or MenuBar moves the location cursor to the component and activates it. If a mnemonic is used for an OptionButton or for a CascadeButton in a MenuBar, pressing **<Alt>** and the mnemonic anywhere in the window or its Menus moves the cursor to the component with that mnemonic and activates it (Section 5.3).

*A mnemonic is generally activatable when the location cursor is within the component that contains the mnemonic. Pressing **<Alt>** and the mnemonic provides a way to activate a visible* *mnemonic when the location cursor is within the window that contains the mnemonic.*

B.5.4 TearOff Activation

Yes   N/A   No

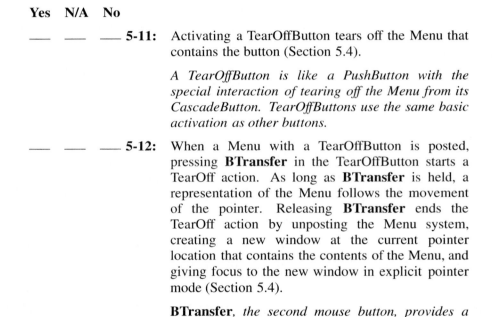

——   ——   —— **5-11:**   Activating a TearOffButton tears off the Menu that contains the button (Section 5.4).

A TearOffButton is like a PushButton with the special interaction of tearing off the Menu from its CascadeButton. TearOffButtons use the same basic activation as other buttons.

——   ——   —— **5-12:**   When a Menu with a TearOffButton is posted, pressing **BTransfer** in the TearOffButton starts a TearOff action. As long as **BTransfer** is held, a representation of the Menu follows the movement of the pointer. Releasing **BTransfer** ends the TearOff action by unposting the Menu system, creating a new window at the current pointer location that contains the contents of the Menu, and giving focus to the new window in explicit pointer mode (Section 5.4).

BTransfer*, the second mouse button, provides a consistent means of activating a TearOffButton.*

B.5.5 Help Activation

Yes   N/A   No

——   ——   —— **5-13:**   Your application uses **<Help>** on a component to invoke any context-sensitive help for the component or its nearest ancestor with context-sensitive help available (Section 5.5).

<Help> *offers the user a consistent mechanism for invoking context-sensitive help.*

B.5.6 Default Activation

Yes N/A No

—— —— —— **5-14:** If your application uses default PushButtons in a window, the current default PushButton is highlighted. When the focus is on a PushButton, its action is the default action, and the PushButton shows default highlighting. If the default action in a window varies, some PushButton always has default highlighting, except when there is no current default action (Section 5.6).

Placing emphasis on the default PushButton in a DialogBox provides the user with a visual cue about the expected reply to the dialog.

—— —— —— **5-15:** When focus is in a window with a default action, **<Enter>** and **<Ctrl> <Return>** invoke the default action. If focus is in a component other than multiline Text, **<Return>** also invokes the default action. These actions have no other effect on the component with the focus, unless the default action has some effect on that component (Section 5.6).

These rules ensure that the means of invoking a default action are consistent across applications.

—— —— —— **5-16:** Except in the middle of a button motion operation, **<Cancel>** anywhere in a DialogBox is equivalent to activating the **Cancel** PushButton in the DialogBox (Section 5.6).

<Cancel> provides a uniform means of canceling a DialogBox from the keyboard.

B.5.7 Expert Activation

Yes   N/A   No

____   ____   ____ **5-17:** If your application supports expert activation, expert actions exist only as shortcuts to application features that are available through another mechanism (Section 5.7).

Expert activation, using mouse double-clicking on buttons, provides a convenient way for experienced users to perform certain tasks quickly. However, new users and keyboard-only users need to be able to perform the same tasks.

____   ____   ____ **5-18:** When the focus is on a button used for expert activation, no default action is available, unless the default and expert actions are the same (Section 5.7).

This rule minimizes possible confusion between default and expert activation.

____   ____   ____ **5-19:** If a component with an expert action is selectable, activating the expert action first selects the component and then performs the expert action (Section 5.7).

A user needs to be able to select a component, even if it has an expert action associated with it.

B.5.8 Previewing and Autorepeat

Yes   N/A   No

____   ____   ____ **5-20:** If your application supports activation preview using **BSelect**, the previewing information is removed when the user releases **BSelect** (Section 5.8).

Activation preview presents the user with additional information that describes the effect of activating a button. This information cannot interfere with the normal operation of the application.

B.5.9 Cancel Activation

Yes   N/A   No

___   ___   ___ **5-21:** Pressing **<Cancel>** stops the current interaction in the following contexts (Section 5.9):

- During a mouse-based selection or drag operation, it cancels the operation.

- During a mouse-based scrolling operation, it cancels the scrolling action and returns the system to its state prior to the start of the scrolling operation.

- Anywhere in a DialogBox that has a **Cancel** PushButton, it is equivalent to activating that PushButton, except during a mouse-based selection or drag operation.

- In a Pulldown Menu, it either dismisses the Menu and moves the location cursor to the CascadeButton used to pull it down, or unposts the entire Menu system. In a Popup Menu, Option Menu, TearOff Menu, or MenuBar, it unposts the Menu system.

- When the focus is in a torn off Menu window, it closes the torn off Menu window.

*These guidelines for **<Cancel>** ensure the consistent operation of the key across applications.*

B.6 Application Design Principles

B.6.1 Layout

B.6.1.1 MainWindow

Yes N/A No

— — — **6-1:** Your application has at least one MainWindow (Section 6.2.1.1).

A MainWindow contains a client area and, optionally, a MenuBar, a command area, a message area, and ScrollBars. The client area contains the framework of the application. The use of a MainWindow ensures interapplication consistency.

— — — **6-2:** If your application has multiple MainWindows that serve the same primary function, each window closes and iconifies separately (Section 6.2.1.1).

For example, a text editor might allow the user to edit multiple documents, each in its own MainWindow. Each window is then treated as a separate application and can be closed or iconified when it is not being used.

— — — **6-3:** If your application has multiple MainWindows that serve different primary functions, each window iconifies separately (Section 6.2.1.1).

For example, a debugger might provide separate MainWindows for editing source code, examining data values, and viewing results. Each window can be iconified when it is not being used, but it is up to the application to decide whether each window closes separately or whether closing one window closes the entire application.

B.6.1.2 MenuBar

Note: These requirements apply only in a left-to-right language environment in an English-language locale. You need to make the appropriate changes for other locales.

Yes   N/A   No

—   —   —   **6-4:** If your application has a MenuBar, it is a horizontal bar at the top edge of the application, just below the title area of the window frame, if present (Section 6.2.1.5).

A MenuBar organizes the most common features of an application. It contains a list of Menu topics in CascadeButtons; each button is associated with a distinct Pulldown Menu containing commands that are grouped by common functionality. The use of a MenuBar yields consistency across applications.

—   —   —   **6-5:** The MenuBar for your application contains only CascadeButtons (Section 6.2.1.5).

When other buttons are included as topics in a MenuBar, they inhibit Menu browsing.

—   —   —   **6-6:** If any of the common Menus are present in the MenuBar, they are arranged in the following order with respect to each other, ranging from left to right across the MenuBar (Section 6.2.1.5):

> **File** Menu
> **Selected** Menu
> **Edit** Menu
> **View** Menu
> **Options** Menu
> **Help** Menu

If a **File** Menu is present, it is the first Menu and is placed at the far left of the MenuBar. If a **Help** Menu is present, it is the last Menu and is placed at the far right of the MenuBar.

The ordering of common Menus in the MenuBar ensures consistency among applications. You can omit any of these Menus if they are not relevant to the application. You can also intersperse other, application-specific, Menus among these Menus.

B.6.1.2.1 File Menu Contents

Note: These requirements apply only in a left-to-right language environment in an English-language locale. You need to make the appropriate changes for other locales.

Yes   N/A   No

          6-7:   If your application uses a **File** Menu, it contains the following choices, with the specified functionality, when the actions are actually supported by your application (Section 6.2.1.5.1).

—   —   —   **New**   Creates a new file. If the current client area will be used to display the new file, your application clears the existing data from the client area. If changes made to the current file will be lost, your application displays a DialogBox, asking the user about saving changes. Has the mnemonic **N**.

—   —   —   **Open...**   Opens an existing file by prompting the user for a filename with a DialogBox. If changes made to the current file will be lost, your application displays a DialogBox asking the user about saving changes. Has the mnemonic **O**.

—   —   —   **Save**   Saves the currently opened file without removing the existing contents of the client area. If the file has no name, your application displays a DialogBox, prompting the user to enter a filename. Has the mnemonic **S**.

— — —   **Save As...**

Saves the currently opened file under a new name by prompting the user for a filename with a DialogBox. If the user tries to save the file using an existing name, your application displays a DialogBox that warns the user about a possible loss of data. Does not remove the existing contents of the client area. Has the mnemonic **A**.

— — —   **Print**   Schedules a file for printing. If your application needs specific information in order to print, it displays a DialogBox, requesting the information from the user. In this case, the Menu entry is followed by an ellipsis (**Print...**). Has the mnemonic **P**.

— — —   **Close**   Closes the current primary window and its associated secondary windows. If your application uses only a single primary window or multiple dependent primary windows, this action is not supplied. Has the mnemonic **C**.

— — —   **Exit**   Ends the current application and all windows associated with it. If changes made to the current file will be lost, your application displays a DialogBox, asking the user about saving changes. Has the mnemonic **X**.

The use of a File Menu with these common file operations yields consistency across applications.

B.6.1.2.2 Edit Menu Contents

Note: These requirements apply only in a left-to-right language environment in an English-language locale. You need to make the appropriate changes for other locales.

Yes   N/A   No

6-8:   If your application uses an **Edit** Menu, it contains the following choices, with the specified functionality, when the actions are actually supported by your application (Section 6.2.1.5.2):

—   —   —   **Undo**   Reverses the most recently executed action. Has the mnemonic **U**.

—   —   —   **Cut**   Removes the selected portion of data from the client area and puts it on the clipboard. Has the mnemonic **T**.

—   —   —   **Copy**   Copies the selected portion of data from the client area and puts it on the clipboard. Has the mnemonic **C**.

—   —   —   **Copy Link**

Copies a link of the selected portion of data from the client area and puts it on the clipboard. Has the mnemonic **K**.

—   —   —   **Paste**   Pastes the contents of the clipboard into the client area. Has the mnemonic **P**.

—   —   —   **Paste Link**

Pastes a link of the data represented by the contents of the clipboard into the client area. Has the mnemonic **L**.

—   —   —   **Clear**   Removes a selected portion of data from the client area without copying it to the clipboard and does not compress the remaining data. Has the mnemonic **E**.

—   —   —   **Delete**   Removes a selected portion of data from the client area without copying it to the clipboard. Has the mnemonic **D**.

—   —   —   **Select All**

Sets the primary selection to be all the elements in a component of the client area.

—— —— —— **Deselect All**
Removes from the primary selection all
the elements in a component of the client
area.

—— —— —— **Select Pasted**
Sets the primary selection to the last
element or elements pasted into a
component of the client area.

—— —— —— **Reselect**
Sets the primary selection to the last
selected element or elements in a
component of the client area. This action
is available only in components that do
not support persistent selections and only
when the current selection is empty.

—— —— —— **Promote**
Promotes to the primary selection the
current selection of a component of the
client area. This action is available only
for components that support persistent
selections.

*The use of an Edit Menu with these common
editing operations yields consistency across
applications.*

—— —— —— **6-9:** If your application uses accelerators for **Undo**,
Cut, **Copy**, and **Paste** in an **Edit** Menu, it uses
either one or both of the models presented in the
following two tables (Section 6.2.1.5.2).

Table B–1. Edit Menu Accelerators, Model 1

Edit Menu Item	Accelerator
Undo	<Alt> <BackSpace>
Cut	<Shift> <Delete>
Copy	<Ctrl> <Insert>
Paste	<Shift> <Insert>

Table B–2. Edit Menu Accelerators, Model 2

Edit Menu Item	Accelerator
Undo	<Ctrl> <Z>
Cut	<Ctrl> <X>
Copy	<Ctrl> <C>
Paste	<Ctrl> <V>

These models provide consistent sets of accelerators for common editing operations in an Edit Menu.

B.6.1.2.3 Help Menu Contents

Note: These requirements apply only in a left-to-right language environment in an English-language locale. You need to make the appropriate changes for other locales.

Yes   N/A   No

6-10: If your application uses a **Help** Menu, it contains either of the following two sets of choices, with the specified functionality, when the actions are actually supported by your application (Section 6.2.1.5.3):

—   —   —   **On Context**

Initiates context-sensitive help by changing the shape of the pointer to the question pointer, described in Section 2.2.2. When the user moves the pointer to a component and presses **BSelect**, any available context-sensitive help for the component is presented, and the pointer returns to its original shape. Has the mnemonic **C**. If this action uses an accelerator, it is **<Shift> <Help>**.

— — — **On Help**

Provides information on how to use your application's help facility. Has the mnemonic **H**.

— — — **On Window**

Provides general information about the window from which help was requested. Has the mnemonic **W**.

— — — **On Keys**

Provides information about your application's use of function keys, mnemonics, and keyboard accelerators. Has the mnemonic **K**.

— — — **Index** Provides an index for all help information in your application. Has the mnemonic **I**.

— — — **Tutorial**

Provides access to your application's tutorial. Has the mnemonic **T**.

— — — **On Version**

Provides at least the name and version of your application. Has the mnemonic **V**.

If your application uses a **Help** Menu, and it does not use the previous set of choices, the **Help** Menu contains the following choices, with the specified functionality, when the actions are actually supported by your application (Section 6.2.1.5.3):

— — — **Context-Sensitive Help**

Initiates context-sensitive help by changing the shape of the pointer to the question pointer, described in Section 2.2.2. When the user moves the pointer to a component and presses **BSelect**, any available context-sensitive help for the component is presented and the pointer returns to its original shape. Has the mnemonic **C**. If this action uses an accelerator, it is **<Shift> <Help>**.

— — — **Overview**

Provides general information about the application window from which help was requested. Has the mnemonic **O**.

— — — **Index** Provides an index for all help information in your application. Has the mnemonic **I**.

— — — **Keyboard**

Provides information about your application's use of function keys, mnemonics, and keyboard accelerators. Has the mnemonic **K**.

— — — **Tutorial**

Provides access to your application's tutorial. Has the mnemonic **T**.

— — — **Using Help**

Provides information on how to use your application's help facility. Has the mnemonic **H**.

— — — **Product Information**

Provides at least the name and version of your application. Has the mnemonic **P**.

The use of a Help Menu with these common help operations yields consistency across applications.

B.6.1.3 Popup Menus

Note: These requirements apply only in a left-to-right language environment in an English-language locale. You need to make the appropriate changes for other locales.

Yes   N/A   No

6-11:   If your application uses any of the common Popup Menu actions, the actions function according to the following specifications (Section 6.2.1.6):

___ ___ ___   **Properties**
Displays a properties DialogBox that the user can use to set the properties of the component.

___ ___ ___   **Undo**   Reverses the most recently executed action.

___ ___ ___   **Primary Move**
Moves the contents of the primary selection to the component. This action is available only in editable components.

___ ___ ___   **Primary Copy**
Copies the contents of the primary selection to the component. This action is available only in editable components.

___ ___ ___   **Primary Link**
Places a link to the primary selection in the component. This action is available only in editable components.

___ ___ ___   **Cut**   Cuts elements to the clipboard. If the Menu is popped up in a selection, cuts the entire selection to the clipboard.

___ ___ ___   **Copy**   Copies elements to the clipboard. If the Menu is popped up in a selection, copies the entire selection to the clipboard.

___ ___ ___   **Copy Link**
Copies a link of elements to the clipboard. If the Menu is popped up in a selection,

copies a link to the entire selection to the clipboard.

Paste   Pastes the contents of the clipboard to the component. This action is available only in editable components.

Paste Link

Pastes a link of the contents of the clipboard to the component. This action is available only in editable components.

Clear   Removes a selected portion of data from the client area without copying it to the clipboard. If the Menu is popped up in a selection, deletes the selection.

Delete

Removes a selected portion of data from the client area without copying it to the clipboard. If the Menu is popped up in a selection, deletes the selection.

Select All

Sets the primary selection to be all of the elements in the collection with the Popup Menu.

Deselect All

Deselects the current selection in the collection with the Popup Menu.

Select Pasted

Sets the primary selection to be the last element or elements pasted into the collection with the Popup Menu.

Reselect

Sets the primary selection to be the last selected element or elements in the component with the Popup Menu. This action is available only in components that do not support persistent selections and only when the current selection is empty.

—   —   —   **Promote**

> Promotes the current selection to the primary selection. It is available only in components that support persistent selections.

The use of Popup Menus with these common actions yields consistency across applications.

—   —   — **6-12:** When a Popup Menu is popped up in the context of a selection, any action that acts on elements acts on the entire selection (Section 6.2.1.6).

In the context of a selection, Popup Menu actions affect the entire selection.

B.6.1.4 DialogBoxes

Yes   N/A   No

—   —   — **6-13:** InformationDialogs do not interrupt the user's interaction with your application (Section 6.2.1.7.5).

An InformationDialog conveys information to the user that does not require immediate attention, so it does not need to be modal.

B.6.1.5 Menu Design

Yes   N/A   No

—   —   — **6-14:** If your application uses a TearOffButton in a Menu, the TearOffButton is the first element in the Menu (Section 6.2.3).

When a TearOffButton is activated, the Menu changes into a DialogBox. The TearOffButton needs to be the first item in the Menu so that the entire contents of the Menu are torn off.

— — — **6-15:** All Menus are wide enough to accommodate their widest elements (Section 6.2.3).

The ability to see the full Label of each Menu element allows the user to browse through a Menu.

B.6.1.6 DialogBox Design

Note: These requirements apply only in a left-to-right language environment in an English-language locale. You need to make the appropriate changes for other locales.

Yes   N/A   No

6-16: If your application uses common DialogBox actions, the actions have the following specified functionality (Section 6.2.4.1):

—	—	—	**Yes**	Indicates an affirmative response to a question posed in the DialogBox.
—	—	—	**No**	Indicates a negative response to a question posed in the DialogBox.
—	—	—	**OK**	Applies any changes made to components in the DialogBox and dismisses the DialogBox.
—	—	—	**Apply**	Applies any changes made to components in the DialogBox.
—	—	—	**Retry**	Causes the task in progress to be attempted again.
—	—	—	**Stop**	Ends the task in progress at the next possible breaking point.
—	—	—	**Pause**	Causes the task in progress to pause.
—	—	—	**Resume**	Causes a task that has paused to resume.
—	—	—	**Reset**	Cancels any user changes that have not been applied to your application. Resets the status of the DialogBox to

the state since the last time the DialogBox action was applied or to the initial state of the DialogBox.

—— —— —— **Cancel** Closes the DialogBox without performing any DialogBox actions not yet applied to your application. Pressing **<Cancel>** anywhere in the DialogBox, except during a cancelable drag operation, also performs the action of this button.

—— —— —— **Help** Provides any help for the DialogBox.

The use of common actions provides a consistent way for the user to respond quickly to DialogBoxes and get back to primary application tasks.

B.6.1.7 Designing Drag and Drop

Yes N/A No

—— —— —— **6-17:** If your application provides any drag and drop help DialogBoxes, they contain a **Cancel** button for canceling the drag and drop operation in progress (Section 6.2.5.4).

The **Cancel** button in the help DialogBox provides a convenient way for the user to cancel a drag and drop operation.

B.6.2 Interaction

Yes N/A No

—— —— —— **6-18:** A WarningDialog allows the user to cancel the destructive action about which it is providing a warning (Section 6.3.2.2).

The user needs to have a way to cancel an operation that can cause destructive results.

B.7 Controls, Groups, and Models

B.7.1 CheckButton

Yes N/A No

— — — **7-1:** If your application uses CheckButtons, each button graphically indicates its state (Chapter 9).

A CheckButton is used to select settings that are not mutually exclusive. The user needs to know whether the button is set or not.

— — — **7-2:** When the user presses **BSelect** in a CheckButton, the CheckButton is armed. If the CheckButton was previously unset, it is shown in the set state. If the CheckButton was previously set, it is shown in the unset state (Chapter 9).

BSelect Press *arms a CheckButton and shows the result of activating it by releasing* **BSelect**.

— — — **7-3:** When the user releases **BSelect** in the same CheckButton that the press occurred in:

- If the CheckButton was previously unset, it is set.

- If the CheckButton was previously set, it is unset.

In all cases the CheckButton is disarmed, and, if the CheckButton is in a Menu, the Menu is unposted (Chapter 9).

BSelect Release *activates a CheckButton.*

___ ___ ___ **7-4:** When the user presses **\<Enter>** or **\<Return>** in a CheckButton, if the CheckButton is in a window with a default action, the default action is activated. If the CheckButton is in a Menu:

- If the CheckButton was previously unset, it is set.

- If the CheckButton was previously set, it is unset.

- In both cases, the CheckButton is disarmed, and the Menu is unposted (Chapter 9).

\<Enter> and \<Return> perform the default action of a window or activate a CheckButton in a Menu.

___ ___ ___ **7-5:** When the user presses **\<Select>** or **\<Space>** in a CheckButton, if the CheckButton was previously unset, it is set. If the CheckButton was previously set, it is unset. In both cases, the CheckButton is disarmed, and, if the CheckButton is in a Menu, the Menu is unposted (Chapter 9).

\<Select> and \<Space> activate a CheckButton.

B.7.2 CommandBox

Yes **N/A** **No**

___ ___ ___ **7-6:** If your application uses a CommandBox, it is composed of a Text component with a command line prompt for text input and a List component for a command history area. The List uses either the single selection or browse selection model (Chapter 9).

This specification ensures the consistent appearance and operation of a CommandBox across applications.

— — — **7-7:** When an element of a CommandBox List is selected, its contents are placed in the Text area (Chapter 9).

This specification provides a convenient way of selecting a previously entered command.

— — — **7-8:** The List navigation actions <↑>, <↓>, **<Ctrl> <Begin>**, and **<Ctrl> <End>** are available from the Text component for moving the cursored element within the List and thus changing the contents of the Text (Chapter 9).

These actions provide a convenient way to choose a command from the List while focus remains in the Text component.

— — — **7-9:** The default action of the CommandBox passes the command in the Text area to the application for execution and adds the command to the end of the List (Chapter 9).

Maintaining a history of commands provides a convenient means of entering often-used commands.

B.7.3 FileSelectionBox

Yes   N/A   No

— — — **7-10:** If your application uses a FileSelectionBox, it is composed of at least the following components (Chapter 9):

- A Text component for displaying and editing a directory mask used to select files to be displayed. The directory mask is a string specifying the base directory to be examined and a search pattern.

- A List component for displaying filenames. The List uses either the single selection or browse selection model.

- A List component for displaying subdirectories. The List uses either the single selection or browse selection model.

- A Text component for displaying and editing a filename.

- A group of PushButtons, labeled **OK**, **Filter**, **Cancel**, and **Help**.

This specification ensures the uniform appearance of a FileSelectionBox across applications.

___ ___ ___ **7-11:** Your application allows the user to select a new directory to examine by scrolling through the List of directories and selecting the desired directory or by editing the directory mask. Selecting a new directory from the directory List does not change the search pattern (Chapter 9).

The method for selecting a new directory to examine needs to be consistent across applications.

___ ___ ___ **7-12:** Your application allows the user to select a new search pattern by editing the directory mask (Chapter 9).

The method for specifying a new search pattern needs to be uniform across applications.

___ ___ ___ **7-13:** The List navigation actions <↑>, <↓>, <**Ctrl**> <**Begin**>, and <**Ctrl**> <**End**> are available from the Text components for moving the cursored element within each List and thus changing the contents of the Text. The contents of the directory Text correspond to the contents of the directory List, and the contents of the filename Text correspond to the contents of the filename List (Chapter 9).

These actions provide a convenient way to choose a directory or filename from the corresponding List while focus remains in the Text component.

— — —— **7-14:** The FileSelectionBox initiates a directory and file search when any of the following occurs (Chapter 9):

- The FileSelectionBox is initialized.

- The user activates the **Filter** PushButton.

- The user double-clicks or presses **<Enter>** or **<Return>** on an item in the directory List.

- The user presses **<Enter>** or **<Return>** while the directory mask Text edit area has the keyboard focus.

The method for initiating a search needs to be uniform across applications.

— — —— **7-15:** Your application allows the user to select a file by scrolling through the List of filenames and selecting the desired file or by entering the filename directly into the file selection Text component. Selecting a file from the List causes that filename to appear in the file selection Text area (Chapter 9).

The method for selecting a file needs to be consistent across applications.

— — —— **7-16:** Your application allows the user to select a new file as many times as desired. Your application does not make use of the selection until one of the following occurs (Chapter 9):

- The user activates the **OK** PushButton.

- The user presses **<Enter>** or **<Return>** while the filename Text component has the keyboard focus.

- The user presses **<Enter>** or **<Return>** while the location cursor is on an item in the file List.

- The user double-clicks **BSelect** on an item in the file List.

This specification results in the uniform operation of a FileSelectionBox across applications.

—— —— —— **7-17:** The FileSelectionBox initiates a directory and file search when the FileSelectionBox is initialized, the user activates the **Filter** PushButton, the user double-clicks **BSelect** or presses **<Enter>** or **<Return>** on an item in the directory List, or the user presses **<Enter>** or **<Return>** while the directory mask Text edit area has the keyboard focus (Chapter 9).

This specification ensures the consistent operation of a directory and file search in a FileSelectionBox.

B.7.4 List

Yes N/A No

—— —— —— **7-18:** Within a List component, your application uses **<↑>** to move the location cursor to the previous item in the List and **<↓>** to move the location cursor to the next item in the List. In a scrollable List, **<←>** scrolls the List one character to the left, and **<→>** scrolls the List one character to the right (Chapter 9).

The arrow keys provide a consistent means of moving the location cursor within a List component.

—— —— —— **7-19:** Within a List component, your application uses **<Ctrl>** **<Begin>** to move the location cursor to the first item in the List and **<Ctrl>** **<End>** to move the location cursor to the last item in the List. In a scrollable List, **<Begin>** moves the horizontal scroll region so that the leftmost edge of the List is visible, and **<End>** moves the horizontal scroll region so that the rightmost edge of the List is visible (Chapter 9).

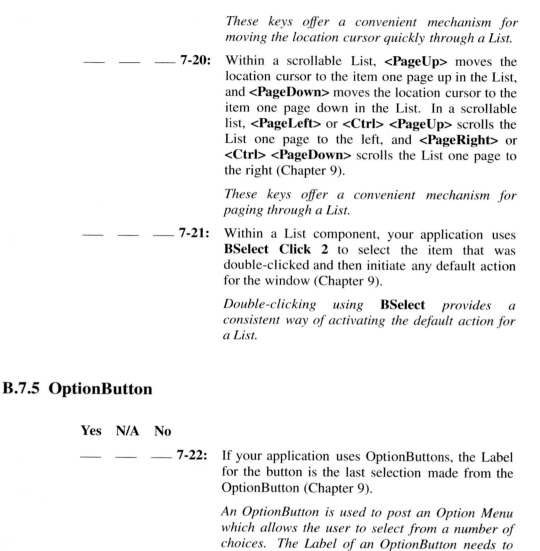

These keys offer a convenient mechanism for moving the location cursor quickly through a List.

— — — **7-20:** Within a scrollable List, **<PageUp>** moves the location cursor to the item one page up in the List, and **<PageDown>** moves the location cursor to the item one page down in the List. In a scrollable list, **<PageLeft>** or **<Ctrl> <PageUp>** scrolls the List one page to the left, and **<PageRight>** or **<Ctrl> <PageDown>** scrolls the List one page to the right (Chapter 9).

These keys offer a convenient mechanism for paging through a List.

— — — **7-21:** Within a List component, your application uses **BSelect Click 2** to select the item that was double-clicked and then initiate any default action for the window (Chapter 9).

Double-clicking using **BSelect** *provides a consistent way of activating the default action for a List.*

B.7.5 OptionButton

Yes N/A No

— — — **7-22:** If your application uses OptionButtons, the Label for the button is the last selection made from the OptionButton (Chapter 9).

An OptionButton is used to post an Option Menu which allows the user to select from a number of choices. The Label of an OptionButton needs to display the most recent selection from the associated Option Menu.

— — — **7-23:** When the user presses **BSelect** in an OptionButton, the associated Option Menu is posted (Chapter 9).

BSelect Press *is a consistent way of activating an OptionButton.*

___ ___ ___ **7-24:** When the user releases **BSelect** within the same OptionButton that the press occurred in, the associated Option Menu is posted if it was not posted at the time of the press. When the user releases **BSelect** outside of the OptionButton, the associated Option Menu is unposted (Chapter 9).

BSelect Release posts or unposts an Option Menu, depending on whether the release occurs inside the OptionButton and whether the Option Menu was posted at the time of the press.

___ ___ ___ **7-25:** When the user presses **<Select>** or **<Space>** in an OptionButton, the associated Option Menu is posted (Chapter 9).

<Select> or <Space> posts an Option Menu from the keyboard.

B.7.6 PanedWindow

Yes N/A No

___ ___ ___ **7-26:** If your application uses PanedWindows, they are composed of any number of groups of components, called Panes, each separated by a Sash and a Separator. The Panes, Sashes, and Separators are grouped linearly, either horizontally or vertically. A Sash is the handle on a Separator between two Panes that is used to adjust the position of the Separator (Chapter 9).

This specification ensures the consistent appearance of a PanedWindow across applications.

B.7.7 Panel

Yes   N/A   No

—   —   — **7-27:**   The $<\downarrow>$, $<\leftarrow>$, $<\rightarrow>$, and $<\uparrow>$ directional keys navigate among components in a Panel (Chapter 9).

A Panel group organizes a collection of basic controls in a horizontal, vertical, or 2-dimensional layout. The directional keys are used to navigate among the controls.

B.7.8 PushButton

Yes   N/A   No

—   —   — **7-28:**   When the user presses **BSelect** in a PushButton, the PushButton is armed. When the user releases **BSelect** in the same PushButton that the press occurred in, the PushButton is disarmed and activated. When the user releases **BSelect** outside the PushButton, the PushButton is disarmed but not activated (Chapter 9).

BSelect provides a consistent means of activating a PushButton.

—   —   — **7-29:**   When the user presses **<Enter>** or **<Return>** in a PushButton that is in a window with a default action, the PushButton is activated. When the user presses **<Enter>** or **<Return>** in a PushButton in a Menu, the PushButton is activated and the Menu is unposted (Chapter 9).

<Enter> and <Return> activate a DialogBox or a PushButton in a Menu.

—   —   — **7-30:**   When the user presses **<Select>** or **<Space>** in a PushButton, the PushButton is activated.

If the PushButton is in a Menu, the Menu is unposted (Chapter 9).

<Select> *and* **<Space>** *activate a PushButton.*

B.7.9 RadioButton

Yes   N/A   No

——— ——— ——— **7-31:**   If your application uses RadioButtons, each button graphically indicates its state (Chapter 9).

RadioButtons are used to represent a panel of mutually exclusive selections. The user needs to know which button in the panel is set.

——— ——— ——— **7-32:**   When the user presses **BSelect** in a RadioButton, the RadioButton is armed. If the RadioButton was previously unset, it is shown in the set state (Chapter 9).

BSelect Press *arms a RadioButton and shows the result of activating it by releasing* **BSelect**.

——— ——— ——— **7-33:**   When the user releases **BSelect** in the same RadioButton that the press occurred in and the RadioButton was previously unset, it is set, and any other RadioButton in the same Panel that was previously set is unset. The RadioButton is disarmed, and, if the RadioButton is in a Menu, the Menu is unposted (Chapter 9).

BSelect Release *activates a RadioButton.*

——— ——— ——— **7-34:**   When the user presses **<Enter>** or **<Return>** in a RadioButton, if the RadioButton is in a window with a default action, the default action is activated. If the RadioButton is in a Menu (Chapter 9):

- If the RadioButton was previously unset, it is set, and any other RadioButton in the same Panel that was previously set is unset.

- The RadioButton is disarmed, and the Menu is unposted.

<Enter> *and* <Return> *perform the default action of a window or activate a RadioButton in a Menu.*

— — — **7-35:** When the user presses <Select> or <Space> in a RadioButton, if the RadioButton was previously unset, it is set, and any other RadioButton in the same Panel that was previously set is unset. The RadioButton is disarmed, and, if the RadioButton is in a Menu, the Menu is unposted (Chapter 9).

<Select> *and* <Space> *activate a RadioButton.*

B.7.10 Sash

Yes N/A No

— — — **7-36:** Within a PanedWindow, your application uses a Sash to adjust the position of a Separator, which adjusts the sizes of the Panes next to it. As a Sash is moved, the Pane in the direction of the Sash movement gets smaller and the opposite Pane gets larger by an equal amount (Chapter 9).

This specification results in the uniform operation of a PanedWindow across applications.

— — — **7-37:** Within a Sash, **BSelect Motion** or **BTransfer Motion** causes the Sash to track the movement of the pointer. In a vertically oriented PanedWindow, the Sash tracks the vertical position of the pointer. In a horizontally oriented PanedWindow, the Pane tracks the horizontal position of the pointer (Chapter 9).

BSelect, *the first mouse button, and* **BTransfer**, *the second mouse button, provide a consistent means of moving a Sash in a PanedWindow using the mouse.*

—— —— —— **7-38:** <↑> and <↓> (for a Sash that can move vertically) and <←> and <→> (for a Sash that can move horizontally) move the Sash one increment in the specified direction (Chapter 9).

The arrow keys offer a uniform means of moving a Sash in a PanedWindow.

—— —— —— **7-39:** **<Ctrl>** <↑> and **<Ctrl>** <↓> (for a Sash that can move vertically) and **<Ctrl>** <←> and **<Ctrl>** <→> (for a Sash that can move horizontally) move the Sash one large increment in the specified direction (Chapter 9).

These keys provide a convenient way of moving a Sash quickly in a PanedWindow.

B.7.11 Scale

Yes N/A No

—— —— —— **7-40:** If a Scale has arrow buttons, your application uses **BSelect Press** in an arrow button to move the slider one increment in the direction of the side of the slider on which the button was pressed and autorepeats until the button is released (Chapter 9).

BSelect Press *provides a consistent means of adjusting a Scale component using the mouse.*

—— —— —— **7-41:** In a Scale trough, if the Scale has tick marks, **BSelect Press** moves the slider one major tick mark in the direction of the side of the slider on which the trough was pressed and autorepeats until the button is released. If the Scale does not have tick marks, **BSelect Press** in the trough moves the slider one large increment in the direction of the side of the slider on which the trough was pressed and autorepeats until the button is released (Chapter 9).

BSelect Press *provides a consistent means of adjusting a Scale component using the mouse.*

—— —— —— **7-42:** Within a Scale slider, **BSelect Motion** causes the slider to track the position of the pointer. In a vertical Scale, the slider tracks the vertical position of the pointer. In a horizontal Scale, the slider tracks the horizontal position of the pointer (Chapter 9).

BSelect Motion *offers a convenient way to adjust a Scale component precisely using the mouse.*

—— —— —— **7-43:** Within a Scale slider or trough, **BTransfer Motion** positions the slider to the point of the button press and then causes the slider to track the position of the pointer. In a vertical Scale, the slider tracks the vertical position of the pointer. In a horizontal Scale, the slider tracks the horizontal position of the pointer (Chapter 9).

BTransfer Motion *provides another convenient way to adjust a Scale component precisely using the mouse.*

—— —— —— **7-44:** If a mouse-based sliding action is in progress, **<Cancel>** cancels the sliding action and returns the slider to its position prior to the start of the sliding operation (Chapter 9).

<Cancel> *provides a consistent way for the user to cancel a mouse-based sliding action.*

—— —— —— **7-45:** In a vertical Scale, **<↑>** and **<↓>** move the slider one increment in the specified direction. In a horizontal Scale, **<←>** and **<→>** move the slider one increment in the specified direction (Chapter 9).

The arrow keys provide a uniform way of adjusting the slider in a Scale component using the keyboard.

—— —— —— **7-46:** In a vertical Scale, **<Ctrl> <↑>** and **<Ctrl> <↓>** move the slider one large increment in the specified direction. In a horizontal Scale, **<Ctrl>**

<←> and <Ctrl> <→> move the slider one large increment in the specified direction (Chapter 9).

These keys provide a convenient way of adjusting the slider in a Scale component quickly using the keyboard.

— — — **7-47:** Your application uses **<Begin>** or **<Ctrl> <Begin>** to move the slider to its minimum value. **<End>** or **<Ctrl> <End>** moves the slider to its maximum value (Chapter 9).

These keys provide a convenient mechanism for setting a Scale to its minimum or maximum value using the keyboard.

B.7.12 ScrollBar

Yes   N/A   No

— — — **7-48:** Within a ScrollBar, your application uses **BSelect Press** in an arrow button to move the slider one increment in the direction of the side of the slider on which the button was pressed and autorepeats until the button is released (Chapter 9).

BSelect Press *provides a consistent means of adjusting a ScrollBar using the mouse.*

— — — **7-49:** In the trough of a ScrollBar, **BSelect Press** moves the slider one page in the direction of the side of the slider on which the trough was pressed and autorepeats until the button is released (Chapter 9).

BSelect Press *provides a consistent means of adjusting a ScrollBar using the mouse.*

— — — **7-50:** Within a ScrollBar slider, **BSelect Motion** causes the slider to track the position of the pointer. In a vertical ScrollBar, the slider tracks the vertical position of the pointer. In a horizontal ScrollBar, the slider tracks the horizontal position of the pointer (Chapter 9).

BSelect Motion *offers a convenient way to adjust a ScrollBar precisely using the mouse.*

— — — 7-51: Within a ScrollBar slider or trough, **BTransfer Motion** positions the slider to the point of the button press and then causes the slider to track the position of the pointer. In a vertical ScrollBar, the slider tracks the vertical position of the pointer. In a horizontal ScrollBar, the slider tracks the horizontal position of the pointer (Chapter 9).

BTransfer Motion *offers another convenient way to adjust a ScrollBar precisely using the mouse.*

— — — 7-52: If a mouse-based scrolling action is in progress, **<Cancel>** cancels the scrolling action and returns the slider to its position prior to the start of the scrolling operation (Chapter 9).

<Cancel> *provides a consistent way for the user to cancel a mouse-based scrolling action.*

— — — 7-53: In a vertical ScrollBar, **<↑>** and **<↓>** move the slider one increment in the specified direction. In a horizontal ScrollBar, **<←>** and **<→>** move the slider one increment in the specified direction (Chapter 9).

The arrow keys provide a uniform means of adjusting a ScrollBar using the keyboard.

— — — 7-54: In a vertical ScrollBar, **<Ctrl> <↑>** and **<Ctrl> <↓>** move the slider one large increment in the specified direction. **<Ctrl> <←>** and **<Ctrl> <→>** move the slider one large increment in the specified direction (Chapter 9).

These keys provide a convenient way of adjusting a ScrollBar quickly using the keyboard.

— — — 7-55: Your application uses **<PageUp>** and **<PageDown>** to move the slider in a vertical ScrollBar one page in the specified direction.

> **<PageLeft>** or **<Ctrl>** **<PageUp>** and **<PageRight>** or **<Ctrl>** **<PageDown>** move the slider in a horizontal ScrollBar one page in the specified direction (Chapter 9).
>
> *These keys allow for the convenient movement of the slider in a ScrollBar using the keyboard.*

— — — **7-56:** Your application uses **<Begin>** or **<Ctrl>** **<Begin>** to move the slider to the minimum value. **<End>** or **<Ctrl>** **<End>** moves the slider to the maximum value (Chapter 9).

> *These keys offer a convenient mechanism for setting a ScrollBar to its minimum or maximum value using the keyboard.*

B.7.13 SelectionBox

Yes N/A No

— — — **7-57:** If your application uses a SelectionBox, it is composed of at least a Text component for the selected alternative and a List component above the Text component for presenting alternatives. The List uses either the single selection or browse selection model. Selecting an element from the List places the selected element in the Text component (Chapter 9).

> *This specification ensures the consistent appearance and operation of a SelectionBox across applications.*

— — — **7-58:** The List navigation actions **<↑>**, **<↓>**, **<Ctrl>** **<Begin>**, and **<Ctrl>** **<End>** are available from the Text component for moving the cursored element within the List and thus changing the contents of the Text (Chapter 9).

> *These actions provide a convenient way to choose an element from the List while focus remains in the Text component.*

B.7.14 Text

Yes   N/A   No

—   —   — **7-59:**   In a multiline Text component, <↑> moves the location cursor up one line, and <↓> moves the location cursor down one line. In a single-line Text component, <↑> navigates upward to the previous component, and <↓> navigates downward to the next component, if the Text component is designed to act like a basic control (Chapter 9).

The up and down arrow keys provide a uniform means of navigation within Text components.

—   —   — **7-60:**   <←> moves the location cursor left one character, and <→> moves the location cursor right one character (Chapter 9).

The left and right arrow keys offer a consistent way of navigating within Text components.

—   —   — **7-61:**   In a Text component used generally to hold multiple words, **<Ctrl> <→>** moves the location cursor to the right by a word, and **<Ctrl> <←>** moves the location cursor to the left by a word (Chapter 9).

<Ctrl> <→> and <Ctrl> <←> provide a uniform way of navigating by words in a Text component. Moving right by a word means that the location cursor is placed before the first character that is not a space, tab, or newline character after the next space, tab, or newline. Moving left by a word means that the location cursor is placed after the first space, tab, or newline character preceding the first previous character that is not a space, tab, or newline.

—   —   — **7-62:**   In a Text component used generally to hold multiple words, **<Begin>** moves the location cursor to the beginning of the line, and **<End>**

moves the location cursor to the end of the line (Chapter 9).

These keys allow the user to move quickly to the beginning or end of a line of text in a Text component.

—— —— —— **7-63:** In a multiline Text component, **<Ctrl> <Begin>** moves the location cursor to the beginning of the file, and **<Ctrl> <End>** moves the location cursor to the end of the file (Chapter 9).

These keys permit the user to move quickly to the beginning or end of a file in a Text component.

—— —— —— **7-64:** Your application uses **<Space>** or **<Shift> <Space>** to insert a space in a Text component. Modifying these with **<Ctrl>** invokes the normal selection function (Chapter 9).

This specification ensures that selection is available from the keyboard in a Text component.

—— —— —— **7-65:** **<Return>** in a multiline Text component inserts a carriage return. **<Enter>** or **<Ctrl> <Return>** invokes the default action (Chapter 9).

This specification ensures that activation is available from the keyboard in a Text component.

—— —— —— **7-66:** In a multiline Text component, **<Tab>** is used for tabbing. In a single-line Text component, **<Tab>** is used either for tabbing or to move to the next field (Chapter 9).

<Tab> *is used for tabbing in multiline Text.*

—— —— —— **7-67:** If a Text component supports replace mode, **<Insert>** toggles between insert mode and replace mode.

By default, the component starts in insert mode, where the location cursor is between two characters. In insert mode, typing a character inserts the character at the position of the location cursor.

In replace mode, the location cursor is on a character. Typing a character replaces the current character with that newly entered character and moves the location cursor to the next character, selecting it (Chapter 9).

These rules ensure the uniform operation of a Text component with a replace mode.

—— —— —— **7-68:** Your application uses **BSelect Click 2** to select text a word at a time (Chapter 9).

Double clicking with the first mouse button provides a convenient mechanism for selecting words in a Text component.

Glossary

acceleration

A temporary change in the mouse pointer gain.

accelerator

A key or sequence of keys (typically a modifier key and some other key) that provides a shortcut, immediately accessing a program function.

activation

Invocation of a component's primary action. For example, the user activates a PushButton by pressing **BSelect** on the PushButton.

anchor

A position in a collection of selectable objects that marks one endpoint of an extended selection range.

application modal

A state of a window in which interaction is limited to that window and windows outside of that window's application.

apply

A label given to a PushButton in some DialogBoxes that performs the action of applying the current changes in the DialogBox without closing the DialogBox.

autorepeat

A means of PushButton activation where a mouse button is pressed and held on a PushButton and the PushButton continues to activate at regular intervals until the mouse button is released.

browse selection

A selection model that allows browsing through single selection collections.

button

A button on a mouse pointing device; mouse buttons can be mapped to the keyboard. A graphical component on a window frame or in a DialogBox that works by pressing it.

cancel

A label given to a PushButton in some DialogBoxes that performs the action of closing the DialogBox without implementing any changes.

cascading Menu

A submenu that provides selections that amplify the parent selection on a Pulldown or Popup Menu.

CheckButton

A component used to select settings that are not mutually exclusive. The visual cue to the selection is frequently that the button is filled in or checked.

click

> To press and release a mouse button. The term comes from the fact that pressing and releasing most mouse buttons makes a clicking sound.

client area

> The area within the borders of a primary window's frame that is controlled by an application.

clipboard

> Any device used to store text or graphics during cut-and-paste operations.

close

> A label given to a PushButton in some DialogBoxes that performs the action of closing the DialogBox. Close is also used as a selection in Menus to close the window associated with the Menu.

control panel

> An area of a window, similar to the control panels in real life, that is used to hold PushButtons and other graphical components.

cursor

> A graphical image, usually a pipe ($|$) or block, that shows the location where text will appear on the screen when keys on the keyboard are pressed or where a selection can be made.

desktop

> *See* **workspace**.

destination

> The location at which transfer actions place data.

DialogBox

> A secondary window that the user can display and that contains application components.

dimmed selection

A selection that is not currently available.

discontiguous selection

A selection model that allows multiple discontiguous selections.

double-click

To press and release a mouse button twice in rapid succession.

drag and drop

A transfer mechanism where data is dragged from a source to a drop site using mouse motion.

drag icon

A graphic that is generated using pixmaps and is moved during a drag operation. The drag icon is composed of a source pixmap, a state cursor, and an operation cursor.

drag transfer

See **drag and drop**.

drop site

An area of the screen on which the user can drop a drag icon.

expert activation

A means of activation where double-clicking on a PushButton activates a different action from clicking the PushButton.

explicit focus

A keyboard focus model that sends keyboard events to the window or component that was specified explicitly with a mouse button or a keyboard event.

focus

A state of the system that indicates which component receives keyboard events. A component is said to have the focus if keyboard events are sent to that component.

focus policy

> The model by which keyboard focus is moved among components. *See also* **explicit focus**, **implicit focus**.

gain

> The ratio of the distance the pointer moves to the distance the mouse moves.

grayed selection

> A Menu selection that is not currently available and so has been dimmed.

help

> A label given to a PushButton in some DialogBoxes that performs the action of providing help for the DialogBox.

highlight

> A graphic technique used to provide a visual cue to the current selection or to the current location of the input focus. Highlighting is frequently accomplished by reversing the video of the selection.

hotspot

> The area of a graphical image used as a pointer or cursor that is defined as the point of the pointer or cursor.

hourglass

> A graphical image used to symbolize the passage of time and provide a visual cue that the application is currently performing an operation.

I-beam

> A graphical image used to represent the location of the mouse pointer in a text entry box and providing a visual cue that text can be entered in an area.

icon

> A small graphical image used to represent a window. Windows can be turned into icons or minimized to save room or unclutter the workspace.

icon box

> A window for organizing icons.

implicit focus

> A keyboard focus model that sends keyboard events to the window or component that the mouse pointer is over.

insertion cursor

> The graphical symbol that provides the visual cue to the location of the insertion point.

keyboard

> An input device consisting of various keys that allows the user to input data, control cursor and pointer locations, and to control the dialog with the workstation.

keyboard focus

> Indicates the window or component within a window that receives keyboard input. It is sometimes called the input focus.

Label

> The text part of an icon or graphical component.

list box

> A component that provides users with a scrollable list of options from which to choose.

location cursor

> A graphical symbol that marks the current location of the keyboard input focus for selection. Typically, this symbol is a box that surrounds the current object.

lower

> To move a window to the bottom of the window stack on the workspace.

maximize

> To enlarge a window to its maximum size.

maximize button

> A control button placed on a window manager window frame and used to initiate the maximize function.

Menu

> A list of available selections from which a user chooses.

Menu system

> A collection of Menus cascading from a single CascadeButton.

Menu window

> An application window used to contain a Menu. Menu windows are transitory.

MenuBar

> A rectangular area at the top of the client area of a window that contains the titles of the standard Pulldown Menus for that application.

MenuBar system

> A collection of Menus associated with a MenuBar and the MenuBar itself.

MessageBox

> The generic name for any DialogBox that provides information, gives the current state of a work in progress, asks a question, issues a warning, or draws attention to an error.

minimize (iconify)

> To turn a window into an icon.

minimize button

A control button placed on a window manager window frame and used to initiate the minimize function.

mnemonic

A single character (frequently the initial character) of a Menu selection. When the Menu is displayed and the user presses the key that corresponds to that character, the Menu selection is chosen.

model keyboard

A fictional keyboard that contains the keys and key labels described by this guide.

modifier key

A key that, when pressed with another key, changes the meaning of the other key. **<Ctrl>**, **<Alt>**, and **<Shift>** are modifier keys.

motion

Movement of the mouse.

mouse

A pointing device commonly used in conjunction with a keyboard in point-and-click, object-oriented user interfaces.

mouse button

A button on a mouse pointing device. Mouse buttons can be pressed, released, moved, clicked, and double-clicked.

multiclick

To click a mouse button multiple times without moving the pointer.

multimotion

To press a mouse button multiple times without moving the pointer and then move the mouse pointer.

multiple selection

> A selection model that allows multiple single selections.

multipress

> To press a mouse button multiple times without moving the pointer.

navigation (traversal)

> An action that causes the focus to move to another component.

no

> A label given to a PushButton in some DialogBoxes that performs the action of answering "no" and closing the DialogBox.

OK

> A label given to a PushButton in some DialogBoxes that performs the action of answering "OK" and closing the DialogBox without implementing any changes.

open

> To start an action or begin working with a text, data, or graphics file.

paste

> Inserting data into an area. Pasting is commonly used in reference to text files where a block of text is cut from one area and pasted into another area.

pause

> A label given to a PushButton in some DialogBoxes that performs the action of pausing the action of the DialogBox.

pointer

> The graphical image that appears on the workspace and represents the current location of a mouse or other pointing device.

pointing device

> A device such as a mouse, trackball, or graphics tablet that allows users to move a pointer about on the workspace and point to graphical objects.

Popup Menu

> A Menu that provides no visual cue to its presence, but simply pops up when a user performs a particular action. Popup Menus are associated with a particular area of the workspace, such as the client area of an application, and a user must memorize where these areas are.

posted

> A state of a Menu where it remains in a visible state even though a mouse button is not being held down. *See also* **spring-loaded**.

press

> To hold down a mouse button or a key.

previewing

> A means of PushButton activation where information about the impending action of a button release is displayed on the button press action.

primary modal

> A state of a window in which interaction is limited to that window and windows that are not ancestors of that window.

primary transfer

> A transfer mechanism where the primary selection is transferred to the destination.

primary window

> A top-level window of an application. Primary windows can be minimized.

Pulldown Menu

A Menu that is pulled down from a client application's title bar.

PushButton

A graphic component that simulates a real-life push button. When a user pushes the PushButton, by pressing a key or a mouse button, an action takes place.

quick transfer

A transfer mechanism where selected data is immediately transferred to the destination.

RadioButton

A graphic component that simulates the buttons on a real-life car radio. Each button represents a mutually exclusive selection. RadioButtons are typically used for setting states or modes.

range selection

A selection model that allows selection of a range of elements.

release

To let up on a mouse button or key that has been pressed. Sometimes it is the press that initiates the action; sometimes it is the release.

reset

A label given to a PushButton in some DialogBoxes that performs the action of resetting the initial state of the DialogBox.

resize

To change the height or width of a window.

resize border

The window manager window frame part that surrounds the client area of an application and that is used to change the height or width of the window.

restore

To return an icon or maximized window to its normal size.

resume

A label given to a PushButton in some DialogBoxes that performs the action of resuming the action of a DialogBox previously paused.

retry

A label given to a PushButton in some DialogBoxes that performs the action of retrying the action whose failure posted the DialogBox.

save

To write changes to a data file to a storage device for safekeeping.

ScrollBar

A graphical device used to change a user's view of the contents of a window. A ScrollBar consists of a slider, a trough, and scroll arrows. A user changes the view by sliding the slider up or down in the scroll area or by pressing one of the scroll arrows. These actions cause the view to scroll up or down in the window adjacent to the ScrollBar.

secondary window

A child window of a primary window.

select

To choose an object to be acted upon or an action to be performed.

selection

The object or action that is selected. Menus are composed of selection items. DialogBoxes contain components, each of which represents a selection.

single selection

A selection model that allows selection of a single element.

slider

> One of the graphical components of a ScrollBar or Scale. The slider is the object that is dragged along the scroll area to cause a change.

spring-loaded

> A state of a Menu where it remains only as long as a mouse button is being held down. *See also* **posted**.

stop

> A label given to a PushButton in some DialogBoxes that performs the action of stopping the work in progress indicated by the DialogBox.

submenu

> A cascading Menu.

system Menu

> *See* **window Menu**.

system modal

> A state of a window in which interaction is limited to that window.

text cursor

> *See* **insertion cursor**.

title area

> The area at the top of the window frame immediately beneath the resize border. The title bar has two functions: it contains a title or name that identifies the window, and it can be grabbed and dragged to relocate the window.

title bar

> The bar across the top of a window manager window that consists of the window Menu button, the title area, and the window-control buttons.

transient window

> A window of short duration such as a DialogBox. The window is displayed for only a short time, usually just long enough to convey some information or get some operational directions.

traversal

> *See* **navigation**.

virtual button

> A model, used by this style guide, which defines mouse button bindings independent of the actual number of buttons on the mouse.

window

> A data structure that represents all or part of the display screen. Visually, a window is represented as a subarea of the display screen.

window decoration

> The frame and window-control buttons that surround windows managed by the window manager.

window frame

> The area surrounding a window. A window frame can consist of a resize border, a window Menu button, a title bar, and window-control buttons.

window manager

> A program that controls the size, placement, and operation of windows on the workspace. The window manager includes the functional window frames that surround each window object and may include a separate Menu for the workspace.

window Menu

> The Menu that appears when the window Menu button is pressed. The window Menu typically contains selections for restoring, moving, sizing, minimizing, maximizing, and closing the window.

window Menu button

> The graphical control button that appears at the left side of the title bar in the window frame.

window navigation

> Moving the keyboard focus among windows.

workspace

> The CRT screen. The area on which the windows of a user's environment appear. The workspace is sometimes called the desk, desktop, or root window.

yes

> A label given to a PushButton in some DialogBoxes that performs the action of answering "yes" and closing the DialogBox.

Index

A

acceleration, 2–10
accelerators, 5–3, 6–42, 6–44, 9–4, 9–5
actions, DialogBox, 6–46
activation, 5–1, 5–3, 5–4, 5–5, 5–6, 5–7, 9–5, 9–21
    basic, 5–2, 5–7, 9–5
    cancel, 9–7
    component, 5–1
    expert, 9–7
    help, 9–6
    Menu system, 3–14
    TearOff, 9–6
active voice, 8–11
active window, 2–2
acts requiring actions, 1–10
add mode, 4–9
addresses, 8–8
affirmative statements, 8–11
alignment
    horizontal, 6–39
    vertical, 6–39
alphanumeric date formats, 8–7
alphanumeric lists, 8–4
anchor, 4–5, 4–7, 4–10
ANS X3.159-1989, 8–1
ANSI C, 8–1

application design, 6–1
application modal, 6–45, 7–5
application title, 7–8
Apply, 6–47, 9–24
arrow pointer, 2–7, 2–9, 9–88, 9–90
    four-directional, 2–8, 9–89
autorepeat, 5–7

B

Balance Beam, 4–6
base, 8–1
basic activation, 5–2, 9–5
basic controls, 6–2, 6–9
    Cascade Button, 6–2
    CheckButton, 6–3
    Label, 6–2
    OptionButton, 6–3
    PushButton, 6–2
    RadioButton, 6–3
    Separator, 6–2
    TearOffButton, 6–3
    ToggleButton, 6–3
basic groups, 6–2, 6–5, A–1
    Menu, 6–5
    MenuBar, 6–5

G

gain, 2–10
graphics, 6–55
graphics tablet, 2–4, 9–59
graphics-like collections, 4–2
group reference, 9–1
grouping
    components, 6–38
    Menu selections, 6–43
    separators, 8–6

H

handles, 7–10
Help, 6–47, 6–60, 9–24
    Menu, 6–16, 6–23, 9–70
help
    activation, 5–4
    application overview, 6–26,
        9–49
    context-sensitive, 1–10,
        6–24, 6–25, 6–60,
        9–48, 9–49
    index, 6–24, 6–26, 9–48,
        9–49
    key bindings, 6–26, 9–49
    product information, 6–26,
        9–50
    tutorial, 6–25, 6–26, 9–49
    using help, 6–26, 9–49
    version, 6–25, 9–49
help activation, 9–6
Help Menu, 9–48

horizontal alignment, 6–39
hot key, 7–2
hotspot, 2–7, 2–9, 9–88
hourglass pointer, 2–8, 9–89

I

I-beam pointer, 2–7, 9–88
icon box, 7–15, 9–53
icon Menu, 7–15, 9–52
iconized window, 7–4
icons, 7–4, 7–14, 8–9, 9–56
immediacy of response, 1–5
implicit focus, 2–2, 2–3, 9–44
Index, 6–24, 6–26, 9–48, 9–49
Information DialogBox, 6–35
InformationDialog, 9–58, 9–75
input, keyboard, 9–59
input devices, 2–1, 2–4, 9–59
input focus, 2–2
interactions, 6–54
interactive methods, 6–8
interapplication, consistency, 1–8
internal window navigation, 2–3
internationalization, 8–1, 8–6, 8–9,
    8–11
    collating sequences, 8–4
    conversion, 8–4
    data formats, 8–5
    date formats, 8–7
    numbers, 8–8
    pre-edit, 8–3
    status, 8–3
    telephone numbers, 8–8

O

object-action selection model, 4–1
OK, 6–46, 9–23
On Context, 6–24, 9–48
On Help, 6–24, 9–48
On Keys, 6–24, 9–48
On Version, 6–25, 9–49
On Window, 6–24, 9–48
Open, 6–18, 9–36
operation
    keyboard only, 2–4, 9–59
    keyboard-based, 2–3
    mouse only, 2–4, 9–59
Option Menus, 6–40
OptionButton, 6–3, 6–9, 9–8, 9–83,
    A–1
Options Menu, 3–2, 6–16, 9–70,
    9–73, 9–83
ordering
    functions, 1–4
    Menu selections, 6–43
ordering Menu selections, 6–43
outline highlight, 3–5
Overview, 6–26, 9–49

P

Pack Icons, 7–16, 9–53
PanedWindow, 6–4, 6–5, 6–40,
    9–63, 9–85, 9–108, A–1
Panel, 6–5, 6–8, 6–10, 9–10, 9–87,
    A–1
panels, control, 6–38

Panes, 6–4, 6–40, 9–63, 9–85
parent windows, 7–4
parts, window, 7–6
Paste, 6–21, 6–29, 9–29, 9–93
paste, 4–20
paste link, 4–20
Paste Link, 6–21, 6–29, 9–29, 9–93
Pause, 6–47, 9–24
pointer navigation, 3–2
pointer shapes, 2–7, 8–9, 9–88
pointers, 2–2, 2–4
    arrow, 2–7, 9–88
    caution, 2–9, 9–90
    designing, 2–9
    four-directional, 2–8, 9–89
    hourglass, 2–8, 9–89
    I-beam, 2–7, 9–88
    mouse, 2–2, 2–3
    question, 2–9, 9–90
    resize, 2–8, 9–89
    sighting, 2–9, 9–90
    track, 2–2
    warping, 2–10
    watch, 2–8, 9–89
    X, 2–8, 9–88
pointing devices, 2–4, 9–59
Popup Menus, 3–2, 6–10, 6–26,
    6–40, 9–6, 9–73, 9–91
positive and negative values, 8–6
POSIX 1003.1, 8–1
pre-edit area, 8–3
    conversion, 8–4
    off-the-spot, 8–3
    on-the-spot, 8–3
    over-the-spot, 8–3
Press, 2–5
previewing, 5–7

S

T

U

V

W

OPEN SOFTWARE FOUNDATION™

INFORMATION REQUEST FORM

Please send me the following:

( ) OSF Membership Information

( ) OSF/Motif™ License Materials

( ) OSF/Motif™ Training Information

Contact Name _____

Company Name _____

Street Address _____

Mail Stop _____

City _____ State _____ Zip _____

Phone _____ FAX _____

Electronic Mail _____

MAIL TO:

Open Software Foundation
11 Cambridge Center
Cambridge, MA 02142

Attn: OSF/Motif™

For more information about OSF/Motif™ call **617 621 7300.**